Adaptation in Contemporary Theatre

Methuen Drama Engage offers original reflections about key practitioners, movements and genres in the fields of modern theatre and performance. Each volume in the series seeks to challenge mainstream critical thought through original and interdisciplinary perspectives on the body of work under examination. By questioning existing critical paradigms, it is hoped that each volume will open up fresh approaches and suggest avenues for further exploration.

Series Editors

Mark Taylor-Batty
Senior Lecturer in Theatre Studies, Workshop Theatre,
University of Leeds, UK

Enoch Brater
Kenneth T. Rowe Collegiate Professor of Dramatic Literature & Professor of English and Theater, University of Michigan, USA

Titles

Authenticity in Contemporary Theatre and Performance
by Daniel Schulze
ISBN 978–1–3500–0096–4

Beat Drama: Playwrights and Performances of the 'Howl' Generation
edited by Deborah R. Geis
ISBN 978–1–472–56787–1

The Contemporary American Monologue: Performance and Politics
by Eddie Paterson
ISBN 978–1–472–58501–1

Drama and Digital Arts Cultures
by David Cameron, Michael Anderson and Rebecca Wotzko
ISBN 978–1–472–59219–4

Social and Political Theatre in 21st-Century Britain: Staging Crisis
by Vicky Angelaki
ISBN 978–1–474–21316–5

Theatre in the Dark
edited by Adam Alston and Martin Welton
ISBN 978–1–474–25118–1

Watching War on the Twenty-First Century Stage: Spectacles of Conflict
by Clare Finburgh
ISBN 978–1–472–59866–0

Adaptation in Contemporary Theatre

Performing Literature

Frances Babbage

Series Editors

Enoch Brater and Mark Taylor-Batty

methuen | drama
LONDON • NEW YORK • OXFORD • NEW DELHI • SYDNEY

METHUEN DRAMA
Bloomsbury Publishing Plc
50 Bedford Square, London, WC1B 3DP, UK
1385 Broadway, New York, NY 10018, USA

BLOOMSBURY, METHUEN DRAMA and the Methuen Drama logo are trademarks of Bloomsbury Publishing Plc

First published in 2018
Paperback edition first published 2019

Cover design: Louise Dugdale
Cover image: Robbie Jack © Corbis Entertainment / Getty Images

A catalogue record for this book is available from the British Library.

A catalog record for this book is available from the Library of Congress.

ISBN: HB: 978-1-4725-3052-3
PB: 978-1-4725-3142-1
ePDF: 978-1-4725-3416-3
eBook: 978-1-4725-2723-3

Series: Methuen Drama Engage

Typeset by Integra Software Services Pvt. Ltd.

For Marcus and Sam, with love

Contents

Acknowledgements

Many people have provided help and guidance in the process of this book's composition. I am especially grateful to the writers, artists and theatre-makers who generously shared their time and resources: Peter Bailey, Tim Etchells, Ant Hampton, Peter Jaeger, Keith Lodwick, Teresa Ludovico, Alberto Prandini, Felix Mortimer, Ans Van den Eede, Wannes Gyselinck and James Yarker. Many thanks to the academic colleagues who have read work in progress, given advice, kept me company at the theatre, or otherwise supported the research: Anna Barton, Joe Bray, Bridget Escolme, Sam Ladkin, Carmen Levick, David McCallum, Bill McDonnell, Marcus Nevitt, Patrice Pavis, Steve Nicholson, Amber Regis, Terry O'Connor, Adam Piette, Sue Vice, Tomasz Wisniewski, Angela Wright and Rachel Zerihan. A period of research leave granted by the University of Sheffield was also of invaluable help. I am very grateful to Mark Taylor-Batty and Enoch Brater for editorial support, likewise to Mark Dudgeon and Susan Furber at Bloomsbury Methuen Drama. Finally, I would like to thank my family and, above all, Marcus and Sam, for their encouragement, love and a fair amount of patience.

Notes

Part of Chapter 2 was previously published as: 'How Books Matter: Theatre, Adaptation and the Life of Texts'. Tomasz Wisniewski, ed., *Between Page and Stage: Between.Pomiędzy* (Gdansk: The University of Gdańsk Press, forthcoming).

Part of Chapter 3 was previously published as: 'Adaptation and Storytelling in the Theatre', *Critical Stages* 12, December 2015. http://www.critical-stages.org/12/adaptation-and-storytelling-in-the-theatre/.

Introduction

This book is about theatre that is made from prose. The history of drama is also the history of prose transformation, and adaptation of this kind is as popular in the contemporary theatre as it has ever been. Today, the theatre reworks not only novels and short stories, but less likely sources such as biography and autobiography, poetry, letters, manifestos and reference works. Beyond theatre buildings, prose literature feeds live art, installations, and site-specific and immersive theatre, thus performance practices which do not automatically assume the existence of a text at all. Theatre is an art self-evidently bound up with adaptation in the widest sense, since repetition, re-presentation and revision are integral to its operations and expected by its audiences. Given the nature of contemporary theatrical production, which values bold and subtle treatments of established plays quite as much as new dramatic writing, and whose sophisticated audiences comfortably accommodate intertextual reference and multimediality, it is not surprising that, in critical terms, the performance of prose literatures today has largely been subsumed within that larger culture of re-presentation rather than singled out for special scrutiny. However, this book seeks to demonstrate that although different forms of intertextuality will necessarily overlap, and no type of adaptation is more important or worthy of attention than another, the consequence of a pluralist perspective has been that too little consideration has been given thus far to what might be uniquely significant in prose adaptation within the theatrical context.

While reinterpretation of dramatic texts is accepted as an essential marker of theatre's vigour and continuing relevance, prose adaptation has always had a much more ambivalent reception. Dramatization of prose fiction, in the theatre and much more so on film, has been perceived as parasitic, as dully derivative, as hubristically ambitious, as opportunistic and money-driven, and as evidence of, and contributor to, the art's stagnation. The performance of prose has been prejudicially received even before the specifics of an adaptation project are considered: at which point the work itself may be criticized as reductive, superficial or a travesty; as lacking in depth, lacking complexity or simply lacking. Such bias still regularly surfaces in popular criticism and continues to be wrestled with in studies of adaptation on screen. Contemporary theatre scholarship does not typically regard prose adaptation as automatically contentious, yet in its analyses tends to slip such work amongst other kinds of intertextual and intermedial practice which can appear, by contrast, as somehow more innovative and vital. This book takes prose adaptation in the theatre as its particular focus in order to present this as practice that is not just artistically legitimate, distinctive and valuable, but one that has been, and continues to be, a lively force of creative regeneration. I argue that the contemporary theatre's appetite for prose texts has engendered significant expansion of performance vocabularies: confronted by the 'problems' posed by the dissimilar forms and conventions of non-dramatic literature, the theatre has been inspired – compelled – to extend its own formal boundaries, in the process confounding the expectations of its audience and newly illuminating the adapted material.

This study seeks to demonstrate how pervasively and variously prose literature is appropriated by contemporary performance. Thus, I consider adaptations inside the theatre and beyond it, in site-specific, promenade and immersive contexts, and in libraries and galleries; adaptations performed solo, in huge multi-company collaborations, and with no 'actor' at all; adaptations which are technologically sophisticated, and others with little or no mediation of this kind; adaptations which are highly physical, and those which place puppets amongst the human cast; and adaptations in postdramatic theatre, including productions which emphasize and display adaptation 'failure'. This book does not attempt to categorize adaptations, or rule that some textual relationships are adaptations and others not. Rather, the term 'adaptation' as applied here embraces any performance project predicated upon, profoundly engaged with and concerned to represent prose literature: on occasion, even these generous definitional boundaries are stretched, I trust legitimately. My discussion of adaptation in contemporary theatre reveals that what is created by this process is only rarely a 'play', let alone one in which a literary source has been squeezed, kicking and screaming, into an alien dramatic mould; instead, the majority of adaptations considered here can be more accurately described as textual re-sitings, within which connections and disjunctions between the contents, forms and contexts of literature and performance are exposed. Prose adaptation emerges from this analysis as the very opposite of easy, parasitic or retrogressive; what becomes increasingly apparent is the difficulty of adaptation, the ingenuity and invention it demands, and the invigorated theatricalities it presents.

The terms of this book combine specificity with considerable openness. I discuss only performance based on prose literature, predominantly prose fiction. This study is not concerned with reinterpretations of dramatic texts; I also exclude adaptations of illustrational sources, like graphic novels or picture books, as well as material borrowings from film, television and digital media. However, while confining itself to sources from prose literature, my discussion does not restrict the categories of prose to be included: this book is not about the challenges of adapting a specific author, nor about dramatization of, for instance, the realist, modernist or postmodernist novel. Instead, this study is self-consciously inclusive in the literary sources considered, an expansiveness which reflects the heterogeneity of adaptation practice, for although canonical texts are certainly appropriated for stage production with regularity, this is not representative of theatrical adaptation across the board. Rather, the multiple and eclectic languages of contemporary performance seek out equally diverse sources of literary inspiration: theatre tackles not just the postmodern but the early modern text; promiscuous in the writing it appropriates, the theatre also readily breaks or disregards generic 'rules'. Within this culture, the act of prose adaptation is curiously positioned, even Janus-faced: the impulse to adapt diverse kinds of non-dramatic literature reflects not only expanding intertextual liberty but also the desire to reengage with narrative structure and the pleasures of story. In recognition of these tendencies in performance, this book's examination of individual case studies is not guided by literary genre, author or period, but by critical questions about the operation of prose adaptation in contemporary theatre which are used to frame each chapter and allow unlike works to be brought into dialogue with one another. In this analysis, I pay close attention to the ways in which the fact or activity of adaptation is exposed in performance; how a production's operation as adaptation intersects with other factors which may have been equally formative; and how far assumptions about adaptations in general, or authors in particular, have influenced a production's critical reception.

While the central object of this study is theatre practice, my discussion is also overtly 'bookish' and addresses a number of significantly literary questions; for example, I consider the physical properties of books and practices of reading, as well as the thematic and stylistic features of individual works. I do this not to privilege the literary above the theatrical, nor to pursue a traditional comparative analysis; nor am I interested in judging the 'success' of adaptations as treatments of the texts they reconfigure. Rather, my emphasis mirrors a fascination exhibited by the adaptations themselves: for recurrently, these are productions which do not move swiftly 'off book' but continue, sometimes during the performance, to grapple with and actively relish qualities such as 'undramatic' literary language, textual ambiguity or editorial dispute, sheer narrative overload, the scent and touch of paper and leather, and the heft of the physical volume. In these adaptations, literature is shown to inflect performance in unexpected ways: far from unimaginatively dependent, the theatre draws creative inspiration from prose writing in aesthetic as well as content-driven ways. Since notably bookish qualities are consciously retained by the adaptations discussed quite as often as they are transformed, this study proposes that certain perspectives more commonly associated with literary analysis may usefully be brought into play in a theatrical context. I thus apply to dramatic adaptation the concept of *ekphrasis*, the capacity and limits of one art form to convey the qualities of another; I discuss whether adaptation could be understood as a practice of edition and what light this perspective might yield; I examine techniques of literary digression, comparing these with modes of theatrical expression that give body to performance without moving narrative 'forward'; I explore literary 'spaces', on the page and in the imagination of readers, and their correspondence or conflict with the physical site of the theatre and practices of immersion; finally, I examine the time-spaces or 'chronotopes' – in Bakhtin's terms – that are formulated by literary texts, and how performance spaces and temporalities respond. However, if this study sometimes looks at performance in a literary way, it also scrutinizes books theatrically. The physical properties of literature shape the aesthetic of many of the adaptations I discuss; writing, erasing and editing are played out live, implicitly questioning the stability of the text; and reading, both aloud and to oneself, is understood as a participatory and creative act. In this way, even before the specifics of individual text–adaptation relations are explored, the performance of prose is revealed by the productions I examine as a complex exchange, one still prone to get irritably beneath the skin of 'reading' audiences, but richly able to give back to literature quite as much as it might seem to take.

Chapter 1 provides an overview of prose adaptation in the theatre, touching selectively on past practices in order to frame an understanding of performance in the present. This opening chapter also identifies preoccupations that have influenced the development of adaptation studies as an interdisciplinary research field and looks closely at arguments traditionally made about dramatic transformations that mask literary bias. Rather than refuting claims about adaptation's characteristic superficiality, reductiveness or misrepresentative effects, I take these objections seriously and try to establish their basis; drawing on a wide range of contemporary examples, I suggest a variety of answers offered by theatre to meet such concerns. Chapter 2 explores the significance of books in performance at a fundamental and material level. I discuss two productions that take place in libraries, *The Quiet*

Volume, by Tim Etchells and Ant Hampton, and *Time Has Fallen Asleep in the Afternoon Sunshine*, by Mette Evardsen, both pieces which pose questions for their audiences about the substance of books and the nature of the author-text-reader encounter. The same chapter examines the impressions made by literary works as performance objects and driving narratives, considering Complicite's *The Street of Crocodiles*, Elevator Repair Service's *Gatz* and finally *The Anatomy of Melancholy* by Stan's Cafe. In Chapter 3, I study that which is perhaps most obviously at stake in adaptation: story, and the means by which it is told. Adaptation, like traditional storytelling, is concerned both to pass on story and to reshape and 'own' this; this doubled process implies a political dimension, also, since narratives may be chosen to reflect or conserve the values of a new audience, or conversely to challenge these implicitly or directly. In this chapter, I explore theatre's negotiation of the charged gap between tale and telling with reference to Kneehigh's *The Red Shoes* and Teresa Ludovico's *I Was a Rat!*

Chapter 4 considers the strategies by which the explicit spaces or landscapes of prose fiction may be translated into theatrical performance. My analysis of adaptation practice shows that articulating such spaces might be less a matter of scenic representation, illustrative or otherwise, than of fluidity and restraint. I discuss the implications of the reader's role, both in contributing to the creation of fictional spaces and imaginatively entering those worlds in lateral relation to their textual occupants. These issues are explored with reference to Complicite's *The Master and Margarita*, and to assess the implications and impact of *literal* 'immersion', Punchdrunk's *The Masque of the Red Death* and Retz's *The Trial*. Chapter 5 presents a series of novels which, by reason of their scale, narrative density or linguistic game-playing, would conventionally be considered 'resistant' to dramatic reconfiguration. However, I argue that in practice the challenges to narrative stability, notions of originality and the possibility of representational wholeness levelled by the postdramatic theatre make this 'language' precisely suited to take on such texts. The chapter also examines conceptual writing as an adaptive and, potentially, a performance form equally invested in the opportunities of textual movement and reassemblage. The case studies used in this chapter are the Hebbel am Ufer's *Infinite Jest: 24 Hours through the Utopian West*, Hof van Eede's *Where the World is Going, That's Where We are Going* and Peter Jaeger's *A Field Guide to Lost Things*.

In establishing the scope and focus of this book, it should be acknowledged that the case studies included are not comprehensively representative of adaptation in performance: prose appropriation is so widely and diversely practised that no sample could achieve this. The temporal, geographical and formal range of work explored is also constrained, inevitably, by my ability to access it. However, the performances discussed in each chapter are intended as representative of the critical dynamics they are used to illustrate; further, my hope is that in combination they will sufficiently convey the vitality of adaptation practice in and beyond the British theatre context. It may also be necessary to state explicitly the perhaps self-evident reality that adaptations in the theatre are not *only* adaptations: in other words, that they are created and received as performance events framed by a plurality of factors unconnected with a literary source. The productions I describe also attract audiences unfamiliar with the texts that inspired their creation, or who will read that literature subsequently, or not at all. It has not been the project of this book to discuss the performances beyond their situation as adaptation, although different spectator relations are acknowledged and referenced at several points in the study. Instead, I privilege the perspective of a spectator who is not pedantically attached to the text but who is actively book-curious, interested in how theatre can 'speak' this language, and in where the process might hesitate or fail as well as where it seems to succeed.

In thinking and writing about adaptation, and in undertaking prose/performance projects of my own, I have found it critically and creatively productive to reflect above all on the slippery, indecisive and to-be-negotiated territory *between* literary source and theatrical outcome. Regarded from this inter-space, text and performance alike become shadowy and unfixed. C. S. Lewis's novels describe something rather like this liminality: the Narnia series is predicated on movement across realms, with the transition often occurring without warning, when falling into the frame of a picture or emerging from a wardrobe door. *The Magician's Nephew* is distinct amongst Lewis's novels for depicting a more substantial interim place, a dreamlike 'wood between the worlds', filled with numerous pools. Digory and Polly each arrive by magic rings from 'our world' and find themselves scrambling out of a pool; other pools, they quickly realize, lead to entirely other worlds. Uncertain whether to go back to the familiar or explore the unknown, they jump into the 'home' pool to ascertain that return is possible:

> At first there were bright lights moving about in a black sky: Digory always thinks these were stars and even swears that he saw Jupiter quite close – close enough to see its moons. But almost at once there were rows and rows of roofs and chimney pots about them, and they could see St Paul's and knew they were looking at London. But you could see through the walls of all the houses. Then they could see Uncle Andrew, very vague and shadowy, but getting clearer and more solid-looking all the time, just as if he were coming into focus. But before he became quite real Polly shouted 'Change', and they did change, and our world faded away like a dream. And the green light above grew stronger and stronger, till their heads came out of the pool and they scrambled ashore. And there was the wood all about them, as green and bright and still as ever. The whole thing had taken less than a minute.
>
> 'There!' said Digory, 'That's alright. Now for the adventure.'[1]

Exploring adaptation seems to me rather like this space of the pool, in which one is drawn in different directions, watching one reality recede as another sharpens into focus. The hazy interplay of worlds described here also recalls the sensation of emerging from deep reading, the brief struggle to reconcile fictional scenes with immediate material surroundings. But the discovery that the 'home' world is only one reality amongst others, and that any of these may be transparent or solid depending on where you are standing, implicitly destabilizes all realities; in adaptation terms, this suggests that no ground, textual or theatrical, should be taken on trust.

1

Adaptation and the Theatre

Adaptation finds a natural home in the theatre. Here, audiences expect and want retellings: reproduction and reinterpretation are central to theatre's *raison d'être*. In the Darwinian sense of the term, adaptation signals that rather than 'a divine design, we have a continuous process': theatre manifests this conspicuously, returning to and ever altering its materials, needing to do so in order to stay alive.[1] The evolutionary trajectory of adaptation, in and beyond the theatre, is less progressive than web-like: adaptations look backwards, without being retrogressive; they extend and forge connections laterally, synchronically; and they also reach forwards, finding fresh means to speak old texts in new times. Each *Three Sisters* redraws and extends the map of Chekhov's play, suggestively interconnecting with stagings prior and anticipated, local and far afield: Benedict Andrews at the Young Vic set it in contemporary Russia, in front of a distinctly Beckettian mound of earth (2012); as adapted by Lucy Caldwell for the Lyric Belfast, Chekhov's drama unfolded in the last years of the Troubles (2016); at the National Theatre, Katie Mitchell's *Three Sisters* saw actors moving in slow motion on a colour-drained stage, amidst ticking clocks and fragile china (2003); the play was reinvented for 1940s Jewish Liverpool as *Three Sisters on Hope Street*, directed by Lindsay Posner at the Liverpool Everyman, with three American-Russian sisters struggling with the experience of displacement (2008); it was replayed through live action, video and multimedia as *Brace Up!*, offering what Elizabeth LeCompte called a 'double portrait of Chekhov and the Wooster Group' (1991);[2] earlier still, Yuri Lyubimov stunned audiences by momentarily opening the external wall of the Taganka Theatre, exposing the dark streets, urban apartment blocks and freezing temperatures of modern Moscow, in ironic and stark contrast to the idealized city of the sisters' dreams (1989).[3] Evidently, the theatre has room for an infinite number and variety of *Three Sisters*, there are never 'enough': they freely accumulate, echoing and contradicting one another, their elements growing entangled in practice and memory with other productions and other media. For Marvin Carlson, the theatre's repetitive compulsions, at every level, make it a site of ghosts:

> Everything in the theatre, the bodies, the materials utilised, the language, the space itself, is now and has always been haunted, and that haunting has been an essential part of the theatre's meaning to and reception by its audiences in all times and all places.[4]

Theatre's repetitive ghosting is likewise noted by Margherita Laera in *Theatre and Adaptation: Return, Rewrite, Repeat* (2014), a collection of interviews with contemporary practitioners and playwrights. Laera suggests further that 'the mechanisms of adaptation and those of theatricality have something fundamental in common, not least in their relationship with temporality'. Adaptation, like theatre, looks back to move forwards, repeating but ever-changing: thus in the theatre, as 'in adaptation's logic, time is no linear progression, but a spiral that keeps turning on itself, causing cyclical reoccurrences while ensuring evolution'.[5] Demonstrating that accumulative, spiralling movement, Laera's collection encompasses radical and in some cases antagonistic theatrical 're-readings', alongside intercultural and intermedial adaptations of diverse kinds. Regarding adaptation broadly as an intertextual practice, Laera outlines a taxonomy that might enable finer categorization within this, differentiating between productions that are inter- or intra-lingual, semiotic, generic, medial, temporal, cultural or ideological. Such terminology valuably assists analysis of what different adaptation projects might be doing, even if those categories very quickly become 'complicated'.[6] Any taxonomy will have its shortcomings: as Laera's case studies show, adaptations in practice exhibit so many variables, so many incompatible comparative terms, that classifications inevitably founder.

Amidst so much circling, evolving and 'ghosted' productivity, it can be difficult to distinguish and critically unpick particular kinds of adaptation practice. In this book I undertake such scrutiny by concentrating exclusively on theatrical treatments of prose literature: predominantly, but not exclusively, adaptations of the novel. 'Intermedial' adaptations of this order fit, but also problematize, Carlson's metaphor of theatre as a 'haunted house', since transforming prose for live performance is quite unlike reproducing a text preconceived as drama. Through its blanks and spaces, a play script has already embedded the invitation to collaborate; most are written in hopeful expectation of not one, but multiple embodiments. Prose is different: a novel is not 'gappy' but appears, at least in a superficial sense, full and finished. Adapting such texts into drama constitutes collaboration that is uninvited, and may even, from the perspectives of some, be unwanted. The theatre's habit of staging novels, however, is as old as the novel itself. In the eighteenth and early nineteenth centuries, the popular Gothic fictions of Horace Walpole, Ann Radcliffe and Matthew Lewis were reborn in drama often in the same year which saw them published as prose; the nineteenth and early twentieth centuries witnessed numerous dramatizations of works by Walter Scott, William Godwin, Mary Shelley, Charles Dickens, Mary Elizabeth Braddon and the Brontës (indeed, Mary Shelley was 'much amused' by a performance of *Presumption; or, The Fate of Frankenstein*, although the story, she considered, was 'not well managed').[7] Regularly, in this period, the theatre kept pace with or actually overtook the literary source. The context of serial publication meant that 'plays often appeared before the novels were complete'; William Rede's adaptation of Dickens's *The Pickwick Papers* was staged in March 1837, with nine instalments of the book yet to be released.[8] Dickens attacks this culture in *Nicholas Nickleby* through the character of Crummles, a 'literary gentleman' – likely a reference to the particularly prolific W. T. Moncrieff – 'who had dramatised in his time two hundred and forty-seven novels as fast as they had come out – some of them faster than they had come out'.[9] Since stage adaptations, unlike novels or plays, were unprotected by copyright legislation, the authors themselves regularly stepped in to pre-empt 'pirated' versions: *Dracula, or the Undead* played fleetingly in the theatre in May 1897 in a version by Stoker eight days before official publication of the horror classic that would be reworked for stage and screen countless times after.[10] Alongside those expeditious dramatizations, emerging at the point of first publication, scholars have explored the continuing afterlife of authors like Dickens, Jane Austen, Henry James and the Brontës in theatre and on screen – and further, in graphic novels, digital media, heritage sites – and the implications of what is less a legacy than a two-way endowment (since adaptations may permanently cast their sources in a different light); such analyses have exposed the extent to which adaptations describe their contemporary context as much as any fictive past, with earlier literatures put to work to illuminate the present world.[11]

Turning prose literature into performance has always excited controversy, drawing charges of plagiarism and parasitism, as well as disparaging assumptions about the inevitably inferior results. While the theatre has a far longer tradition of recycling its narratives and materials – Shakespeare's extensive appropriation of pre-existent sources is a much-cited case in point – the rise of the novel in the eighteenth century permanently altered concepts of and attitudes towards dramatic adaptation. For as Colin MacCabe notes, the novel was not just an emerging genre, 'but a genre that claimed that its fictions were new: for the novel declares the importance that its stories are original in its name'.[12] This recognition helps to explain why scholars such as Allardyce Nicoll, chronicling the history of theatre in the nineteenth century, claimed that the popularity of novel dramatizations – a practice which 'did not demand the highest of talents' – was contributing to the drama's wider 'decline', with playhouses turning to straightforward borrowings as opposed to 'original' dramatic literature.[13] Yet even if the plots and scenes of novels could sometimes lazily be capitalized upon, the history of adaptation in the theatre suggests a more complex, and more mutually fruitful, relationship between performance and literary prose. Novelists have variously benefited from theatre: for example, Montcrieff had some justification, in his response to Dickens's anger at 'plagiarism', for arguing that the latter had lifted many of his characterizations directly from the stage;[14] Henry James, while famously unsuccessful in writing plays, consciously employed 'dramatic' techniques to powerful effect in the narrative style of works including *What Maisie Knew, The Awkward Age* and *The Turn of the Screw*; and prose authors from all periods – Henry Fielding, Jane Austen, Oscar Wilde, J. B. Priestley, Iris Murdoch, Sarah Waters – have shown theatre to be a richly suggestive theme.[15] But theatre, for its part, has found far more to gain from and draw upon in prose literature than a fount of pre-formed scenarios. Not least, the challenges posed by certain elements of novels, and indeed, by entire literary genres, have obliged the theatre to adopt ingenious strategies in order to accommodate these, and, further, have impelled rethinking and extending the representational capacities of performance itself. For while it has often been claimed that adaptation 'struggles' to retell narratives not conceived as drama, it can be counterclaimed that this medial difference is precisely what necessitates creativity in the act of reinvention.

The single example of the Gothic novel will serve to demonstrate how theatre might deal in practice with issues of literary 'difficulty', with the resistance that prose puts up to drama. The early stage versions of these novels, of the late 1790s, were produced amidst lively dispute about what content could be staged and how. The grisly scenes and mysterious apparitions that made the fictions of Radcliffe and her contemporaries so popular could not be retained in the theatre without offending polite sensibilities, or, just as seriously, attracting critical ire for daring to represent 'ridiculous deviations from common sense and common experience'.[16] In a climate of considerable hostility to the dramatic 'marvellous', such elements of the novels were often erased in adaptation, but were also frequently burlesqued as comedy; in this way, even where sequences *as written* appeared dramatically unworkable, the theatre still found strategies to present these under a different guise.[17] Questions around the viability for dramatic adaptation of Gothic literatures have been differently answered in the contemporary theatre, not least by exploiting the potential of participatory methods such as promenade and immersion. Grid Iron's 1997 adaptation of Angela Carter's Gothic Bluebeard tale 'The Bloody Chamber' was designed as a promenade, presented originally in Edinburgh's catacombs and, in revival, at the London Dungeons; rather than physically reproducing the horrors Carter describes – whether the forcible 'deflowering' of the young bride, or the mangled corpses of her predecessors – the production allowed the audience to infer that menace from the haunting qualities of the sites themselves.[18] It is possible to see from these brief illustrations how the very intractability of prose literature in dramatization can itself inspire theatrical resourcefulness; after all, as Steven Berkoff observed of his own boldly physical interpretations of Kafka in the late 1960s and early 1970s, taking on 'the impossible' fruitfully imposes 'a demand upon the imagination'.[19] But the example of Grid Iron's promenade production also draws attention to the fact that the appropriation of prose literature in the theatre can today assume all sorts of guises. Thus, of dramatic adaptation in the twenty-first century, we can ask not just how such literature is treated onstage, but how this is handled *off* stage: in site-specific and immersive theatre, in gallery installations, performances in libraries, or in the open air. Evidently, adaptations look very different in these spaces: but attending to transformations of literary prose in such forms and contexts, as this book does, illuminates the diversity of the contemporary theatre's adaptive practices, exposing different 'intermedial' tensions but equally, new and unexpected opportunities.

The adaptations considered throughout this study, in partial reflection of the complex manifestations of theatrical adaptation more broadly, together evidence the extraordinary inventiveness with which theatre has responded to the implicit provocations of literary source texts. By examining the ways in which individual adaptation projects consciously exploit qualities of liveness, performer-audience relationship, physicality, *mise-en-scène* and ephemerality – qualities which powerfully distinguish the theatre itself – it becomes apparent how sharply live performance differs as a context for re-presenting prose literatures from the more extensively considered field, in adaptation studies, of drama on film. The dissimilar representational codes and mechanisms of stage and screen have also significantly shaped the reception of adaptation in each context. In particular, film's capacity for and tendency towards aesthetic naturalism has allowed great opportunities in adaptation but attracted criticism for the same reason. For example, as Christine Geraghty has shown, Schlöndorff's *Swann in Love* (1984), adapted from Proust, was praised for 'painstaking' and sumptuous historical 'authenticity' but also accused of 'indulging in nostalgia for an idealized past and the commodification of costumes and sets'; the film's rich recreation of period and place simultaneously laid it open to criticism of seeming to value surface at the expense of depth, and in consequence digressing from the 'spirit' of the source.[20] Theatre, by contrast, is not inherently a naturalistic medium and rarely strives for verisimilitude of the cinematic kind; instead, stage drama signifies much through little, its relative poverty fundamental to its pleasure. Identifying the multiple layers of the performance event serves to highlight the singularity of theatre, as well as its unlikeness to cinema. A theatre production offers up meaning at the level of dramatic action: that is, the fiction that an audience is invited to 'believe' in, at least to some extent. Simultaneously, the production communicates through its performance action: the representational mechanisms used to convey, and sometimes to contest, the dramatic fiction. The gap between the levels of drama and performance is visible to the audience and understood by them; indeed, the disjunction between idea and expression is not simply accepted but celebrated as the very space of theatrical creativity. The production's manipulation of this dynamic also influences meaning-making on the additional level of event action: around impressions of atmosphere, participation, occasion, economics, collectivity (or the lack of it), excitement or boredom. In any production, the theatre will strive to make positive use of the potential in these multiple, interdependent layers. But intermedial adaptation provides the opportunity to reexamine this construct and its implications: and as I shall argue, the theatre's illustrative and representational 'inadequacies' – what it *cannot* and does not try to do – make it, paradoxically, an especially fertile and promising context for adaptation of literature.

The ability of adaptation to exploit gaps and friction between the levels of drama, performance and event can be illustrated with reference to the RSC's *The Life and Adventures of Nicholas Nickleby*. This show, which opened at London's Aldwych Theatre in 1980, as Christopher Innes puts it, 'moved the artistic goalposts' for stage adaptation, as well as being an extraordinary and award-winning piece of theatre in its own right; additionally, two years later, the filmed production was the centrepiece in the launch of British television's then innovative and experimental Channel 4.[21] David Edgar turned Dickens's 800-page novel into just over eight hours of performance time, presented in two parts by a cast of forty-nine actors who all remained on stage throughout. Between them, Edgar and co-directors Trevor Nunn and John Caird strove to tell the story of Nicholas's adventures while drawing attention, as they did so, to the semi-impossible undertaking of theatrical adaptation. Edgar gave the actors Dickens's narration as well as his dialogue, and retained virtually every character in the novel; in practice this meant that most performers had numerous roles, some of which were conjured only within the space of a few lines. Roger Rees as Nicholas was the eponymous centre of the production, yet both the script and Brecht-influenced direction made telling his story a communal and collaborative task; appropriately so, since for Dickens, too, the 'life and adventures' are not narrowly those of the hero but a means of exploring the life of a society and time. The adaptation displayed a kind of self-conscious bravado in taking on the novel in that manner and at that length, demanding that the spectators, likewise, commit to this and be seduced by it. For many who saw the Nunn-Caird production or subsequent revivals, the RSC's production was experienced as a masterpiece: one could leave at the end, exhausted yet exhilarated, equally impressed by the imagination and ambition of the theatre as by Dickens's novel. Critical response to the show was predictably more mixed. Reflecting on the RSC's undertaking, decades later, Stephen Lacey remarks upon an uncomfortable disjunction between Dickens's bleak depiction of grinding poverty and brutality and the triumphant, ultimately celebratory achievement of the production, epitomized by its subsequent Broadway transfer and accompanying commercial success.[22] It would seem harsh to take the project to task for accessibility or economic viability (although popular success is often read as evidence of adaptive 'dumbing down'); but more usefully, Lacey's observation – which suggests that, in this case, performance competed with drama in the service of event – exposes the ways in which theatre's distinctive formal structures and expressive mechanisms carry risks for adaptation as well as possibilities.

Theatre studies has for the most part treated adaptations of prose literatures as effectively inseparable from a wider, long-standing practice of borrowing and reinvention, the exception being where scholars have, as noted previously, focused on the dramatic afterlife of novels, short stories or verse narratives by particular (usually canonical) authors. While this form of intermedial adaptation is an important part of theatre's larger re-interpretive culture, keeping prose adaptation thus marginalized – or generalized – passes up the opportunity to apply to this practice the kinds of arguments and analyses that have shaped discussion of prose adaptation in other dramatic media. Drama on screen has played a central role in the development of adaptation studies as a critical discipline; in this context, theatre, by contrast, has remained very much on the margins. This book proposes that many of the questions typically posed about dramatic adaptation on film (and also addressed, less frequently, in contexts such as video games and theme parks) can productively be asked of theatre too: for although, as already observed, the two art forms are distinctively unlike one another, they also have preoccupations and practices in common.[23] In adapting prose fiction, theatre and cinema alike must bring new dimensions to the narrative that are visual, aural and material; must establish the scope and scale of the *mise-en-scène*; must consider not just how to represent what is only described, but *whether* to represent what is *not* described; must determine how best to balance the length and density of the prose and the duration of the performed representation. As well as such drama-specific concerns, typically tested against film within adaptation studies, more fundamental arguments have been made about adaptation per se that have been less fully explored in a theatrical than a cinematic context: issues about what adaptation 'owes', if it owes anything, to its source or sources, and about what the new context affords as well as what it might 'take'. In the rest of this chapter, therefore, I take some key concerns of adaptation studies and locate these within the context of the theatre. In doing so, I look closely at charges frequently levelled against dramatization, considering their relative applicability to theatre as well as a number of critical counterarguments. Since adapting novels for live and filmed performance has always been relatively – but regularly – belittled, I have found it valuable to explore in some detail the prejudicial assumptions behind that denigration; I do so not in order to 'defend' a practice that should not need it, but because those attitudes expose tensions inherent in intermedial translation which can in turn be read not as inhibitors to adaptation, but as a basis for experimentation and invention. Theatre, as I show here through a wide range of examples, can contribute distinctively to debates about dramatization of prose literature within adaptation studies and through this could play a far more compelling role in shaping such arguments than it has thus far.[24] For while theatre's dimensions of liveness, ephemerality, spatiality and changeability make its outputs singularly difficult objects of study (as well as less easily shareable than their screen counterparts), these very qualities shape adaptation practices uniquely, meaning in turn that theatre's example can re-inflect and refresh the terms of the debate.

Adaptation studies: A critical context

Adaptation studies developed in the twentieth and twenty-first century as a discipline, or interdiscipline, of the humanities, born of scholarship within and between study of film, literature, translation, drama and new media. Of these contributing fields, screen studies has, as noted, most decisively shaped debates about adaptation in theory and advanced frameworks through which adaptations in practice might be received and understood. Theoretical analyses by early scholars like André Bazin and George Bluestone in the 1940s and 1950s, to the contributions of Geoffrey Wagner, Morris Beja, Dudley Andrew and David Bordwell in the 1970s and 1980s, to later twentieth- and twenty-first-century studies by Brian McFarlane, Deborah Cartmell and Imelda Whelehan, Sarah Cardwell, James Naremore, Robert Stam and Alessandra Raego, Kamilla Elliott, Thomas Leitch, Christine Geraghty, Colin McCabe and others, has together shaped a complex and nuanced appreciation of literary and cinematic 'languages' while continuing to fuel arguments about medial distinction and/or interdependence.[25] The prominence of film as a driver within adaptation studies is partly explained by the persistence with which cinema has historically drawn on literature for inspiration, and simultaneously by the apparent obligation upon film, as the younger art form, to defend the aesthetic value and legitimacy of adaptive 'writing' on screen. In the twenty-first century, with film studies long established as an institution in its own right (rather than an 'offshoot' of English literature) and screen adaptations subjected to analysis as rigorous as that applied to any other kind of movie, it may be difficult to grasp retrospectively why the practice of adaptation on film should have needed justification in the first place. Yet arguments about the relationship between film and literature date back to the beginnings of cinema itself: scholars and practitioners in both disciplines have long grappled with questions about the uniqueness of each 'language' and what they share; the complexity of concept or subtlety of articulation each medium can achieve; the distinctive qualities of experience film and literature shape for their respective audiences; their different contexts of production, reception and circulation, and how these in turn affect interpretation and judgement.

The earliest films, based in the technology of magic lanterns (at their peak of popularity in the Victorian period) and the Kinetoscope, were 'extremely simple' studies of movement and image sometimes no more than a minute long, but as David Bordwell and Kristin Thompson note, 'narrative form also entered the cinema from the beginning' – meaning in practice from 1903–1904 onwards – and quickly became the most prominent and fast-growing type of film in the commercial industry.[26] Mutually accommodating co-existence of literature and film became impossible once the latter had asserted itself firmly as a narrative art as much as a visual and aural one.[27] Since filmmakers turned with increasing frequency to novels and short stories as sources of narrative, controversy fired up further. In her now-classic essay 'The Cinema', first published in 1926, Virginia Woolf acknowledged and admired the nature and potential of 'movie reality', but was fiercely critical of the film industry's appropriation of other art forms, and above all, of literature:

> All the famous novels of the world, with their well-known characters and their famous scenes, only asked, it seemed, to be put on the films. What could be easier and simpler? The cinema fell upon its prey with immense rapacity, and to the moment largely subsists upon the body of its unfortunate victim. But the results are disastrous to both. The alliance is unnatural. Eye and brain are torn asunder ruthlessly as they try vainly to work in couples.[28]

In Woolf's account, literature is identified as the authentic and vulnerable body; cinema, by contrast, is the encroaching parasite, full-blooded only through its greedy draining of the life of others. Despite the tone of the passage quoted, the essay in its entirety is not opposed to cinema per se; Woolf considered the screen extraordinarily powerful, but dangerous since the new medium had been born 'fully-clothed. It can say everything before it has anything to say'. Instead of looking towards literature to find 'something to say', Woolf urged experimentation with expressive capabilities she considered uniquely filmic – a suggestive abstraction of the visual far removed from everyday reality, a distinctive kind of 'dream architecture' – but remained insistent that for the future health of both art forms, everything 'accessible to words and to words alone, the cinema must avoid'.[29] Woolf's exhortation that the new medium should explore the full potentiality of the filmic was then, and still remains, of value.[30] Yet the hierarchical and binaristic terms in which that recommendation was couched are plain and proved problematically contagious. In Woolf's essay, the novel is judged authoritative by its anteriority, with film the young pretender; works of literature are represented as aesthetically and conceptually coherent, whereas film is seemingly content with tearing off bits and pieces; finally, and perhaps most damningly, Woolf's conception of the demands that literature and film made on 'brain' and 'eye', respectively, carries a potentially prejudicial subtext about (verbal) depth versus (visual) surface.

These 'objections' to cinematic adaptation, arguably suggestive of deeper anxieties about film encroaching on literature's territory, have been extensively contested within screen studies and broadly discredited, even if their traces still visibly run through popular as well as scholarly debates. While it is difficult to dispute claims of literature's historical seniority, equating age with superiority is hardly defensible; moreover, the novel – the literary form most commonly at stake in adaptation – is not so very much older, usually dated from the beginning of the eighteenth century (although antecedents have been identified from considerably earlier).[31] The argument that literary texts are coherent 'works', whereas films – which borrow not only from narrative sources, but from other arts and the culture more broadly – are dependent or parasitic 'intertexts' is profoundly undermined by structuralist and poststructuralist analysis, which insists that 'every text is an intertext', the structure and meaning of which can only be established when it is viewed within an (indeterminably) vast web of intertextual influence. It follows from this proposal that assumptions about authorship and originality are equally rendered suspect. Barthes described the writer, not as the originator but the 'orchestrator' of a text that is, inevitably, a 'tissue of quotations', a composition built from the already written.[32] As well as kicking away any pedestal from which literature could look down upon film, this way of seeing crucially reframes how adaptations, in any medium, are perceived; if every text is a construction moulded out of other texts, adaptations cannot be unnatural or parasitical but are rather the embodiment of the way in which textual production already occurs, albeit in overt and heightened form.

Theories of intertextuality do not obviously help to counter loaded assertions about the conflicting demands made by each medium on brain or eye. This alleged distinction was to some extent fostered by early work in film theory, crystallized by George Bluestone's influential 1957 study *Novels into Film*. Bluestone's arguments were influenced by the need to free film from any perceived obligation towards 'fidelity' in adaptation. As Nöel Carroll emphasizes, for Bluestone film was crucially an 'art form [with] its own domain of expression and exploration [...] determined by the nature of the medium'; since literature and film were not hermeneutically comparable, the artworks shaped by each medium should be treated as individually coherent and non-dependent.[33] Bluestone's insistence on film's unique expressive capabilities did not, of course, suggest that the brain was any less engaged when viewing a film than when reading, but rather that the receiver's mode of processing content was wholly different in each case. For Bluestone, the novel was 'a linguistic medium, the film essentially visual'; words on a page had to be 'filtered through the screen of conceptual apprehension', whereas by contrast 'the moving image comes to us directly through perception'.[34] In a discussion of no fewer than twelve 'fallacies' that have prejudiced reception of novels on screen and, by their dogged persistence, inhibited the broader development of adaptation studies as a critical field, Thomas Leitch unpicks the flaws in what might initially seem an unexceptionable basis for medium comparison. The fact that film more obviously makes perceptual apprehension central to its communicative system does not, Leitch emphasizes, assign conceptual appreciation exclusively to the field of literature. Moreover, while images on screen might fairly be called 'percepts', a film's 'visual codes' are just one element of an artwork which also invokes 'auditory codes, narrative codes, fictional codes, and a rhetoric of figuration', the entirety requiring 'as much conceptual initiative and agility as interpreting the verbal (and narrative and fictional and figural) signifying systems of a given novel'.[35] Despite their formal differences, Leitch concludes, books and films alike deal in both concepts *and* percepts: each engages the thinking brain while additionally influencing us on an impressionistic and sensory level. Leitch also draws attention to the ways in which repeated film viewing further undermines the supposed distinction: films as well as novels are 'endlessly rereadable', with each revisit enabling increased conceptual appreciation, without necessarily a corresponding decrease in the work's perceptual impact.[36]

Adaptation studies: A theatrical context

How far are attitudes and biases that run through debates about film's use of literature still pertinent for adaptation in the theatre? In certain respects, the contexts, aspirations and communicative mechanisms of film and theatre are divergent and their distinctions partially explain why the latter has been somewhat less vigorously challenged on its adaptive practices, but correspondingly also why theatre as a critical discipline has supported, rather than vitally shaped, the advance of adaptation studies. First, storytelling and ritual enactment are amongst the oldest arts, predating the communication of narrative in written form; thus while a specific adaptation project might yet be taxed with trampling on hallowed, pre-laid, literary ground, theatre itself has authoritative claims as a space historically defined by narrative (re)telling. Second, following on from this, the dramatic theatre has traditionally been considered a verbal art quite as much as a visual one, even if the balance between word and spectacle is differently weighted from period to period, style to style and culture to culture. In the theatre the relationship between text and performance has proved fraught and contested: in the staging of plays, never mind the performance of prose, word and spectacle have regularly been perceived as in conflict.[37] Third, as already emphasized, theatre's intertextuality is inherent, self-evident and unapologetic: returning to narratives, telling these again and differently, employing quotation, juxtaposition, parody and collage are all fundamental to its modus operandi and its rewards.

However, theatre, like film, is also evidently visual, aural, embodied and scenic, and reliant upon action as much as narration. Consequently, adaptations of novels in the theatre, likewise, are criticized for offering spectacular 'surface' in place of literary 'depth'; alternatively, those same productions may be praised for the way in which the perceptual impact of spectacle becomes a means of accessing conceptual depth. These attitudes, and the tension between them, are well demonstrated by invoking Woolf again, here with reference to the critical reactions prompted by Katie Mitchell's *Waves*, directed at the National Theatre (2006). Woolf's last novel is deeply preoccupied with the operations of consciousness, still more so than is her earlier work; *The Waves* is poetic and lyrical, without dialogue and with no guiding narratorial shape, seeming to take place inside the mind, or a series of minds. In the effort to find a stage language that could re-voice the distinctive characteristics of Woolf's novel, Mitchell made extensive and innovative use of multimedia: the eventual production incorporated pre-recorded film alongside video feed of real-time stage action, with additional sound effects created live by the actors. However, discussing the adaptation on its subsequent New York transfer, Charles Isherwood found the result 'fundamentally disappointing' precisely because, in his view, the qualities that made Woolf's novel so remarkable were lost. His account of the production, what it staged and what it could not show, ironically catches something of the bitterness of Woolf herself on adaptation:

> With unflagging energy and speed [the actors] scuttle around the stage, grabbing props from shelves at the side, moving video cameras in and out of position, standing at the ready to create a sound effect at precisely the right moment to match an image. [...] Their labors are impressive certainly, but they are also sorely distracting from the more necessary task of staying attuned to the reflections of the novel's half-dozen characters [and] rarely did any image seem to justify by its beauty, inventiveness or emotional weight the labor involved in manufacturing it before us live.[38]

Isherwood's terms sharply convey the impression that in *Waves*, surface obscures depth – more precisely, that busy exteriority frustrates appreciation at the interior level. We might rephrase this, recalling Leitch's terms, to say that for Isherwood the perceptual impact of *Waves* actively inhibits conceptual access to the material being treated; this spectator's brain and eye (and ear) are 'torn asunder', to the detriment of his understanding of the whole. However, for some other reviewers of Mitchell's production, the jarring effect produced by the different systems in operation was central to its adaptive success. Lyn Gardner in the *Guardian* describes feeling 'as if you've mistakenly wandered into someone else's head and are drowning in an internal monologue in which the whispered banality of the everyday knocks hard against the deepest unarticulated desires'.[39] For Ben Brantley, writing in the *New York Times*, the performers' 'labor' is not a distraction from more important reflections, but meaningfully draws audience attention; self-consciousness of the means of production is appropriate for a writer 'always painfully aware of the inexactness and artificiality of art: that her words, however fine-spun, could only approximate what she wanted to say'.[40] The potency of the clamour created by the different levels of communication and kinds of activity, the 'disconcerting split sensation'[41] that resulted, made the production for many critics a landmark, not just for stage adaptation, but by extension of the boundaries of contemporary theatre more broadly.[42]

It would be tempting to dismiss Isherwood's perspective on *Waves* outright as merely indicative of a conservative preference for the literary over the spectacular, word over image and, finally, source over adaptation. But while his position does to some extent imply the persistence of that bias, the problems he posits 'against' stage adaptation of novels raise substantial questions about this practice that merit further scrutiny. Alongside *Waves*, Isherwood considers in his article – combatively titled 'Pages That Weren't Meant for Stages' – Steppenwolf's *Kafka on the Shore*, based on Haruki Murakami's novel, as well as two adaptations inspired by Dostoevsky's *The Brothers Karamazov*, by Chicago's Looking Glass Theatre, and by Peter Brook at the New York Theater Workshop (all 2008). The inclusion of Dostoevsky in this line-up demonstrates that Isherwood's argument is not simply about theatre's capacity, or incapacity, to stage the modernist novel but about the transposition of prose literature to performance in principle. Isherwood identifies several problems he considers inherent in the process of transfer, hinging on the fundamentally unlike operation of each medium. The first is to do with the expansive nature of literary form, a scope and scale that must of necessity be compressed in adaptation: that compression means reduction, not just in length or number of characters, but of conceptual significance, since the necessity of cutting down leads theatre-makers to emphasize narrative – plot, incident, activity – rather than what the narrative stands for: its weight and import, both within the bounds of the fiction, and in our processing of this. This perceived problem of conceptual reduction is exacerbated by another casualty of the process, regarded as the inevitable corollary of translation into theatre: the removal of the literary author's 'shaping consciousness', the singular vision which frames and makes sense even of narratives that, like Murakami's, are intended to be dreamlike and disorientating. Drama's necessary attention to action means de-emphasizing or sacrificing this narratorial perspective; further, the collaborative nature of theatrical creation brings in a host of other 'authors' and the consequent effect of dilution or, alternatively, fragmentation (without Murakami's overarching voice, the disjointed events staged in *Kafka on the Shore* seemed to Isherwood 'arbitrary' and thus 'impenetrable'). The 'shaping consciousness', conveyed here as vital to an authentic and informed reception of the text, is beyond the boundaries of what adaptation can achieve because in the end, it is only accessible to us through reading:

> Reading is an inward, intimate experience, a quiet communion between one imagination and another. The reader is the author's active collaborator. Words are just signifiers after all. The images and experiences they evoke are brought into being in the mind of the reader. Books happen inside us; theatre happens to us. The difference may be subtle – both can of course move us in similar ways – but it is crucial.[43]

For Isherwood, theatre's attempts to stage prose literature almost invariably fall down for these reasons: the inevitability of reduction, the emphasis on exteriorities and corresponding diminution of significance, the substitution of multiple perspectives for the author's singular vision, the significantly different affective and conceptual structures of book-reading and performance-watching. The arguments are, of course, not his alone; press reviews of stage adaptations regularly reflect such concerns, often invoking them at the start and end of commentaries as an implicit perceptual frame.

Thus Michael Billington's review of Simon Reade's 2013 *Pride and Prejudice* at the 'novel-hungry venue' Regent's Park begins by regretfully noting the loss of the author's 'persistent, ironic voice', and concludes that even a well-staged adaptation 'inevitably offers diluted Austen'; the same critic's review of the Bristol Old Vic's *Jane Eyre* (2015) opens with the assertion that 'All adaptations of classic novels sacrifice gradations of time and the authorial voice', and that this particular production, although 'full of wit, resource and invention', gives a 'headlong rush' through the novel that conveys 'theatrical skill rather than the moving accumulation of detail you get in great fiction'.[44] A review by Charles Spencer, discussing *The Portrait of a Lady* at Bath's Theatre Royal (2008), similarly invokes the inevitable superiority of the source: 'Without James's narrative voice, the piece often seems like Jane Austen without the wit, or a Merchant Ivory film without the scenic locations'; in this particular instance, the stage adaptation is ultimately dismissed for reducing James's novel into 'dramatised historic chick-lit'.[45] It is not only reviewers who voice such perspectives, but sometimes authors too. The novelist Milan Kundera described stage adaptations as 'nothing more than a kind of *Reader's Digest*', a process of reduction that deprives the original 'not only of charm but also of sense'; he goes further, asserting that 'if the sense of a novel survives rewriting, that indirectly proves its mediocrity'.[46] Whether subtly judgemental or actively damning, such commentaries demonstrate the ways in which the critical reception of adaptations promulgates a familiar discourse of loss, lack and 'sacrifice' which frequently drowns out less conservative perspectives and, of necessity, sets the new work at a disadvantage.

The 'problems' often associated with theatrical adaptations that I describe here might be refuted on the basis that the underlying premises are false; the claims could be undermined by the introduction of specific examples testifying to the contrary; it could also be countered that if adaptations do 'reduce' novels, some are actively improved by that treatment. Alternatively, we could take the view that these criticisms do have some substance and might indeed have a bearing on theatrical adaptation at the levels of creative process, performance and spectator reception. Given how frequently such complaints resurface in discussions about adaptation from verbal to visual dramatic form, I suggest it is most productive to examine each concern seriously: in doing so, we can ask not simply whether claims of incompatibility are justly founded, but if, should they prove to be so, those differences must in practice be obstacles.

Adaptations are reductive

It seems initially reasonable to suppose that in the course of turning a substantial novel into a theatre production of, say, two to three hours, much would have to be excised: the plot simplified, 'minor' characters removed, the fictional timeframe more concisely focused. In his manual *Page to Stage: The Craft of Adaptation*, Vincent Murphy reinforces the point that 'producing pressures force most new scripts to stay under two hours running time, with a small cast that includes a local or national celebrity if the show hopes to run more than five weeks' and that adaptations 'tend to follow the current model of scripted plays'.[47] There is a kind of violence implied by such a process, in which the literary body is ruthlessly cut down to allow what remains to fit into the mould of a play. It would be possible to point to instances of this almost surgical approach to adaptation; however, reflective and further-reaching examination of theatre practice reveals alternative and more imaginative relationships with source texts that collectively belie this assumption about how adaptation works (indeed Murphy, a professional playwright, is keen to show how often, and how successfully, theatre breaks the 'rules'). A particularly vivid counterexample is represented by Elevator Repair Service's *Gatz* (explored further in Chapter 2), a production in which the whole of Fitzgerald's novel is read aloud on stage; this resulted in a running time of seven hours or more, and thus extraordinarily heavy demands on audience as well as performers. The bold strategy that *Gatz* adopts evolved through the company's creative and interrogative engagement with the book: the question for the makers became not, how to reshape the source material to meet the requirements of the 'target' medium, but how the latter might alter its own shape to accommodate what it was about *The Great Gatsby* the artists considered most important. This example, an extreme case in point, demonstrates that adaptation in the theatre *need* not reduce, by cuts, the text appropriated. The decision to retain and speak all, or almost all, of a text will remain the exception in stage adaptation but it is not unique; Forced Entertainment's *The Notebook*, considered later in this chapter, as well as Brook's *The Grand Inquisitor* (the single relatively successful example of stage adaptation Isherwood acknowledges), likewise demand that their audiences experience performance unfolding at the pace of prose, with the pleasures and attendant frustrations that accompany this.

Where theatre productions refuse to make literary sources more 'manageable' – or where resistance to such modification is rendered overt, and substantially shapes audience experience – they illustrate the tensions inherent in adaptation per se. Further, they invite us to reflect precisely on questions of reduction, absence and erasure. This must be so, no matter how 'unabridged' the treatment. Acknowledging that every word of *The Great Gatsby* has been retained, for example, is not the same as *having* all of it, or even of reading the novel oneself; the time-bound nature of theatre, although in this case unusually stretched, conveys rather the feeling that Fitzgerald's book is running through our collective hands like so much sand. The company understands this, meaning that this adaptation is as much, or more, about the attempt to capture the whole work as the effective achievement of this in practice. This, in turn, is not a reflection of theatre's particular constraints, but rather of the limits in any effort of apprehension, including that of the lone reader: each encounter with the literary source – solitary or communal, reading or watching, skimming the text or following it word by word – must always be incomplete in the meanings it yields. From this perspective, all readings, including the readings that adaptations provide, may fairly be termed 'reductive'. But whereas Isherwood elides two senses of this word, suggesting that in the process of reducing (cutting down) its material physically, adaptation inevitably reduces (lessens) the original's conceptual force, post-structuralism reminds us that the import and meanings of a text always exceed any reading of it; from this perspective, the reductions imposed by theatre in adaptation need not be considered in principle as more partial, problematic or treacherous than those of individual readers.

Yet if theatrical adaptation is a kind of reading, it is plainly of a different order to the 'quiet communion' Isherwood describes. His terms notably idealize the relations of reader with author, in a conjured scene within which meanings flow, untrammelled, through the channel of the book. Nonetheless, the difference in context of consumption is materially important: the impression formed of a book in the reading process is typically allowed to remain unvoiced, subjective and indeterminate; by contrast, an adaptive reading of the same work in the theatre is articulated, objectively present and, to an extent, fixed. It might be more accurate, therefore, to regard adaptation as closer to critical interpretation than private reading, since adaptation, like criticism, re-frames the text, proposing that we read it not neutrally, but in a specific light. In seeking to persuade audiences of the legitimacy and value of this proposal, certain features of the work appropriated – speeches, figures, images or actions – are subjected to particular scrutiny, or 'imaginative flights', while other elements recede or disappear.[48] In one way, then, adaptation can prompt impassioned and sometimes hostile responses, not necessarily because of *how* a source is read, but *that* it is read at all. In the theatre, or on screen, the decisions taken in the process of shaping the adaptation's *mise-en-scène* are starkly, solidly exposed to the audience: the impact of this exposure might be received as welcome illumination, but may equally be resisted as implicitly foreclosing alternative interpretations and relationships.

The evident plurality and proliferation of adaptations in general should in itself signal the contingency of any theatrical reading; titular claims to be definitive ('the Real True Story') are typically tongue-in-cheek. But in addition, individual productions may take steps to declare their adaptation's partiality and unfixity. This could be said of Mitchell's *Waves*, which by displaying the labour and temporality of meaning-making drew attention, as Brantley observed, to the felt inadequacies of expressive language (including, here, those of the theatre itself in re-articulating Woolf's novel). Something similar is manifest by Stan's Cafe, although to a very different aesthetic end, in the company's handling of Robert Burton's unwieldy, category-defying compendium *The Anatomy of Melancholy* (see Chapter 2). Here, the actors visibly grapple on stage with the task of adaptation, a fair reflection – albeit reframed performatively – of the challenges the project presented in the rehearsal room. These actors appear to change their minds in the moment about what elements to keep, what to discard, what to censor (as not 'fit'); this kind of live editing highlights the tensions in adaptation's necessary selectivity, while simultaneously mimicking the fluid status of a book which was itself repeatedly revised, extended and reissued. Exposing the contingent status of any text, perhaps especially those most solidly canonical, can also be comically liberating. In *Mr Darcy Loses the Plot* (2016), devised and performed by the two-woman theatre company Lip Service, a frustrated Darcy breaks free of Austen's half-finished *Pride and Prejudice* to wander haplessly through Du Maurier's *Rebecca*, Gaskell's *Mary Barton* and even Beatrix Potter's *The Tale of Jemima Puddleduck*. Something more than a mashup, an adaptation of this kind also teasingly underlines the precarity of text and writing; Darcy tries out other narrative possibilities at a point when 'his' novel is still incomplete. Beyond interweaving Austen with other authors, the production also references other adaptations: frequent mention of Darcy's prowess at 'outdoor swimming' gestures knowingly to Colin Firth's performance in this role (BBC, 1995) and conveys how adaptations actively restructure our relationship with 'the original'.

An alternative and radically different strategy that reveals the contingency of adaptation's readings is made possible in the use of interactive and immersive performance forms. The kind of audience experience offered by a Punchdrunk production, for example, allows the spectator-participant considerable freedom to forge her own route – spatial and physical, but consequently also interpretive – through the 'work'. In Chapter 4, I consider in detail the operation and implications of this structure with reference to *The Masque of the Red Death*, the company's adaptation of several short stories by Edgar Allan Poe. In such a production, the spectator is well aware that for all she sees, as much or more is 'missed'; in this way, the immersive form conveys the superabundant potential of the text(s) while also disclosing the manifest gaps in any and every reading. The sensory fullness and sheer scale of Punchdrunk's work also point to qualities inherent in theatrical production which imply a potent counterclaim against charges of adaptation's 'reductions'. For if adaptation reduces, it also expands: in the immersive example, that expansion is literalized in the form of architectural spread (we range over many floors, in multiple rooms), but also revealed as an increase in density; 'information' filters through to all the senses, meaning that theatre can say many things at once in a way quite unlike the double-edged significance of a written line. A show like *The Masque of the Red Death* makes the opportunities of multi-layered communication especially palpable, but more fundamentally it accentuates the ways in which theatre, like music, is an art form inherently able to strike complex chords as well as single notes. The most minimalist and least overtly 'theatrical' adaptation – for example, Brook's *The Grand Inquisitor*, described (favourably) by Isherwood as a 'ritual staging of a moral essay' – likewise accrues supplementary meanings by virtue of physical and situated embodiment. The issue remains, however, whether theatre's medial expansion functions to support, or to inhibit, spectator 'reading', engagement and experience.

Adaptations are superficial

To ask whether adaptations of prose into drama are 'superficial' is not to suggest that their purposes are trivial, or their results set to be banal. Rather, drama and theatre *can* be considered superficial to the extent that the medium necessarily turns our attention towards surfaces. In adaptation, the process of realizing the *mise-en-scène* involves decisions about what to make visible and audible; and if everything that is staged accrues significance, it is equally true that audiences only access that significance through what is done and shown. This returns us to Bluestone's argument, and Leitch's 'fallacy', about concept versus percept: in other words, about the dissimilarity – and potentially, the discordant clash – between ideas and thoughts on the one hand, and impressions received through the senses on the other. Here, as with the charge that adaptations are 'reductive', the notion of 'surface' comes profoundly loaded. Discussing nineteenth-century stagings of Sir Walter Scott's novels, Philip Cox demonstrates how contemporary reviewers (and Scott himself) regarded dramatization as a concession to 'the comprehension of a vulgar audience', a process which effectively allowed *Ivanhoe*, for example, to filter down from 'high' to 'low' culture.[49] In this period, Cox argues, the mechanics of drama, acting and the stage were critically invoked in order to promote, by contrast, the assumed superiority of prose and poetry:

> the fact that the theatre is dependent upon what could be termed more 'superficial' modes of representation goes some way to account for its decline in status as a 'serious' art form at a time when the construction of inner truth and depth appeared increasingly to bestow artistic worth.[50]

However, if theatre reveals the appropriated text(s) by means of visual, aural, embodied and scenic surface, the evidence of adaptation in practice demonstrates that this need not imply a diminished – or even a delayed – relationship with conceptual 'depth'. Adaptation studies has wrestled extensively with the nature of these medial distinctions, their effects on readers and/or audiences, and the value judgements frequently attached to them. In that debate, proponents of dramatic adaptation have had to deal with double claims of prose literature's advantage. First, it is regularly argued that since literary form can express interiority, thereby exposing the contradictions and complexities of character motivation individually, relationally and in context, it can communicate the underlying significance of action and experience. This capacity of prose fiction is taken to mean that a novel (for instance) is able to convey a more insightful perspective on its own internal action than can pertain once that content has been exteriorized as drama – since in the new medium, it is assumed, it is not possible to retain this privileged vision without recourse to 'literary' devices, such as voiceovers, or onstage narration.

Second, while prose literature is considered to offer readers *more* meaning, it is also conversely distinguished for its ability to say *less*: to be more selective, and leave more interpretive possibilities open, than dramatic embodiment can allow. Adaptations risk erasing or overwriting the conscious absences of literary language, as Jonathan Miller explains: 'In some mysterious way, the description of a scene [in a novel] appears to be fully occupied by what it describes and never appears to lack what it fails to mention.' By contrast, when directing film adaptations, Miller observed that each frame became immediately and 'inescapably loaded with unnecessary detail'.[51] It follows from this assumption that adaptation into visual form must rub up, sometimes problematically, against the preconceptions of reader-audiences. In a provocative piece for the *Guardian* about the BBC's acclaimed 2005 dramatization of *Bleak House*, the novelist Philip Hensher announced that he had refused to watch it simply because 'one doesn't want it in one's head'; the overlaid images of specific contemporary actors onto Dickens's characters would subtly corrupt the novel for him, interposing 'another imagination [...] between the author's and the reader's: one nothing to do with either'.[52] This reading encounter, like Isherwood's 'quiet communion', may seem suspiciously smooth: is the flow of ideas and imagery otherwise untroubled by the impositions of culture, education and history? Nonetheless, the complaint that adaptation brings in a quantity of sensory impressions that have 'nothing to do' with a book is fairly founded: the difficulty is less that dramatization imposes illustrations that clash with pre-imagined versions, but that it fills in spaces that the reader did not experience as a gap.

These two different, yet interrelated perceptions of dramatic adaptation's representational limits – that drama lacks prose literature's ability to communicate interiority, and simultaneously that the process of translation into visual performance (on screen or stage) emphasizes exteriority beyond that which a *reading* audience wants or needs to know – describe a perverse and problematic double bind. Linda Hutcheon insists that commonly claimed distinctions between 'showing' and 'telling' are simply clichés: defending film, she draws attention to the capacity of the close-up to create psychological intimacy and express 'powerful and revealing interior ironies'; referencing the stage, she proposes that opera effectively conveys thoughts and internal conflicts given the accepted convention that 'characters on stage do not hear the music they sing'.[53] Robert Stam considers that recurrent insistence on medial dissimilarity manifests a kind of 'iconophobia', in his words a 'deeply rooted prejudice against the visual arts'.[54] Yet this attitude does not only degrade and distort the visual medium; at the same time, the perspective on how prose literature works is also reductively conveyed. Readers do not *only* understand character and thought by being informed of this through the narration, but also by inferring information from, precisely, 'exterior' clues. Nonetheless, for Isherwood's *Waves*, or Hensher's *Bleak House*, dramatic embodiment constitutes an active barrier to meaning; the spectator or viewer who values the book 'as literature' must somehow shut this out, or else pierce *through* the scenic display in order to access the 'real' meanings concealed behind it. This in turn evidently reinforces the anti-adaptation stance of both, in which enactment is seen only as an unsatisfactory and inadequate means of 'getting at' great literature, which can only ever be properly appreciated by reading. This perspective problematically implies a narrow motivation for adaptation in the first place – that it seeks to serve the source in some way accurately or 'faithfully' – and at the same time radically devalues the expressive capabilities of the new medium.

Against the position that regards the exteriority of drama as a source of unwarranted and unhelpfully digressive signification, I propose the counterargument that theatre's inherent preoccupation with surface can be positively exploited in adaptation, not merely in the sense of bringing 'to life' the physical characteristics of a fictional environment, but precisely to address the tension between interior and exterior realities and to problematize the distinction between them. The flexible representational conventions of physical theatre, for instance, allow productions to treat actors as objects and objects as actors; making the mutability of performance elements prominent in this way correspondingly implies that anything and anyone on stage can become eloquent. This quality of latent fluency is powerfully exploited in Complicite's *The Street of Crocodiles*, discussed further in Chapter 2. In this adaptation, the quantities of books strewn in the space and manipulated by the cast are not only props which reference the protagonist's mode of employ under the Nazis ('sorting' books for saving, or burning); further, books are used by the company to shape an evocative physical language that accentuates their sensory qualities, their weight or fragility while evoking their potency as channels for knowledge and memory. The complex and layered texture of this production does not invite spectators to seek out underlying meanings that are masked by the live 'display'. Instead, the close attention of actors to material surfaces is itself made fascinating, signalling that, as with Proust's madeleine, the wealth of meaning and the qualities of surface are understood as interdependent and inseparable. It is not easy, the audience recognizes, for 'things' to release their significance, nor for adaptation in the theatre to transmit the potency of meanings contained in its appropriated texts; as discussed in Chapter 2, intermedial adaptation must engage in a kind of *ekphrasis*, whereby one order of expression is voiced – with self-conscious inadequacy – through the medium of another. Opportunities for reflection on the interrelationship of form and content, exterior and interior, arise from the combination in Complicite's production of eloquent physicality and a great deal of quiet (yet not empty) space. The audience is given glimpses of Schulz's fictional world, more than they are told about it; the fragmented quality of the dialogue, evident in the published play script, shows that verbal text is a thread running through the production, and not its driver. This highlights the way that *Street of Crocodiles* allows its audience 'thinking time' – and indeed, this capacity is one which theatre in general is well able to exploit. For while stage adaptations do not usually voice the unspoken thoughts of characters directly – although they might elect to do so, as *Gatz* does – drama inevitably and valuably includes gaps and spaces in which we may infer such thoughts, and think our own.

Conversely, the presupposition that prose literature, or any artistic medium, can 'go inside' the mind in the first place may itself be resisted. A modernist text like Woolf's *The Waves* might convey stream of consciousness, but in the process does not make those workings transparent or graspable. Likewise, the 'thought process' and actions of the protagonist in Kafka's *The Trial* become as obscure and puzzling for the reader as the judicial system appears to K himself. How should, or could, thought of this order be dramatized? The internally conflicting multimedia and live systems in *Waves* suggest one way to convey the instabilities and illogicalities of consciousness; in Retz's immersive adaptation of Kafka (discussed in Chapter 4), the necessity to 'make sense' of the escalating, nightmarish action is largely displaced from the dramatic character onto the spectator-participant. A more recent novel, Agota Kristof's *The Notebook* (1986), works rather differently on the reader in its interplay of exteriority and interiority. Kristof was obliged to leave her native Hungary in 1956, when Soviet-imposed government policies became forcibly repressive, and that experience of exile and disenfranchisement is reflected in *The Notebook*. The novel is presented as a fictional record of the lives of identical twin brothers sent away from home to live with their grandmother in a remote village towards the end of the Second World War and through the early years of communism. The most striking feature of the book – aside from its brutally harsh depiction of human behaviour under an oppressive regime – is that it is told entirely in the first person plural, meaning that for the reader the children, Claus and Lucas, are literally as well as figuratively inseparable. Their record of events, the boys decide, will contain no opinion, speculation or imagination – '[w]ords that define feelings are very vague' – but only 'what is, what we see, what we hear, what we do', in other words the 'faithful description of facts'.[55] This rule results in a peculiarly naïve, uncannily doubled voice which leads the reader into horrifying territory – abuse, perversion, violence, degradation – without judgement and without emotion. The boys train themselves to handle pain and punishment, since they must master this in order to survive. Their actions are always rational: they set explosives that horribly disfigure the priest's housekeeper, having recorded in the notebook her mockery of a starving prisoner within a 'human herd' marched through the village by officers; they slit the throat and torch the house of an elderly neighbour, at her request.

Forced Entertainment's adaptation of *The Notebook* (2014) – highly uncharacteristic for the company, as an adaptation of a literary text – finds ways to mirror in theatrical terms this seemingly translucent narrative surface. Two male actors wear identical suits, jumpers, spectacles and boots; on an otherwise empty stage, they read two hours' worth of text aloud from matching exercise books, voices synchronized and articulation passionless. They do not mimic childish mannerisms, but appear as adult men relating an account of wartime chaos through the words of fictional children (a story that also, or alternatively, suggests fragmentation of the self through trauma). The alienated delivery makes it possible for spectators to tolerate, and occasionally find humour in, accounts of atrocities which, expressed emotively, would be simply repugnant; at the same time, that aesthetic removal serves as a permanent reminder that – 'truthful' record or not – we cannot gain access to the children's minds. Our guides, in the book and onstage, purport to tell the world as it is, yet remain themselves inscrutable, and in this way, the presentational form adopted by the adaptation re-produces the self-conscious exteriority of Kristof's prose, as well as its disturbing effects. If theatre relies on outward display, that reliance precisely serves this adaptation: given only 'what is, what we see, what we hear, what we do', the burden of interpretation and moral judgement rests squarely on the audience's shoulders.

Adaptations misrepresent

Adaptations inevitably 'misrepresent' their appropriated sources as they present them, since the process of adaptation involves change, distortion and artifice. Of course they will do so; as Leitch states, 'whatever their faults, the source texts will always be better at being themselves'.[56] Nonetheless, even though adaptations *must* deviate from their sources, notions of misrepresentation have powerfully influenced scholarly and popular adaptation discourse, crystallized in the notion of 'fidelity'. Within adaptation studies, the concept of fidelity towards the textual source has radically shifted, in critical debate, from a position which broadly assumed that faithful re-creation was the desired end, towards critical deconstruction of what fidelity could possibly constitute in practice (especially when this involves a shift of artistic medium), to still more fundamental contestation of the value in introducing such terms in the first place. Throughout this trajectory, scholars have noted with concern the moralistic language that has marked this debate, a tendency Brian McFarlane highlights here: 'Fidelity is obviously very desirable in marriage; but with [...] adaptations, I suspect playing around is more effective.'[57] Seeking partly to counter insistence on fidelity, comparative theorists in film studies such as Geoffrey Wagner and Dudley Andrew developed new critical models which validated a diversity of relationships between adaptation and source. Such models – Wagner's *transposition*, *commentary* and *analogy* (1975), and Andrew's *borrowing*, *intersection* and *transformation* (1980) – served broadly to demonstrate and justify adaptations being quite like, less like and markedly unlike their sources. By granting adaptation license for creative invention, comparative models troubled the principle of fidelity to some extent. Wagner argued that of these adaptive relationships, the closest to the source (transposition) was in principle *least* valuable, lacking independent artistic integrity, and in practice 'typically puerile'.[58] Andrew claimed similarly that while the skeleton of a literary work could broadly be retained in the new medium (here, film), its more vital 'spirit' would not necessarily stay attached; in the majority of cases, he suggests, adaptations are more usefully examined for their 'fertility not their fidelity'.[59] However, despite the laudable aim of moving evaluation beyond fidelity, comparative theory remained limiting insofar as the literary text still structured the analysis. As Sarah Cardwell observes, comparative interpretation stumbles precisely where the differences between adaptation and source are most marked; the more radical the divergence, the less meaningful comparison becomes.[60] Additionally, assessment of closeness to and difference from a source is even more problematic when translation moves from one medial context into another; for as adaptation's objectors have always been at pains to point out, visual imagery, spoken dialogue or music are 'not the same' as narrative prose.

Repeated efforts to erase considerations of fidelity from adaptation discourse have not been successful, however, even though this concept has been thoroughly worked over, deconstructed and re-framed. Laera brusquely resists the issue in her editorial – 'Faithful or unfaithful to what, anyway?' – but this does not prevent questions about fidelity resurfacing in several of the book's interviews.[61] In other publications, the very titles of essays such as J. D. Connor's 'The Persistence of Fidelity: Adaptation Theory Today' (2007) and Casie Hermansson's 'Flogging Fidelity: In Defense of the (Un)Dead Horse' (2015) demonstrate the continuing force of this concept, although in quite different ways. Connor complains that fidelity's persistence is critically stifling, not because it is used as a criterion to assert value, but because in practice 'questions of quality' are avoided by overattention to similarity.[62] By contrast, while critical of the 'now-anachronistic' strategy whereby fidelity is set up as a ritual 'straw man', Hermansson argues that the concept is still fruitful, above all because adaptations themselves regularly invoke it.[63] Both perspectives have weight, as does Christine Geraghty's straightforwardly valuable reminder that '[f]aithfulness matters if it matters to the viewer'.[64] In other words, analysis has progressed well beyond the assumption that an adaptation *ought* to resemble its source, and even that it *can* do so, in any meaningful sense; nonetheless, so long as artists and audiences are passionately invested in the material treated, questions about semblance, commitment and authenticity remain pertinent, if still contestable.

In the theatre, as in the cinema, the critical response to adaptations demonstrates the persistence of such concerns, although not in the form of knee-jerk demands for 'fidelity'. We can see this, for example, in reviews of the National Theatre's 2012 production of *The Curious Incident of the Dog in the Night Time* (2003), adapted by Simon Stephens. Mark Haddon's award-winning detective novel, distinctive above all for the voice of its protagonist-narrator (a teenage boy with Asperger's syndrome), was acclaimed for its humane and humorous representation of autism, as well as for its intricate plotting and skilful handling of 'difficult' themes. Given the nature and reputation of the source, it is not surprising that reviews of the stage production, across a two-year period, almost invariably reflect on its proximity to the novel, seeking in this not imitation, but certainly, consideration. Charles Spencer in the *Telegraph* draws on the traditional discourse of fidelity, observing that the production 'manages to be theatrical while remaining entirely true to the spirit of the book'.[65] Susannah Clapp in the *Guardian* steps further back from this position, to comment that the central actor (at this stage of the run, Luke Treadaway) 'takes us into the real achievement of the book and play'.[66] Also in the *Guardian*, a year later, Alexis Soloski considers that the production effectively countered elements of tweeness in the source, noting with approval that 'Stephens and director Marianne Elliott handle the novel with care, and a little distrust'.[67] Stephens himself, interviewed in 2012, emphasized that 'what was important to [him] was the certain fidelity and loyalty to the original writer's vision'; his own contribution was 'entirely to do with structure and with the design of the language rather than the invention of the language', which, Stephens notes, remained '85 per cent' Haddon's.[68] What emerges from such commentary, in this example, is the perceived obligation not to imitate the original but to establish what qualities of the novel mattered most to author and readers, and rearticulate this dimension respectfully in the production; Stephens's words imply that not to do so would constitute *bad* faith.

However, sometimes adaptations display their deviation from the source in significant and advertised ways. One of the inherent limitations of fidelity as a criterion is that it disallows criticism of the original; yet even source texts that are profoundly admired by their adapters may contain elements that are troubling or outright objectionable. Such aspects may be radically rewritten or can be more subtly problematized for a new audience, and theatre is a forum with rich potential to exploit what Linda Hutcheon calls adaptation's pleasurable 'palimpsestuousness': meaning, the ability of audiences to relish the familiar, simultaneously with the changed.[69] As observed previously, the 'problem' of reduction in dramatic adaptation may be countered by the opportunities that come with formal expansion. In performance, articulation of meaning may become palimpsestic precisely by drawing on, and juxtaposing, different significatory systems in the same moment. In Chapter 3, I discuss how this layering operates in Kneehigh Theatre's 2010 *The Red Shoes*, adapted from Hans Christian Andersen. In this production, even before an ending which actively resists the judgemental conclusions of the original, the visual aesthetic – the performers' shaved heads and almost robotic dancing – and the Klezmer-influenced live music critically reposition the story told; the *mise-en-scène* itself urges that we (re)read this fairy tale about difference and punishment in a larger, historically attuned, 'real world' context. Kneehigh's production is thus not 'faithful' to its source, but surely does not 'betray' this either. Patrice Pavis offers a helpful perspective on directorial positions that may be applied here. For Pavis, artists staging new productions of pre-existent texts do not *either* surrender to what (they believe) that text 'means to say', *or* substitute their own vision in its place; more usually, he observes, experiments in contemporary practice

> do not take any certainty as a starting point, but [...] invent a framework of enunciation, and a tuning and adjustment which will bring out unexpected solutions from the text, which only acting and staging can invent.[70]

Pavis's words describe an attentive, dialogic interrelationship between new 'authors' and textual source. Whether the material is play or prose, its re-animation through theatre – a process which exposes 'solutions' that may only be discoverable in this live context – suggests the vital role played by adaptations in helping to negotiate the dynamics and dependencies of past and present, old words/worlds and new.

Theatre's negotiation of textual interdependence may be made deliberately visible in adaptation and can be a means of structuring the perspective and experience of audiences. Hof van Eede's *Where the World is Going, That's Where We are Going* (2012), examined in Chapter 5, is avowedly so preoccupied by the necessity to do justice to the source text – Diderot's *Jacques the Fatalist* (1796) – that the two actors remain frozen, postdramatically, on the brink of their task: in consequence, the audience must derive entertainment not from an adaptation 'proper', but from the performers' anxieties, prevarications and digressions. In the same chapter, I consider Peter Jaeger's *A Field Guide to Lost Things* (2015), a work of conceptual, poetic writing also performed by the author as a durational reading. Jaeger's *Field Guide* is a highly selective, systematized re-reading of Marcel Proust's *Swann's Way* (1913), which adopts as a tenet Walter Benjamin's claim that Proust made 'the fidelity of things' his central subject. The durational form used by Jaeger to present his *Field Guide* also reflects in performance the demands notoriously made on the reader by Proust's linguistic style; in source and adaptation alike, therefore, fidelity in a different sense is tried as readers and audiences are required to adjust their attention to slow-paced textual rhythms, in submission to the impress of the form itself. In these two examples, Hof van Eede and Jaeger are similarly preoccupied by the appropriated source and acknowledge a duty towards this which is undertaken with an overt sense of labour – although the results differ markedly, not least in that all Jaeger's words are Proust's (albeit in translation) while virtually none of Hof Van Eede's are Diderot's. Both works provoke questions about originality and imitation, proximity and distance, depth and banality, 'good' and 'bad' writing. Adaptation in performance does not just prompt such questions, it enables them: the project of adaptation cannot avoid engaging in such debates, but can also, as here, draw energy from them.

This diverse range of examples from theatre practice, and the larger questions pursued in this chapter, expose adaptation in two major senses of the term: first, adaptation as product, the displayed outcomes of the intermedial encounter; and second, adaptation as process, the movements and workings of the encounter itself. Adaptation practices in the contemporary theatre do not, I suggest, remotely resemble the rapacious, deadly 'attack' on literature by film that Woolf so graphically (not to say snobbishly) depicted. Theatre productions of the kind I describe – the outcomes of the adaptation process – are hardly skeletal frames, or blood-sucked carcasses; nor, as we have seen from press reviews, do adaptations lazily ride on the back of a source's literary reputation, even if they wished to do so. Rather, theatre-makers and the adaptations made appear ceaselessly fascinated by their source texts; respectful of them, although rarely deferential; and sensitive to distance and dislocation. The process of adaptation is not one of 'making fit', in the sense of chopping, reducing and squashing literary prose into a rigid dramatic mould: instead, 'fitness' becomes a relationship to be negotiated, not only within making and rehearsal, but often exposed to the audience during the performance itself. In the creative meeting between text(s) and makers, the multiple authorial voices are as likely to find themselves in competition as in harmony, and may do nothing to resolve or disguise this; however, at least some amongst adaptation's plurality of 'readers' – not least, from within the audience – will inevitably regard the result as a form of betrayal, joining the outraged howl of Jacques's Master (according to Kundera): 'Death to people who rewrite what's already been written! I'd like to see them skewered and barbecued. They should have their balls and their ears cut off…'[71] In the next chapter, I explore the meanings books seem to release to readers, theatre-makers and audiences, as well as the potency in meanings withheld, or otherwise ungraspable; the material allure of books, and the potential of this quality in performance; and the tensions between private and public theatrical 'readings'.

2

Performing Books

This chapter considers what the dimension of performance, of liveness, can bring to a book: further, it asks what a book – and beyond this, *bookness* – might bring to performance. I examine distinctive ways in which books can 'matter' in adaptation practice as well as how elements of textual materiality can inform performance itself. Through this, I argue that attention to the form of books as well as to their content can invigorate not just theatrical practice but also adaptation in theory, since a more layered analysis of books and bookness in adaptation in turn extends understanding of the ways in which different orders of text speak to and with one another. The chapter considers five performances in detail: *The Quiet Volume*, by Tim Etchells and Ant Hampton, and *Time Has Fallen Asleep in the Afternoon Sunshine*, by Mette Evardsen, both intimate events designed for a library setting; Complicite's *Street of Crocodiles*, the company's acclaimed and vividly theatrical interpretation of the fiction and life of Bruno Schulz; *Gatz*, by the American theatre group Elevator Repair Service, an award-winning seven-hour production in which F. Scott Fitzgerald's *The Great Gatsby* is read aloud on stage in its entirety; and finally, *The Anatomy of Melancholy*, adapted by Birmingham-based Stan's Cafe from Robert Burton's seventeenth-century medical compendium. These five performance pieces, vastly different in character, testify to the potency not simply of narratives but of books themselves as talismanic yet vulnerable objects, and celebrate the capacity of readers to make any text meaningfully their own. Additionally, as I discuss, the explicit articulation of 'bookness' in all of these productions serves to underline the distinctive qualities of each medium in play – literary work on the one hand, and theatrical performance on the other – and to expose and exploit points of friction between them.

The matter of books

The Quiet Volume is an audio installation designed for libraries, collaboratively created by British artists Tim Etchells and Ant Hampton. Since its inception in 2010, the piece has been presented at around fifty libraries across the world. *The Quiet Volume* is described by its makers as 'autoteatro', meaning a work generated by the audience themselves, following a series of instructions or cues, and performed to one another. Here, participants attend (and perform) as a pair: often, therefore, together with a friend. With headphones on and audio synchronized, they enter the reading room and sit at a reserved table, on which lie a red and yellow notebook and two matched piles of novels: José Saramago's *Blindness*; Agota Kristof's *The Notebook*; and Kazuo Ishiguro's *When We Were Orphans*. A voice whispers in the ear, encouraging covert observation of the library's 'real' users and attention to the room's various sounds: instructed to do so, each opens the notebook on the table and – when the whisper is abruptly broken off, and the written word takes over – 'you find yourself reading after all'.[1] This moment, several minutes into a piece that runs for just under an hour, brings into sharp focus the central preoccupation of *The Quiet Volume*: what happens on the page, and what happens in the heads of readers. The whisper is unobtrusive, a voice barely there, the speaker's gender and age uncertain: yet when a line *heard* must suddenly be continued in reading's 'silence' the impact of its loss is joltingly registered. Throughout, the piece plays games with its performer-participants, troubling their progress through the notebook with unexpected white spaces (and no reassuring announcements that 'this page is intentionally left blank'), badly behaved fonts and abruptly fading print.[2] The audio track and notebook instructions together explore the idea of reading, building the activity's anticipation. While reading is often described as if it were a disembodied, dreamlike absorption, here the physicality of the act is emphasized. The hands that are 'busy everywhere' in the library, turning pages and tapping keyboards, are also perpetually 'massaging temples, touching scalps, rubbing eyes, fiddling with ears, noses, pencils'. Hands have bodies, and bodies have lives:

> Hands more used to writing than reading, with chalk, on blackboards, endlessly. Hands feared by others. Cupped hands. Frozen hands. Confused hands. Hands that moved together with a shrill voice. All those hands held in the air. Hands that held other hands. Hands that held books all their life until one day they started shaking. Hands shaking other hands, firmly. Nicotine-stained hands. Hands in rubber gloves. Skilled hands. Wet hands, with rippled fingers. Small, soft hands with fingers like sausages. Hands that protected, or protested.

The participants study their own hands, the map of skin against the grain of the page, their partner's hand mirroring the action to their right or left across the desk: 'Now press your palm down into the paper as if you were, somehow, trying to enter the page, or trying to pass through it into some other space. Keep pressing down [...] until the skin changes colour, until your hand perhaps shakes a little.'[3] In this way, almost half of the performance time passes before touching the volumes that have waited, closed, on the desk. When these are finally opened, the act of reading has been established as acutely physical and hyper-sensory, echoed first of all in Saramago's narrative about a bizarre epidemic of blindness that hits the inhabitants of an unnamed city; but a few minutes in, the reader is pulled away and turned back towards the notebook, obliged to linger, fuzzily, on the 'dazzling white [...] snowfield' of an empty page. Such games continue with the other novels too. Kristof's is turned upside down, the alienating visual image used to stir memories of learning to read; later, the sentences on the page differ, subtly but disturbingly, from the words whispered ('Lucas takes a ~~bottle~~ carton of goat's milk and walks to the priest's house. The congealed food ~~stands on~~ lies all over the kitchen table').[4] From Ishiguro's fiction about war-torn Shanghai, the reader is pointed to another book, Gabriele Basilico's collection of photographed cityscapes, and asked to contemplate which rush of traffic might be Saramago's city, which devastated office buildings Ishiguro's, which rubble Kristof's. When finally the books are closed, the images faded and the headphones removed, the participants return to daily, unfiltered sound, and their own audible breathing. Instructed by the notebook, they pause for a moment, and then leave.

The Quiet Volume is clearly not an adaptation in the familiar sense, but it is a piece of theatre generated by and founded upon an encounter with books and reading. The work's punning, almost self-cancelling title draws attention to the potency of the book silently to contain or restrain a clamour of words, as well as to the peculiar character and fullness of the internal reading 'voice'. From the first moment, the page is exposed as a difficult space, but also a playful and generative one; as Ric Allsopp has put it, the page visibly and palpably becomes 'a surface on which the processes of representation can be assembled – not a *tabula rasa*, but a complex ground'.[5] Where Barthes's proposition that 'every text is an intertext' could seem too abstract or unconditional, here the structure of the autoteatro ensures that participants understand this claim materially and physically: the solidity of the book as object is undermined and made slippery; the words accumulated and distributed across its pages are displayed as contingent and uncertain. At one point, participants are asked to imagine an alternative kind of filing system in the library, for which individual drawers would contain every instance of a cut up word: a drawer for 'trees', 'knifes' or 'toenails', meaning that the one marked 'clouds' would contain factual clouds extracted from a pilot's manual alongside fictional ones 'from *Wuthering Heights*, beyond them a great confusion of clouds from Joseph Conrad, Chinua Achebe and Doris Lessing'.[6] In this way, the reader-participants are led to detach words from authors, to blur distinctions between fictional and factual, 'great literature' and pragmatic writing: to see language, in other words, as malleable and up-for-grabs. This work of pleasurable destabilizing is taken further through the way in which *The Quiet Volume* also probes the presupposition that reading is fundamentally a private experience, like Hensher's meeting of minds, or Isherwood's 'quiet communion'. By contrast, the participant here must negotiate the teases of the text, the companionable but non-identical engagement of their fellow reader, and the muted hubbub of the library: implicit or explicit, such interventions remind us that literature and reading do not exist within a sealed-off space but one marked by many kinds of disturbance. *The Quiet Volume* thus provocatively prepares the ground upon which we might begin thinking about theatrical adaptation, with texts shown as fluid and alterable, sound and image beginning to render words audible and visible, and individual readings subject to the pressure of other interpretations, and the interruptions of a wider world.

The peculiarly concentrated energies of the library are differently harnessed by the Norwegian live artist and dancer Mette Evardsen in *Time Has Fallen Asleep in the Afternoon Sunshine*, an 'intimate scenario for an audience of one', first performed in 2010 in Leuven, Belgium, and presented at Birmingham's Fierce Festival in 2012. At Evardsen's invitation, local volunteers had agreed to memorize a chapter or more of a book of their choosing. The event took place in Birmingham Central Library: visitors made a half-hour appointment with a work chosen from a list – a library of 'living books' – for a one-to-one recital of a single chapter. The piece was inspired by Ray Bradbury's *Fahrenheit 451* (1953), a book about the disappearance of books. Bradbury's science fiction novel imagines a dystopia in which literature is banned. When the narrative opens, most books have already been eradicated; any volumes discovered subsequently are seized and burned. Bradbury had learned that 451 degrees Fahrenheit is the temperature at which paper starts to burn: his title thus invokes the inflammatory qualities of texts and writing at the metaphorical and the literal level. In the novel, an underground community is dedicated to learning entire books by heart so they may be preserved for future generations. The theme of memorizing, of texts vitally 'contained' in minds and bodies, is appropriated by Evardsen in her performance piece. Bradbury's exiled book-lovers, self-described 'bums on the outside, libraries inside', explain themselves to the conflicted 'fireman' Montag:

> We're nothing more than dust-jackets for books, of no significance otherwise. […] Why, there's one town in Maryland, only twenty-seven people […], is the complete essays of a man named Bertrand Russell. Pick up that town, almost, and flip the pages, so many pages to a person. And when the war's over, some day, some year, the books can be written again, the people will be called in, one by one, to recite what they know and we'll set it up in type until another Dark Age, when we might have to do the whole damn thing over again.[7]

Fahrenheit 451 explores how books matter to us and how the effects of their absence may be registered. Bradbury's motif of legalized book-burning seemed at the time he was writing to hint at themes of state censorship, but the author insisted this was a misinterpretation; his overriding concern was the way in which the increasing popularity of television threatened to kill an interest in reading. Interviewed in 2007 on receiving the Pulitzer Prize (the first time the award had been made to a writer of science fiction), Bradbury reiterated his fears about the impact of television, with its pernicious stream of 'factoids': 'They stuff you with so much useless information you feel full.'[8] Engrossed in inane TV programmes, the majority of the population depicted in *Fahrenheit 451* has stopped asking questions about the world; they are too dazzled by colour and deafened by noise. By contrast, the resistance movement fights to preserve not just specific books, but the principle of the book: the unique demands that the literary form makes of a reader and the rich argumentation implicit in books en masse. What is at stake for Bradbury in this dystopia is not only knowledge that could be lost to future generations; books and reading have for him a still more profound function, as he has explained elsewhere:

> I am a librarian. I discovered *me* in the library. I went to find *me* in the library. Before I fell in love with libraries, I was just a six-year-old boy. [...] I graduated from the library when I was twenty-seven. I discovered that the library is the real school.[9]

Books are described as spaces that structure the creation of self; by extension, therefore, *Fahrenheit 451* anxiously predicts the blunted, depthless identities that an exclusively televisual diet might produce.

Bradbury's antagonistic pairing of television against book reading, like Woolf's condemnation of cinematic 'attacks' on literature, looks decidedly conservative today, as well as left far behind by significantly more complex systems of text/image production and dissemination. His binary derived from the assumption that people accustomed to manageable bites of text, helped down with plenty of pictures, would become increasingly unwilling to make the more substantial intellectual commitment that a work of literature was understood to require. Television viewers may be cheaply 'stuffed', yet are perpetually in need of feeding; by contrast, book reading emerges as a form of investment demanding time and patient concentration, but which ultimately yields more sustaining dividends. The argument might as easily have been turned around: instead of proceeding from an unshakeable assumption of literature's superiority, one could have presupposed that the multidimensionality of television would in time stimulate and extend the receivers' ability to perceive and comprehend complex narratives and layered representations. Indeed, Bradbury's anxiety about television's effect did not mean he eschewed the medium altogether; he wrote several *Alfred Hitchcock presents ...* teleplays, as well as working with John Huston on the screenplay for Huston's 1956 adaptation of Melville's *Moby-Dick* (an invitation Bradbury initially hesitated to accept precisely because, he admitted, he had 'never been able to read the damn thing').[10]

Evidently, the rise of the screen did not mean the end of literature, even if the former has played a part in significantly restructuring our relationship with reading. Bradbury was asked in 2010 to comment on e-books, specifically the Amazon Kindle:

> Those aren't books. You can't hold a computer in your hand like you can a book. A computer does not smell. There are two perfumes to a book. If a book is new, it smells great. If a book is old, it smells even better. [...] You have to hold it in your hands and pray to it. You put it in your pocket and you walk with it. And it stays with you forever.[11]

Given the preoccupations of *Fahrenheit 451*, Bradbury's response is unsurprising. In the novel, books as material objects are fast disappearing, yet as each one is absorbed into the brain and body of a human being, it acquires the quality of a muscle memory and correspondingly attains the profound significance the author describes here. This issue of passionate attachment to a book – to individual books, the principle of the book and the material substance of books – has rich implications for adaptation in the theatre. In a twenty-first-century context, it is more plausible as well as more productive to take from *Fahrenheit 451* not Bradbury's privileging of verbal above visual, or narration above enactment, but rather his representation of a distinctive type of fascination. At the heart of this is the recognition that books (are) matter: in other words, that everything books 'mean' is bound up – literally – within their physical volume but simultaneously escapes and exceeds that space, since the matter of books becomes animate only through acts of reading (and remembering, and sharing). This paradoxical combination of the book's containment and overflow, the conceptual and corporeal levels of readerly engagement, is equally that which Etchells and Hampton explore in *The Quiet Volume* and likewise Evardsen in *Time Has Fallen Asleep in the Afternoon Sunshine*.

Where Bradbury insisted that reading books required a unique variety of persistent engagement – one that television seemingly placed under threat – the same quality is reimagined by Evardsen as an encounter between voice, text and listener in a coming together that is leisurely and at the same time enjoyably laborious. The title of Evardsen's work is taken from Bradbury's novel but is itself a quotation from another text: *Dreamthorp: essays written in the country*, by the nineteenth-century poet Alexander Smith. Smith's line alludes to a state of stasis, a suspended moment in which the hands on the church clock, he writes, 'seem always pointing to one hour'.[12] The intimate performances that took place in Birmingham's library seemed to call for a related kind of attention from the listener-audience: a willingness to let each recital take the time it needed and a degree of tolerance, on both sides, of overlong pauses, stumblings, even actual errors. Reviewer Lyn Gardner describes her own spectatorial experience, having elected to hear Natsume Soseke's *I am a Cat* (1905–06), as 'curious', a well-chosen word that doubly denotes the peculiar and intriguing. For Gardner, the experience was

> not the same as being read to, but similarly pleasurable, [and] as much about the act of memory itself as [...] about the story – about effort. The human books do not perform in any way, but neither are they completely neutral, because they cannot help but imprint themselves on the book, almost as surely as the writer: in every cough and

> hesitation, and in the second-by-second struggle to remember, the ever-present possibility of forgetting.[13]

Those volunteer readers are not performers in a conventional sense, but are inevitably more than the 'dust jackets' Bradbury's rebels claim to be; they also represent a level of implicit interpretation and explicit embodiment beyond *The Quiet Volume*'s whisperer. Gardner emphasizes also what her experience felt like in context, within the space of the library: how inert by comparison seemed the unopened books on the shelves, and yet how this recital suggested by implication that all books were potentially 'living things' that might, at a given moment, leap from the wall and tip out their contents. What a cacophony that would produce! In *Fahrenheit 451*, Montag's boss, Beatty, reminds one woman who is protesting against the destruction of her treasured books why the law has had to be put in place: 'Where's your common sense?' he asks: 'None of these books agree with each other.'[14] Refusing to see reason, she throws herself into the flames, to be consumed together with her library.

In Bradbury's novel, the motives for learning the text are central to the plot; were the rebels not to do this, the books would be forever lost. *Fahrenheit 451* does not contain scenes of recitation, but the possibility of it is implied; we, like Montag, are invited to imagine each member of the resistance as a walking text, a vulnerable receptacle for words and meanings. In *Time Has Fallen Asleep in the Afternoon Sunshine*, the reason for memorizing has been detached from the narrative and in consequence it becomes a strangely dislocated and illogical task, yet a committed one: the books have been learned 'by heart'. Committing chapters of prose to memory is difficult, and not only for the 'non-actor'; the listener cannot but register that oddness. Richard Hornby has described the process by which actors learn lines in the theatre as one in which the text on the page 'gradually disappears': first, the script is 'held in your hands' while you 'walk through the role'; later, the lines become speeches located 'in place and time', once the production has taken shape; ultimately, in performance, 'the lines simply come out by themselves, feeling as spontaneous to the actor as they sound to the audience'. For Hornby, the actor has by this point 'conquered' the playwright and 'stolen' the words.[15] While his account of acquired naturalness might not characterize every performance aesthetic, the trajectory that moves from foreign to familiar, the externally perceived to the internalized, broadly describes the activity of theatrical line-learning. But this is not what happens in *Time Has Fallen Asleep in the Afternoon Sunshine*, since the texts were not written to be spoken and there are surely too many lines; the activity of recitation is studiedly signalled as bound to falter, if not fail. Evardsen's actors, by all accounts, have not stolen the words; rather, they have been caught holding words that are not theirs, or awkwardly dropping them, breaking them. The books selected by the actor-participants are not absorbed into, or (in Bradbury's terms) burned up by, the adaptation; instead the performance frames them with self-conscious precarity.

As a project of adaptation, *Time Has Fallen Asleep in the Afternoon Sunshine* could be considered both loyal – the project takes an element in Bradbury's novel very literally – and liberated, given that Evardsen admits no obligation to adapt the work as a whole in any conventional sense. The 'curious' piece resulting from this approach provocatively represents one way adaptation might circumvent the critical standoff between yearnings for fidelity on the one hand, and recommendations to throw off the shackles of a source text in the name of creative freedom on the other. The unusual course taken by *Time Has Fallen Asleep in the Afternoon Sunshine* does not, perhaps, lay down a pattern that adaptation practice more generally might adopt: nonetheless, Evardsen's work illustrates in sharp, almost miniaturized focus, the possibility of holding the two sides of the fidelity/creativity equation in pleasurable tension.

Scenes of reading

(i) Schulz/Complicite: *The Street of Crocodiles*

In the context of adaptation practice, it is often supposed that while directors and (re)writers begin with an attachment to a book, they must then necessarily detach themselves from this to a significant degree in order to let the adaptation find a life of its own in the new form. However, it is intriguing to pursue an opposite route: to explore instead the consequences – aesthetic, experiential – of allowing this attachment to *persist*. Thus, rather than proceeding from assumptions about which elements of a literary work can or cannot be translated into theatre, the writer or director might alternatively be fired by curiosity about what theatrical shape an adaptation might ultimately assume if seemingly untranslatable literary qualities are retained, as far as possible, 'intact'. In an 1845 essay on the perceived decline in American drama, Edgar Allan Poe argued that the surest route to artistic reinvigoration would be for theatre-makers to 'burn or bury the "old models", and to forget, as quickly as possible, that ever a play has been penned [...], to consider *de novo* what are the capabilities of the drama – not merely what hitherto have been its conventional purposes'.[16] Adaptation from one medium to another issues precisely this invitation: as argued in the previous chapter, those aspects of a book that on the surface do not 'fit', or will not 'work', represent opportunities for theatrical innovation.

In Chapter 1, I referred to Complicite's *The Street of Crocodiles* (1992), a production inspired by the fantastical collection of linked stories by Bruno Schulz, first published in 1934. The production strengthened the company's already fast-growing reputation, introducing their work to the British theatrical mainstream even while their aesthetic exuded 'a kind of otherness'.[17] *The Street of Crocodiles* marked an important moment in terms of stage adaptation, also: the fluidity and invention that characterized Complicite's stage world seemed implicitly to uphold, but in revitalized performance language, the claim Berkoff had made two decades earlier: that no work of prose literature lay beyond the reach of the theatrical imagination. In the show's opening moments, Cesar Sarachu, in the role of Joseph (a character in many ways resembling Schulz himself), carefully picked up a book. He pressed it tightly to his chest; he caressed it; then, raising it to his face, he inhaled its unique scent. And when the actor (as Joseph, as Schulz) breathed in this book and leafed through its pages, other actors playing characters from Schulz's stories began to materialize in dreamlike fashion before the audience: one forced her way out of a packing case, in the process dislodging further heaps of books; another walked impossibly down a vertical wall, reading all the while; others rolled, or floated, heads buried in books, in words, as if they were only half-present on the stage, their bodies shading off into the text they had crawled out of. Director Simon McBurney states in the programme that with this adaptation the company had 'attempted to create a peculiar theatre language, a fabric that might hold some of the scents falling from the jacket of Schulz's prose'.[18] This metaphor was translated physically to the production: Joseph remembers when he *smells* the book he is reading. The moment Sarachu lifts the text up to his face is already multi-layered: 'Joseph' breathes in the essence of paper and ink and by this means allows the reanimation of his memories of childhood and family; at the same time, Complicite, as artists, try to catch the sensuous qualities of Schulz's writing, willing that this fragrance should touch and scent the theatrical work they have made in response.

Sarachu's action implicitly poses a question: how far can the materiality of a literary text have gravity, and productive vitality, in stage adaptation? There is a certain perversity attached to this enquiry, given that scholars in the field of adaptation studies have justifiably come to regard 'over-attachment' to a source with profound suspicion. When what had been the dominant discourse of 'fidelity' in adaptation theory was at last thoroughly unsettled – if, as the previous chapter argues, never fully ousted – critical emphasis shifted in large part to the creative integrity of the new artwork, now absolved from the imperative to refer back, endlessly and deferentially, to the source, or sources, that inspired it.[19] It is hard to take issue with this general critical redirection, for after all, who would want to see subservient treatments? Devices such as voiceovers on film, or onstage narrators, regularly suggest less a considered gesture of commitment to the source than a failure of imagination, indicative that no more complete solution to the challenges of medium translation could be found. But since lack of imagination is scarcely a charge that could be levelled at Complicite, what significance can be found in the desire, physically embodied by Sarachu, to hold on so insistently to the *matter* of the book?

Where Etchells and Hampton turn the audience into readers, and Evardsen frames an intimate listening encounter, Complicite require us to be absorbed by the *performance* of literary fascination. In what ways might such representation offer potency? To grasp the incipient impact of an actor onstage, immersed in a book, it is helpful to reflect on the sensation of 'watching reading' in the context of ordinary life. The sight of somebody absorbed in a book pricks the curiosity of the onlooker first of all to know what that person is reading – not to have this summarized, but as it were to peer over the shoulder and see the same page, to follow the text as it is read, line by line. Generally, circumstances ensure this is impossible; but even if it were not, the experience gained would not be 'the same' because the second reader would not enter the identical imaginative space that the first reader has already reached. Recalling a childhood habit of quietly extracting narrative content in bookshop aisles, Francis Spufford observes of such 'intangible shoplifting':

> I have not ceased to be amazed at the invisibility I depend on. Other people can't see what so permeates me, I accept that, but why can't they? It fills me. The imbalance between what's felt and what shows means I carry the sensory load of fiction like a secret.[20]

Unsurprising, then, that the spectacle of a reader 'lost' in a book prompts a sense of double remove: first, because the other cannot see what he or she is looking at; second, because the page is in any case no more than a sign pointing towards the space where that reader 'is' mentally.

The implications of this account of reading-in-the-world for the theatre are clearer if this activity is relocated in an aesthetic context. In art historian Garrett Stewart's 2006 study of representations of readers and reading in painting, *The Look of Reading*, the author demonstrates that only rarely are viewers of such artworks allowed to glimpse the content of what a painted figure is looking at (be this novel, letter, or something else entirely). Instead, Stewart argues, the image of reading piques curiosity by deliberately withholding that knowledge from us, and in the process provoking a kind of bodily *frisson* by rousing what we, the viewers of the work, understand that the reading experience provides. Yet as Stewart remarks, the recurrence of representations of reading in art initially seems puzzling, since if 'reading is where you go to be elsewhere', why should artists 'labor so intensely to evoke the unpicturable space'? Stewart observes, rightly, that '[s]tasis, blankness, introversion […] are not normally the stuff of scenic drama'.[21] Central to Stewart's theoretical explanation for this phenomenon is the intriguing and persuasive claim that representation of the *look* of reading recruits a form of 'narrative energy': studying the image of a reader engaged with a text, the viewer is led to feel the tension between the static visuals of the canvas, and the (implied) momentum of a verbal text, albeit here only the painted sign of one. Reading is, crucially, durational: both the pleasures of reading, and the import of what one reads, are characteristically qualities released not instantaneously, but in the course of the activity. While viewers of visual art will need some time to examine the different elements within a painting, in the end the simultaneity of the whole is available against which to measure their conclusions. The point of this comparison of the two media is not to set visual 'surface', to its disadvantage, against narrative 'depth' – a distinction which, as argued in the previous chapter, is surely fallacious – but rather to propose that representation of one kind of art form within another, especially where these function in manifestly different ways, draws attention to the frustrations and failures of representation as well as the capabilities implicit within each.

The critical term for the depiction of one type of art by another is *ekphrasis*, the word derived from the Greek *ek*, meaning out, and *phrasis*, to speak. Perhaps the most frequent exemplifying context for *ekphrasis* is literature, an instance being where a poetry or prose text describes in detail the characteristics of a work of visual art. Here, one aesthetic language is being used to describe the qualities of another – or conversely we might imagine that one language is itself striving to 'speak out' from within another – always in the knowledge that this endeavour will fall short of achieving truly satisfying expression. Stewart's work traces a reverse *ekphrasis*, then, whereby a visual medium seeks to articulate the distinctive structure of experience offered by the narrative arts. This notion of *ekphrasis* can usefully be applied in the context of theatrical adaptation, not least to illuminate the performance of reading and 'bookness'. Although staged reading is not a simple equivalent of painted reading – drama is visual and verbal, and (more explicitly than with fine art) the experience of its audience is durational – it will be apparent that many of the same representational tensions are upheld when the two art forms are brought together. Further, when books are prominent and scenes of reading occur within stage adaptation, those differences are intensified further, since adaptation as a practice always implicitly extends the invitation to discover something new both about the source and the medium that has taken this over. When Complicite's spectators watch Joseph inhale the distinctive odour of his book – a volume that both is and is not Schulz's *The Street of Crocodiles* – that gesture rouses the desire to share the character's nostalgic journey while emphasizing the uniquely personal dimension of his relationship with the text/object: the audience is drawn in, yet also gently shut out.

Clutching onto the book in this way, the character Joseph – simultaneously the actor, and by extension McBurney and the company – invests it with extraordinary power. The conviction that printed words might become animate if one wants it enough is also, not coincidentally, an impression that permeates Schulz's writing. The narrator's visionary, if unstable, father in *The Street of Crocodiles* insists, repeatedly, that there 'is no dead matter', that apparent 'lifelessness is only a disguise behind which hide unknown forms of life'; in truth, he asserts, the 'whole of matter pulsates with infinite possibilities', 'entices us with a thousand sweet, soft, round shapes which it blindly dreams up within itself'.[22] Obsessed by birds, the father pores over his ornithological textbooks, the intensity of his gaze causing 'feathery phantasms [...] to rise from the pages and fill the room with colors'.[23] In Complicite's hands, the leaves of books ripple and flutter, take shape as if about to escape the performers' grasp altogether: here, it is not the case that actors straightforwardly manipulate objects, in an appropriation that only works one way; rather, the physical properties of the objects themselves influence the movements of human bodies in a process of reciprocal exchange.

Elsewhere in Schulz's writing, the narrator's description of an immense map of the shoddy yet alluring district known as the Street of Crocodiles gives way, without narrative demarcation, to a description of physically traversing the district itself by the reader, although the route that we are led along remains throughout disconcertingly papery: the grey buildings recall the 'black-and-white photographs [of] cheap illustrated catalogues', their large windows 'ruled like the pages of a ledger'.[24] Schulz's authorial voice renders more pronounced a sensation that, according to the phenomenologist critic Georges Poulet, distinguishes the experience that reading always offers. For Poulet, a book

> is not shut in by its contours, is not walled-up as in a fortress. It asks nothing better than to exist outside itself, or to let you exist in it. In short, the extraordinary fact in the case of the book is the falling away of the barriers between you and it. You are inside it; it is inside you; there is no longer either outside or inside.[25]

Poulet's words might recall the subtly negotiated relations between readers and books tested by Etchells and Hampton, and by Evardsen; but in addition, his depiction of the fragile borders between 'worlds' aptly describes Complicite's practice too. The work of the Lecoq-trained company has always exploited the potential fluidity between actors, objects and spaces: in their productions, 'props' become animate and behave as if they were living things; correspondingly, human actors are fully capable of dissolving into their environment. Complicite's theatre, more than most, has found ways to stage a dreaming aesthetic; and yet, in the moment to which I keep returning – when Sarachu inhales the scent of the book – those barriers Poulet describes do not fully 'fall away'. The physical matter of the book remains, resting in the actor's hands as the material connection between the space the production inhabits –

here and now – and an elsewhere of both Schulz's and Complicite's imaginings. The text itself appears to occupy this felt gap between the constrained time frame of stage performance and the fluid, variable and hence immeasurable space through which readers can elect to travel for any literary work. That gap – between places, times, durations, bodies, texts, minds – is the essence of adaptation's inherent frustration, yet it is also adaptation's pleasure. Like an 'exact' translation, an ideal adaptation is impossible: but spectators may still be teased by glimpses of a perfection of sorts, and might be elsewhere sustained by the artists' evident desire to revivify a text, the commitment to task and material, even where they expose how far this remains elusive or only fleetingly achievable. In *The Pleasure of the Text*, Barthes describes the charged vitality of the gap, asking:

> Is not the most erotic portion of a body where the garment gapes? [...] [I]t is intermittence [...] which is erotic: the intermittence of skin flashing between two articles of clothing [...]; it is this flash itself which seduces, or rather: the staging of an appearance-as-disappearance.[26]

This account suggests that a gap, in the context of theatrical adaptation, could legitimately be registered not as a locus of inevitable disappointment, inferiority and loss ('All stage adaptations of literature must sacrifice ...') but of excitement and possibility. Fundamental to the satisfaction of the performance in Birmingham Central Library is understanding the struggle in a recital which imperfections make more poignant, not less; similarly, Complicite's Joseph and the watching audience are brought to understand that they can only gain intermittent entry to the remembered, narrativized world.

(ii) Fitzgerald/Elevator Repair Service: *Gatz*

In adaptation terms, Elevator Repair Service's *Gatz* (2006) might seem to be striving as far as possible to defy the gap between literary source and theatrical performance – or at least, to reduce the size of this very significantly. As with *Time Has Fallen Asleep in the Afternoon Sunshine*, a book is here not so much adapted, as adopted: in *Gatz*, Fitzgerald's entire novel (rather than an opening chapter, as in Evardsen's project) is read aloud with every 'he said' and 'she said' retained.[27] The company embarked on the adaptation in the early 2000s with the aim of making their own version of *The Great Gatsby*, starting out – somewhat superficially, they acknowledge – by 'looking [...] for sections with a lot of dialogue'. Vexation quickly followed: the literal focus on speech had the effect of silencing what to them was the most important 'voice' in the novel, that of the narrator; evidently great quantities of text would have to be cut if they continued to force the book into the shape of a play. However, Fitzgerald's novel is written in the first person, in the character of Nick Carraway, and from this perspective, every word of the book could legitimately be considered 'dialogue'. This recognition led ERS to follow this logic to its conclusion: they would preserve *all* the text. *Gatz* began as a re-picturing of Fitzgerald's novel but grew ever more detailed to the point where the resulting adaptation is, rather like Schulz's map, difficult to distinguish from the territory it represents. By conventional standards, the production, at more than seven hours, is far too long. But director John Collins justified their decision very simply: the novel, they found, 'could not be reduced or improved or re-imagined, it just had to exist in the form that it came to us'. The company decided, they said, 'to bring reading onto the stage, not make a play, but make a book a theatrical experience'.[28]

Gatz is set in a drab, cluttered office: instantly familiar, yet with the nature of its business deliberately, hazily, unspecific. When his computer fails to boot up, an employee, played by Scott Shepherd, picks up a copy of *The Great Gatsby* found in his desk, and as if for want of anything better to do begins to read it aloud, and does not stop (Bradbury would surely have approved of the anti-technological trajectory). Shepherd does not enact what he reads, and nor do the rest of the cast, who play other members of office staff, explicitly take on roles within Fitzgerald's story; rather, the workaday routine action that continues to revolve around Shepherd's office worker/reader – who stands for Nick, without directly representing him – becomes increasingly infected by the contents of the book being read. Spectators are led to regard one employee as Tom Buchanan, another as Daisy, a third as Gatsby: the blurry, unremarkable workplace is gradually transformed (in the words of one reviewer) into a 'dreamlike meeting ground' in which 'the more intense passions of the novel's figures can bleed through, emotionally, into the humdrum world that today's readers inhabit'.[29] The spectators' recognition that what they are watching is not a dramatization of *The Great Gatsby*, but Shepherd (as an office worker) reading *The Great Gatsby*, immediately frees the production from any expectation that narrative events will be enacted and, further, that the actors 'are' – and so should ideally resemble – Fitzgerald's characters: indeed, as Barthes noted of the garment's 'gape', the exposed deficiencies or breakdowns of the metatheatrical game are part of its pleasure, meaning that spectators, like Shepherd's reader, can supply what is missing through their imagination.

In one way, the bold conception behind this production evocatively reflects how reading sometimes affects us. A book in which we are truly absorbed can seem temporarily to construct a world more real, more substantial and often more desirable than the one seen when we look up from the page. *Gatz* consciously invokes that experience; while those seven-plus hours pass in 'real time', the hands of the onstage clock are frozen – not 'asleep in the afternoon', but at 9.38 on an otherwise ordinary morning, as if the rest of life, and its accompanying rules, had been momentarily suspended. But even though ERS's production takes spectators through Fitzgerald's novel word for word, it will be clear that *Gatz* offers something infinitely removed from the normally solitary activity of reading. In her analysis of the show, Catherine Love remarks on 'how many of [her] fellow spectators arrived armed with pillows, flasks, and snacks, clearly prepared for what was perceived to be an arduous – if attractively novel – theatregoing marathon'.[30] The pillows might connote the comfort of bedtime reading, but the rest of it looks more like support mechanisms for a student assignment 'all-nighter'; the whole paraphernalia suggests an event poised finely between indulgence and endurance. Watching *Gatz* cannot be 'like' reading by and for oneself, but the production reflects and celebrates the kind of experience books can and do inspire: a collapse of resistance, or 'barriers' (in Poulet's terms); a sensation of doubled existence; obsessive attention not solely on narrative, character or structure of language, but with the tactility of the text. Not just any edition of a book: *this* one. And while its focus on reading and preoccupation with the physical text makes the show not conventionally dramatic, it is nonetheless insistently, even defiantly, theatrical. This quality is most immediately displayed in the central performance of Shepherd who, after years of touring the work, had become able to recite the entire novel; while here he reads rather than recites, half an hour from the end he closes the book and simply carries on with the text where reading had left off. Shepherd's virtuosity in the role, noted in virtually every review of the show, as Love argues, 'places him at the top of an implicit hierarchy of labour within the performance, while the less prominent, repetitive labour of some of his fellow performers shares more in common with the daily grind of the average office worker': Shepherd is framed as 'the Reader', but Fitzgerald's text is read, through the adaptation process, by the entire company.[31]

The Street of Crocodiles and *Gatz* pursue divergent paths in adapting the literary works that inspired them, yet each production gives the physical substance of books a distinct and potent gravity that is revealing about literature, theatre, and the pleasures and tensions exposed when one aesthetic collides with another. Preoccupation with textual 'matter' persists in the work of both companies, evidently. Elevator Repair Service's work *Arguendo* ('for the sake of argument'), which opened in 2013, builds a performance text out of court transcripts and American legalese; a visual motif of this production is the incorporation of projected text – endless pages of it – that swirl and zoom in and out of focus in ways that seem to mirror the bewildering and perverse circularity embedded in the language itself. Complicite, too, have steadily pursued their fascination not simply with adaptation of literature, but with the appearance and disappearance of books and the power of words on paper and screen. In 2012, the company mounted a version of Mikhail Bulgakov's sprawling, multi-layered cult novel *The Master and Margarita* (written between 1928 and 1940, but unpublished until 1967).[32] Here again, the text behind the adaptation is itself highly self-referential, a book centred on the activity of writing and that questions the durability of literature. In Complicite's production (considered further in Chapter 4), characters – and by extension, spectators – travel across 1930s Moscow by means of a huge projected map that, Schulz-like, zooms in and out with the dizzying facility of Google Earth; later, under the devil's influence, the city's buildings scorch, crinkle and disintegrate as easily as if they were made of paper. When the new Soviet literary establishment MASSOLIT rejects the Master's novel – since it deals with the 'undesirable' theme of a conflicted Pontius Pilate – its author hurls the only copy of his work into the fire. But as Satan later assures him, 'manuscripts don't burn': on cue, a desk drawer flies open of its own accord to reveal the stack of paper magically intact.

The claim that 'manuscripts don't burn' has been much quoted subsequently, and variously understood. The phrase has been thought to signify that works of literature can never truly be 'destroyed' by forces of censorship (an interpretation resonant in the case of both Bulgakov and Schulz), or more generally to suggest that a text is etched as deeply in the mind as on the page.[33] Both these meanings are reflected in Bradbury's *Fahrenheit 451*: the matter of a book, his novel implies, exceeds the physical form in which this is contained and burning the book as object will not destroy its soul. Yet at the same time, the vulnerability of physical books – and physical bodies – is tangible since it is only through some form of material embodiment that this inner life becomes accessible. In an era in which public libraries must fight to remain open, the stages on which *The Quiet Volume* and *Time Has Fallen Asleep in the Afternoon Sunshine* play out are less peacefully secure than they once appeared. Adaptation is the art of actively negotiating this relationship of form and content: in contemporary theatre, adaptation seeks ways to manoeuvre (that which it regards as) the substance of a book in its complex transmission between author and reader-spectator, and between the context of origination and a new space of reception. I argue that this means in practice that adaptation assumes not simply an interpretive but an editorial role.

Adaptation as edition

Thus far in this chapter, I have considered different ways in which adaptation handles its attachment to literary texts in a complex allegiance not just to authorial content but to the shape, heft and texture of the book in material form. The peculiar significance perceived to adhere to this physical book – in its silent containment of 'other' spaces, voices, lives, times and interactions – helps to illuminate the prominence of books on stage in adaptations, the ways in which their pages are read silently or aloud, caressed, breathed in, manipulated and projected. In the second part of this chapter I continue to explore the relationship between authorial text and material object, but focus that enquiry through the concept of edition: in other words, the particular shape in which a text is presented and published at a given point in its longer history. Arguments about the task of the editor and the function of an edition have radically shifted over time; I show here how an awareness of these positions may usefully extend the critical vocabulary applied when considering the distinctive 'editions' that theatrical adaptation puts forward.

In an essay titled simply 'What Is a Book?' Roger Chartier and Peter Stallybrass answer their question by tracing arguments produced historically in literary, philosophical, political and legal analyses, around the status of books, authorship and ownership. From this, two major and mutually contradictory perspectives emerge about what constitutes a book. There is first the 'platonic' view, which argues that a work of literature transcends any possible material incarnation of it; second, there is the 'pragmatic' view, which holds that a work has no existence beyond the forms in which it is read or received.[34] These two opposing positions have variously shaped book production and literary analysis, but there remains a friction between the supposed 'immateriality of texts and the materiality of books', which, the authors observe, also colours the dynamic between readers and the texts they appropriate. Chartier and Stallybrass cite the Argentinean author Jorge Luis Borges, who in a 1978 lecture insisted he had no interest in the physical aspect of books, caring only for the words they contained and the ways in which these had been received and interpreted. Yet in his autobiography, Borges used very different terms in relation to *Don Quixote*, a book that had influenced him deeply:

> I still remember the red bindings with gilt titles of the Garnier edition. Eventually, after my father's library was broken up and I read *Don Quixote* in another edition, I had the feeling that it was not the real *Don Quixote*. Later, a friend obtained for me a Garnier copy with the same engravings, the same footnotes and the same *errata*. For me, all these things were part of the book; in my mind, this was the real *Don Quixote*.[35]

Here, the value attached to a specific 'pragmatic' edition – the version of *Don Quixote* Borges had grown up with – is felt to outweigh that of the 'platonic' literary work. This example demonstrates what intuition suggests, that the form a book takes matters: at the very least, it matters at the ground level of individual readers.

Edition is defined by the OED as 'one of the differing forms in which a literary work (or collection of works) is published, either by the author himself, or by subsequent editors'. It is also explained as 'the action of producing, or bringing into existence', with the verb to edit (Latin *editus*, past participle of *edere*, to put forth) meaning to publish or 'give to the world'. Clearly, if the job of putting forth a text is variously understood and executed, then this in turn may provoke dispute about the efficacy and authenticity of different editions. In his introduction to *Palimpsest: Editorial Theory in the Humanities*, George Bornstein explains that until the early 1980s the view largely prevailed in Anglo-American editing that the aim of literary edition was to produce the definitive or 'best' text of a work, 'usually theorised as an ur-text marred by subsequent corruption in transmission'.[36] Elsewhere, Paul Eggert uses similar terms to outline this traditional perception of the literary work as 'an aesthetic object [needing] only to be cleaned of the textual detritus acquired over the decades and centuries in order to stand now, in effect, outside of history'.[37] Yet the solidity of this position was already being undermined by poststructuralist arguments: in his seminal essay 'From Work to Text' (1971), Barthes showed how texts are always unstable, existing as a 'process of demonstration' that is 'experienced only in an activity of production'. Therefore, said Barthes, '[i]t follows that the Text cannot stop (for example on a library shelf); its constitutive movement is that of cutting across (in particular it can cut across the work, several works)'.[38] That Bornstein titles his own collection *Palimpsest* makes clear that this plural, stratified conception has reshaped editorial theory also. The palimpsest is multi-layered, a document on which the markings and annotations of earlier periods are faded but unmistakable; the fact that such a document would originally have been produced on semi-transparent vellum or parchment paints an evocative image of part-erased words still visible beneath each new impression. Bornstein explains that persuasive arguments for textual contingency gradually produced a sea change in editorial theory, broadly characterized as a movement away from the emphasis on producing a definitive text towards acceptance of a multiplicity of valid versions. This altered view was underpinned not only by theoretical insistence on textual 'openness', but by acknowledging a history of literary production which demonstrated that a work could and did exist in multiple versions – sometimes even bearing the mark of several different authors – each with its own temporal and intentional legitimacy.

The concept of a text as always and inherently intertextual was consolidated and extended by Jerome McGann in the early 1990s in his important work *The Textual Condition*. Here, McGann unpicked further the implications of these ideas for critical editing. Texts, he argued, 'represent – are in themselves – certain kinds of human acts'; this view of text as activity helps to explain why, according to McGann, every text 'has variants of itself screaming to get out, or antithetical texts waiting to make themselves known'.[39] The textual condition is represented by McGann as one of movement, with the meaning of any work (or word) constituted through its usage. Thus, he insists, the existence of multiple and potentially conflicting versions of a work is not what produces textual instability, rather it is a symptom of it: for McGann, 'variation is the invariant rule of the textual condition'.[40] From this perspective, no edition of a book can be definitively 'authoritative', or transparent; instead, every edition, 'including every critical edition, is an act of reimagining and redefining a text's audience(s) and its ways of interacting with those audience(s)'.[41] This position might seem by extension to undermine the authority of all publication, embracing instead a kind of limitless, anarchic textual play; yet McGann's argument is rather that we should look for authority and integrity within the activity of edition, rather than in any neatly bound(aried) outcome. This analysis describes and advocates a perceptual shift from notions of *a* 'work of art' to the *work* of art, that is, towards a continual, energetic, interventional (re)shaping process.[42]

Thus, adaptation can, I propose, itself be read as a practice of edition. Several aspects of the arguments rehearsed above are useful in deepening understanding of adaptation both as an activity and as an outcome brought under critical scrutiny. Adaptation appropriates, frames and 'puts forth' its source text(s); individual adaptation projects may assert a recuperative purpose – an aim, for instance, to make visible a significance embedded in the text that subsequent layers of interpretation have hitherto obscured – or may draw attention to their own contingent status, their deliberate and specific topicality. Such contrasting accounts of the relationship of adaptation to its source are also reflected in the changing shape of adaptation criticism, discussed in Chapter 1: while the value of an adaptation was at one stage (and still is often) measured primarily against the text it appropriated – in which context it was typically found wanting – that privileging of the 'source' has increasingly been countered by arguments that adaptations *had* to establish independent creative purpose and coherence if they were to be other than dully derivative. Beyond this, the notion of text as palimpsest – multi-layered, open and in flux – is already inherent in the activity of adaptation. The critic Michael Alexander first coined the term 'palimpsestuous' in his analysis of Ezra Pound's poetry, which, he showed, contained numerous embedded allusions to and fragments of earlier works.[43] This intimate borrowing – the 'incestuous' dimension in the act of layering – will often be intuited by readers even where individual references are not consciously registered or their sources identified. The palimpsestuous, or palimpsestic, character of adaptation has been underlined by other scholars since: as noted, it is a quality explored by Hutcheon in *A Theory of Adaptation*, and is drawn on elsewhere by Milan Pribisic and Thomas Leitch.[44] The concept of the palimpsest is most fruitful here when it is used to frame adaptation not in terms of a work in isolation – as if a single adaptation is 'laid over' an original work – but as an accumulation of activity as a result of which the sharp distinction between source and reworking is brought into question.[45] The same thinking supports a contemporary understanding of edition, recognizing this not as the attempt to produce a fixed 'best' version but as intervention in an ongoing process, a contribution that itself influences the meaning and shape a text assumes over time. Any edition, then, should be regarded as temporary and imperfect: and while this is inherently true for any text, the works of some authors, as I discuss next, pose extraordinary and immediate problems that editing must grapple with if never finally resolve.

Burton/Stan's Cafe: *The Anatomy of Melancholy*

In 1621, clergyman and Oxford scholar Robert Burton published his encyclopedic, influential and popular work *The Anatomy of Melancholy*. This book when first issued was already more than 350,000 words; Burton's last and lengthiest version ran to well over 500,000. In a 2001 essay, literary critic Nicholas Lezard described *The Anatomy of Melancholy* as 'the book to end all books', a tribute that acknowledges not simply the great size of the compendium but encompasses its mode of production, structure, scope and complexity of purpose.[46] Burton was the librarian of Christ Church College, and the library's rich collections – in the disciplines of philosophy, classics, history, geography, literature, religion, the sciences – were the fundamental source of his information; in line with the mode of academia that prevailed at this time, Burton delighted in an ability to travel the world without leaving the comfort of his study, to bring back 'the "rich pearls, outlandish wealth, gums, jewels, and spicery" of scholarship'.[47] *The Anatomy of Melancholy*, then, is the result of deep and comprehensive plundering of thousands of other works, each in turn appropriating multiple other sources; in one sense, perhaps, Burton's book simply manifests fundamental assumptions of academia writ large. The plurality of routes by which Burton undertook his 'anatomizing' of the melancholic state – a condition generally experienced as morbid but also, he showed, philosophically productive – resulted in a work thickly studded with references to the learning that underpinned it. Historian Noga Arikha likens the book, with its 'dense network of embedded quotations, a seemingly infinite set of hyperlinks', to the infinite textual production of the internet; Burton's vast project, Arikha suggests, 'could seem a testimony to the ultimate vanity of human knowledge, as melancholy as the endless sea of information that our screens indifferently project to our digital onlookers' tired eyes'.[48] Acknowledging the daunting breadth of the landscape he covers, Burton self-consciously takes on the role of editor-guide. He announces in a 'satirical preface' that he will borrow the voice and character of Democritus Junior, traditionally known as the 'laughing philosopher', who regarded human follies with sympathy and tolerance.[49] According to Burton, Democritus himself tended towards melancholy yet would walk through the streets of the town and 'laugh heartily at such variety of ridiculous objects, which there he saw'.[50] That appreciation of the absurd colours the work throughout, and Burton's handling of his subject, in keeping with his adopted persona, is as humorously entertaining as it is seriously intended.

The concept of melancholy as explored in this work is founded on humoural theory, which had developed in the fifth century BC and still dominated Western medical thinking centuries later.[51] According to this view, the body produced the four fluids or 'humours' of black bile, yellow bile (or choler), phlegm and blood; each element was connected to a specific temperament – broadly characterized as melancholic, aggressive, peaceful or lively – and preponderance of any would manifest as an unhealthy and potentially dangerous imbalance. Every aspect of one's life was thought to affect the proportionate relationship of the humours; Burton's anatomizing of his theme correspondingly tackles the ways in which melancholy is exacerbated – but may also be treated – by diet, physical activity, climate, intellectual engagement, sleep, love relations and more. The listing of causes of melancholy in the book is so prolonged and expansive that the condition begins to look pretty well inescapable. At the same time, the reader must find a way through advice suggesting, for example, that too little exercise stimulates melancholy, but so too does an excess of it; that wine can be hurtful to some, but is a good physic to others; that it is wise in a man to marry a prostitute, since then he need not be tortured by fear that she is unfaithful; that Sutton Coldfield in Warwickshire healthfully combines a barren placidity with excellent air in Spring; and that a sufferer must place confidence in his physician, since while the efficacy of treatments remains hotly disputed, nothing is more damaging to the melancholic condition than a lack of faith. *The Anatomy of Melancholy* is thus already an inherently editorial work, in that its author strives impossibly to contain and catalogue a sprawling mass of frequently contradictory ideas and information: Burton's 'head [had] been filled to self-cancelling overflow by the bibliography of his day', and throughout, his text draws attention to the shifting status of medical and popular understanding.[52] The book assumed the contingent status of the version in literal terms also; Burton published five rewritten and progressively expanded editions during his lifetime, with many more issued subsequently both in print and online.

For all its author's jokes, dry asides, and the adopted persona through which the entire commentary is channelled, *The Anatomy of Melancholy* remains a decidedly unlikely source for theatrical adaptation. Its enquiry is systematic (moving from definitions to symptoms, causes and possible cures), but Burton's work – essentially a textbook – has no *dynamic* shape and cannot drive its material towards a conclusion; the content is overwhelmingly factual, even if the authority of those facts is called into question; and the tone of the whole, in the words of Democritus, is undeniably 'somewhat tart'.[53] Despite these potential obstacles – and perhaps to a degree because of them – the Birmingham-based theatre company Stan's Cafe created a stage adaptation of the book, which had its premiere in 2013. Stan's Cafe is best described less as a company than a group of artists who, under the direction of James Yarker, have since the early 1990s regularly collaborated to make work in a variety of forms including performance, film, installation, dance and community event. Previous projects have wrestled explicitly with the demands of finding a structure able to articulate extraordinary content. Notably, in *Of All the People in All the World* (2003) the artists used grains of rice, poured in heaps of wildly varying sizes, as physical representations of abstract human statistics describing population, economic distribution and opportunity: in this installation the extreme simplicity of form – as well as the use of rice, an essential foodstuff – contrived speakingly to expose inequities and invite debate. *The Anatomy of Melancholy* presents a quite different challenge: and yet the same question about how dry content may be translated into potent performance action remains pertinent to the undertaking.

Given what has been said about the many difficulties Burton's work instantly throws up, it is striking that Stan's Cafe choose to adhere very closely to the literary form of the original. The show is performed by a cast of four, of whom one (Gerard Bell) plays the role of Burton/Democritus throughout. Flip-charts, sheets of card and a large projection screen are used by the actors to demonstrate directly the *Anatomy*'s elaborate structure (signalling 'The First Partition', for instance, and within this, 'Section 1 – Definitions', 'Section 2 – Causes'). The production runs at close to three hours, and while this *relative* brevity was the result of significant cutting – given the exhaustive length of the original – the impression conveyed in performance is still that of virtually unbounded space given to Burton's words. The actors distribute the text between them, but the language itself is altered very little and the demands this makes on the audience are considerable. A programme note advised the spectators: 'The show is long and full of content. Don't worry if you find yourself drifting off and thinking of something else. This is natural – just enjoy those thoughts and when they end come back to the show for more.'[54] Yarker explained that when collaboratively devising the piece, the group agreed on the principle that they would only use the original text, apart from 'changing self-reflexive comments from the book so they refer to audiences rather than readers'.[55] This rule enables the material to retain its historical distance, the otherness of its linguistic register. In performance, this means that the audience must attune themselves gradually to the unfamiliar expression, but also that when elements in the commentary do exhibit potential contemporary relevance, this connectedness is experienced more pointedly: observations about 'university heads [who] as a rule pray only for the greatest possible number of freshmen to squeeze money from', or parents who are cruelly stern, or remiss, or who 'dote so much upon their children, they crush them to death' can be registered by a modern audience without the need that these be updated.[56]

While I propose that adaptation in general may be examined through the trope of edition, Yarker describes this as an explicit premise of Stan's Cafe's production. Noting that Burton's book grew organically through several different versions, their own adaptation could be regarded, he suggests, as 'merely a new edition'.[57] The approach the group take to the text in performance further emphasizes the activity of editing, by highlighting cuts, citations and translations from Latin. Sometimes this operates to comic effect, as when the actors announce but then withhold aspects of the material. Thus when the flip chart displays 'Member 2 – Of the Body and Soul: Subsection 1 – Digression of Anatomy', the opening speaker, Craig Stephens, is hastily interrupted:

> **Craig** Before I proceed to define the disease of melancholy, I hold it not impertinent to make a brief digression of the anatomy of the body …

Graeme Remember we did hold it impertinent and decided I would proceed directly to an explication of the humours.

Gerard Indeed.

Craig Well remembered.

At this, the chart is flipped forward once more to reveal 'Subsection 2 – Humours and Spirits', and here, as at many other points in the show, pages of text are torn out of their manuscripts and discarded.[58] The decision to use four actors, who dispute amongst themselves the selection and wisdom of the information they are charged to convey, aptly physicalizes the internal contradictions that Burton's work made no attempt to disguise; the cast's small disagreements, whether directly verbalized or only hinted at in raised eyebrows and sidelong glances, are equally suggestive of editorial differences in the handling of the material. Apart from Bell as Burton/Democritus, the actors do not play characters, but nor are they 'themselves', nor are they 'neutral': rather, they are functions that support and at times inhibit the editorial putting forth of Burton's work. In his discussion of printed (as opposed to electronic) critical editions, Paul Eggert comments on the status of scholarly notes, which, like 'attendant lords', are intended to 'swell the royal progress of the text we are reading but [...] remain strictly subservient to it. They are meant to make its old-fashioned or other-worldly decorums legible for us'.[59] Eggert's formulation effectively describes the actors' delicate negotiation of their task. Typically they function smoothly, standing formally at the margins of the text; yet elsewhere, they seem to dig in their heels and draw attention to themselves in multiple subtle ways, much in the way that notes, as Eggert observes, sometimes 'seem to have a will of their own'.[60] The costumes and the space the actors inhabit likewise describe their interstitial place. They are in Jacobean dress, but at least one wears trainers with it; the clutter of the stage is dominated by seventeenth-century scholarly apparatus of various kinds, heaps of books and a human skull, but also includes a can of Carlsberg, crisp packets, post-its and a plastic snake. Such deliberate anachronisms underline the status of these contemporary actor-editors as 'interlopers' within 'the textual field of the work', at the same time suggesting confusion of the divide distinguishing rehearsal from performance.[61]

The production opened at Warwick Arts Centre in March 2013 and toured the United Kingdom during the following twelve months. Critical response was somewhat mixed: typically reviewers admired the ambition of the project and enjoyed the eccentricities of the source material, but there were several hints that the work had not – or not yet – found a fully satisfactory shape in performance. Those critics who perceived insufficiencies in the adaptation put these down to the explicitly 'bookish' qualities of the production itself. Thus, reviewing the performance at Oval House, Alexandra Coghlan enthusiastically described Burton's work as 'just that kind of against-the-grain eccentric that could lend itself to radical, slash-and-burn theatrical reinvention'; however, Coghlan argued, in practice the measured and inclusive attitude of the adaptation to its source could not effectively sustain audience interest in the original's 'plotless, discursive, digressive musings'.[62] Gardner for the *Guardian* took a similar line, finding the production overly dry but agreeing that '[w]ith serious editing, there could be something intriguing here'.[63] 'Editing', here, seems simply to mean cutting: editing *down*, in other words. Gardner implies that the company's reluctance to cut more ruthlessly evidences the misguided attempt to stay 'faithful'; perhaps, like Coghlan, she would have preferred 'slash-and-burn'. However, editing in this limited sense was not the aim of the adaptation. The company's treatment of Burton did not set out radically to reinterpret his work; nor did they attempt to shape a performance structure or style that would compete with the appropriated text. In fact, there was a conscious wish to preserve something of the original's linguistic overload and allow the book's 'endless sea of information', in Arikha's terms, to wash over spectators as it does the reader. If spectators do temporarily drift away on this textual tide, notes Hannah Tookey, the show's exhibited essay-like structure (the screen, the charts) provides 'a clear bookmark to pick up watching from'.[64] Nicola Fordham Hodges, in *Disability Arts Online*, described the impossibility of keeping abreast of the show's logorrhea:

> This play is dense with wonderful erudite quotations, flicked before us on flash cards almost too fast to read, let alone for a reviewer to write down. In the end I gave up. This play doesn't take itself too seriously: neither should I. The characters themselves screw up chunks of their scripts and chuck them on the stage.[65]

To make the point that the performance does not take itself entirely seriously does not undermine the commitment of the adaptation project behind it: as still another reviewer – Jo Beggs – puts it, the rejected pages are 'ripped boldly, yet with respect'.[66] The actors grapple with the impossible task of first, passing on a voluminous and rambling body of words; second, of attempting (following Burton) to catalogue and anatomize a resistantly enigmatic human condition. In performance, the actors seem to hint at the hopelessness and hubristic folly of their enterprise. They work their way through the vast text – sorting, tentatively cutting, translating, annotating – with the air of dusty scholars: there is room for gentle jokes, mild disagreements and minor corrections, but no appetite at all for slash-and-burn.

Reflecting here on Stan's Cafe's performance, my intention is not primarily to refute the criticisms made by less complementary reviews. Manifestly, an adaptation of Burton's book could be approached wholly otherwise: mimicking ERS's model with *Gatz*, extensive quantities of text might indeed be retained verbatim, but juxtaposed with performance action that had its own internal laws and life; it is harder to hypothesize, perhaps, what would become of Burton in the hands of Complicite. Equally, alternative approaches to adapting *The Anatomy of Melancholy* might result in a production experienced as more reliably entertaining, or stylistically experimental, or critically interventionist. I suggest, however, that Stan's Cafe's treatment of the work is most usefully regarded as a practice of edition. As I have shown, editing is a complex and loaded project that goes far beyond 'cutting'. The thoughtful editor hopes to make a text public, (re)issuing this in a considered and carefully framed form. Interference with that text will generally be kept minimal: invisibility of editing is not possible, nor is it desirable, but nonetheless the editorial function positively acknowledges its literal marginality. The integrity of such a practice, McGann argues, resides less in the editorial product than in the activity itself: 'edition' in this sense is explored as a critically engaged process – a fluid project in motion – rather than as something that must be judged by its necessarily partial and inadequate outcomes. In this light, perhaps, the production discussed here is not precisely *an* edition, 'successful' or otherwise. Instead, *The Anatomy of Melancholy* in performance *is* edition: curious of its material yet wary of too-hasty intervention, seeking connectedness, yet sensitive to distance and difference.

The Anatomy of Melancholy, *Gatz* and *The Street of Crocodiles* in the theatre and *Time Has Fallen Asleep in the Afternoon Sunshine* and *The Quiet Volume* in the library together present a far more complex and nuanced picture of the relationship between literature and performance than is popularly attributed to adaptation. In each case, the production regards the book as a site that allows and resists intervention, even as the text itself is exposed as contingent and multi-vocal, rather than stable and singularly authoritative; nowhere is this clearer than in Burton's extraordinary project. The theatre draws out preoccupations and characteristics not just of specific books, but the book as object and the book received through the reading process. The intervention made by performance is used to highlight tensions between the seemingly disembodied literary narrative and the rooted physicality in the act of reading, and to complicate that distinction as books become things and reading becomes performance. In turn, books are seen to lend their curious qualities to the performances that explore them: from an almost hypnotic focus on a single word or the paper's grain in *The Quiet Volume*, to inhalation of ink in *The Street of Crocodiles*, to the reams of print in *The Anatomy of Melancholy*, it seems as if performers, performer-participants and audiences are seeking ways, as Etchells and Hampton put it, 'to enter the page, or trying to pass through it into some other space'. The *ekphrasis* of adaptation is operable in both directions: while the theatre strives to make books speak, so too are books reframed to expose their incipient theatricality.

3

Story: Adaptation and the Act of Telling

This chapter considers the ways in which an appreciation of the concerns and critiques attached to story and storytelling can be used profitably to reframe understanding of theatre's own (re)tellings, in performance practice and in adaptation studies. An adaptation need not, of course, be narrative-led: whatever priorities might seem to drive the literary source, its adaptation may be more powerfully influenced by the formal demands imposed by the material, or by other agendas – cultural, political, economic – to which 'story' becomes subordinate. Equally, the chosen text might itself entertain the possibility of story only to resist this, by fracturing the telling, withholding its anticipated rewards, or by reinventing the 'rules' of narrative organization and development. Embedded playfulness of this kind is seen in extreme form in Denis Diderot's digressive *Jacques, the Fatalist* and in David Foster Wallace's sprawling multi-narrative novel *Infinite Jest*, both of which I discuss in Chapter 5. Further, as we have seen, prose adaptation in the theatre does not only mean adaptations of fiction: the previous chapter considered the theatrical treatment by Stan's Cafe of what is a treatise or reference work, if *The Anatomy of Melancholy* can meaningfully be categorized at all. Nonetheless, while acknowledging both that dominant assumptions about linear narrativity are undermined by examples of novels at least as far back as the mid-eighteenth century and thoroughly unsettled in the twentieth and twenty-first century, and that adaptation practice today seeks out ever more unlikely sources for inspiration, it remains notable how frequently 'story' *is* emphasized in that process above other factors. Practitioners and playwrights gesture towards story to signal the continued potency of a source text or its rediscovered relevance and timeliness; persistently, the borrowed work is pictured as a 'story that needed telling', sometimes as a means of enabling another yet more urgent narrative to be heard.

The philosopher and literary critic Richard Kearney has argued, here drawing on Aristotle, that the art of storytelling is 'what gives us a *shareable world*'. Kearney continues:

> It is, in short, only when haphazard happenings are transformed into story, and thus made *memorable* over time, that we become full agents of our history. […] Without this transition from nature to narrative, from time suffered to time enacted and enunciated, it is debatable whether a merely biological life (*zoe*) could be considered a truly human one (*bios*).[1]

In this light, the apparent centrality of story in adaptation is unsurprising. If storytelling is understood, as Kearney suggests, as a practice of articulation that seeks to shape human experience and imagination in purposeful and profoundly interconnected ways, then storytelling through adaptation can in turn be regarded as an adherence to, and perpetuation of, the same desire. For while the appropriative move that adaptation necessarily makes is sometimes perceived as parasitic, a more generous interpretation of the adaptive impulse is precisely to see in this an affirmation of belief in the shareable. Adaptation proposes often unexpected connections between forms, genres, periods, styles, authors, preoccupations, cultures, languages – and in the case of adaptation for the theatre, as Mike Alfreds phrases it, between the 'world of the written story and the world of its performance'.[2] Such negotiations will inevitably be marked by tensions as well as opportunities.

My opening paragraphs display a degree of linguistic slippage between 'story' and 'narrative'. While these terms are very often used interchangeably (and habitually feature within each other's definition), a common distinction is that where a story may be self-contained, a narrative hints at a larger purpose: the latter term implies not only story content but the mode of telling and, perhaps, the motive for doing so. Its etymology is based in the classical Latin *narrare*, to relate or recount, and post-classical *gnarus*, meaning knowing or skilled; in that period and in the Middle Ages, to narrate also meant to plead in a court of law and to recite the verdict of a jury; thus, as J. Hillis Miller explains, '[w]ithin the concept of narration are obscurely inscribed the ideas of judging and interpretation'.[3] Jean-François Lyotard's application of the phrase 'grand narrative' (or metanarrative), outlined in *The Postmodern Condition*, implicitly underpins this interpretation. For Lyotard, the grand narrative is a characteristic feature of the period of modernity, exemplified in the operations of the Enlightenment project. The grand narrative (here of Enlightenment progress, rationality and individualism) attempts to sweep up, recast and explain individual stories according to its own validating philosophy; rejection of and incredulity towards these universalizing narratives is, according to Lyotard, one of the defining markers of postmodernity. If we accept that 'narrative' carries at least the germ of this connotation, the individual story – or 'little narrative' – can be an important form of resistance in the face of the totalizing power of the 'grand'. The practice of adaptation is positioned ambiguously against these terms, however. The storytelling impulse within adaptation is richly generative, encouraging us to listen for difference within appropriated texts as well as commonality. But at the same time, one could protest that the pressures of the adaptation form and context may force the source material into a pre-established mould. To take a popular example, the steady appetite of UK viewers for televised costume drama is appeased by successive adaptations of (predominantly) nineteenth-century realist novels; Sarah Cardwell has shown how such productions 'are marked out as different from other television programmes in several ways, and are often characterised as an escape, a refuge, both from run-of-the-mill television and from the present (our contemporary world)'.[4] Cardwell's own study effectively highlights distinctions between the approaches taken by individual adaptations; nonetheless it could be inferred from this illustration that the 'grand narrative' of classic adaptation, which demands satisfaction of certain generic requirements – visual spectacle, star casting and, typically, a certain ideological conservatism – risks overwriting the particularities of discrete literary works.

The implications and impact of 'grand' and 'little' narratives, and the vulnerabilities attached to this relationship and exposed by the adaptation transaction, are issues addressed in the first half of this chapter. The second part of my discussion concentrates in detail on two adaptation projects, both of them ensemble productions: Kneehigh Theatre's *The Red Shoes* (mounted in 2000, revived in 2010); and *I Was a Rat!,* collaboratively produced by the Birmingham Repertory Theatre, Nottingham Playhouse and New Wolsey Theatre, together with the Italian company Teatro Kismet (2013). The matter and the manner of traditional storytelling permeate these shows in different ways. Kneehigh's production takes a fairy tale by Hans Christian Andersen as its source; Philip Pullman's novel for children rewrites and subverts a traditional tale, the identity of which is withheld from the reader for much of the book. Through analysis of these adaptations, as performance events in their own terms and as readings of different and distinct orders of text, I explore how the theatre encounters and might tackle the sometimes fraught relationship between 'preservation' and 'transformation'; how stage production reinterprets the storyteller's art of both sustaining and disrupting narrative progress; finally, how these acts of telling necessarily perform a doubling (at least) of fictional and actual, elsewhere and immediate, described and embodied, that in turn demonstrates how, as a forum for adaptation, the theatre has unique formal abilities that can help to keep stories of all kinds contingent and open.

Storytelling as adaptation: Adaptation as storytelling

To regard the literary basis of adaptation primarily as a story might seem to imply, naively, that the formal or contextual attributes of a work are somehow inconsequential. In practice, however, it does not follow that such considerations will be neglected. Rather, the privileging of story is typically a popularizing move that conveys the promise of accessibility, entertainment and engagement. 'Story' announces a journey of the imagination, an undertaking to rouse curiosity, stir emotions and feed an appetite for discovery. Crucially, story also stands for a place in which different kinds of audience might come together, a common ground, not because a story means the same to everyone but because anyone can tell, listen, remember and retell a story and in so doing can make it significantly their own. Highlighting the communication of story as the central preoccupation of an adaptation may also indicate a desire to be free from the 'trappings' of a text – its associations, expectations and histories of reproduction and reception – and thus clear a space within which it might become possible to tell and/or receive that story *as if* for the first time. Finally, proposing a connection between theatre today and an older performance tradition of oral storytelling acknowledges the distinctive character of traditional tales as widely and immediately comprehensible on the level of surface narrative, yet simultaneously capable of yielding multiple and rich interpretive possibilities for culturally mixed audiences of all ages. Undertaking to 'retell' a source text in this way – fairy story or literary fiction, familiar or more obscure – is an inclusive gesture that implicitly probes the borderlines of narratives and leans towards an expansion rather than 'fixing' of communicative space.

Evidently, the twin elements of a work of literature and the adaptations it inspires are not straightforwardly the equivalent of a traditional folk or fairy tale and its re-emergence in historical and cultural variants. A novel by a single, named author (still living or otherwise) is not so fully and freely available for adaptation as a popular narrative whose roots are unknown and whose boundaries are uncertain; indeed, the more strongly a text is considered the product of a specific author-creator, the more cumbersome the critical baggage attached, at all stages, to any project of adaptation. Fairy tales, however, already have the quality of fragments: they are 'shards of story' and consequently seem to invite and even require intervention in a way that is not equally true of a work originated as literature.[5] Yet if one accepts even in part Barthes's claim that any text is 'a multidimensional space in which a variety of writings, none of them original, blend and clash', and that ultimately an author's power is only 'to mix writings, to counter the ones with the others, in such a way as never to rest on any one of them', then the distinction between literary and popular narratives becomes less fundamental.[6] From this perspective, any work of literature stands as a contribution to, and intervention in, an ongoing history of textual production and transmission: its covers are not opaque but translucent, its pages already scribbled on in other hands. Just as importantly, accepting a degree of correspondence between these practices – adapting literature for performance on the one hand, and popular storytelling on the other – can be helpful to us, since the connection draws attention not only to an ancient and still vibrant tradition of narrative (re)circulation that manifests cross-culturally, but one that is directly constructed by the dual and potentially conflicting imperatives of preservation and transformation. The theory and practice of adaptation are self-evidently marked by precisely this tension: inescapably so, since to consider any work in terms of adaptation is immediately to acknowledge an intertextual relationship or dependency.

The American academic Jack Zipes has been one of the most attentive and assiduous commentators on the evolution, dissemination and mutation of the classical fairy tale from its roots in oral storytelling, demonstrating through several studies from the late 1970s onwards the shifting cultural and political meanings these narratives can serve to reinforce and at times contest. Zipes demonstrates not simply that such tales are malleable, altered by context and open to ideological use and abuse; he argues that transformation is and has always been integral to the storyteller's task. Since it is impossible to establish the original or authentic version of popular tales, this drive towards reinvention may have arisen more from necessity than choice:

> [Storytellers] all have had to build on the past, on tradition, on stories handed down over the ages. They have had to translate from different tongues to facilitate understanding and create meaning. But what distinguishes the great writers and storytellers is that they write and tell with a conscious effort to grab hold of tradition as if it were a piece of clay and to mold it and remold it to see what they can make out of it

> for the present. [...] Nothing is inanimate in their hands and mouths. They are animators, breathing life into all things and all beings. They don't worship the past and tradition, but demand that the past and tradition justify themselves in the present. In turn, they ask that their remolding of the past and tradition be questioned.[7]

By this account, to undertake 'storytelling' is to connect with an existing body or bodies of tales, handed down through and changed by generations; active participation in the telling process is an almost shamanic act that combines appreciation of the rituals of the past with revivifying creativity in the present. Crucially, Zipes associates the element of tradition as much with the stance of telling as with the stories themselves. When taking up a tale its new narrator has an obligation to be curious and even actively distrustful, since to pass on any story without questioning what is at stake within it is to betray rather than uphold the telling tradition.[8]

How might this representation of the storyteller's task be used to reframe understanding of adaptation, both in general and within the theatre? First, to participate authentically in this tradition would require adapters to approach their sources with a combination of fascination (why else are they drawn to it?) and scepticism; re-makers could not allow their obsession with a text to blind them to its 'faults'. That such a perspective *would* be adopted might seem axiomatic, given that today, in practice and in theory, adaptations and critics have advanced from a place where what Wagner disparagingly termed mere 'transposition' of a source is demanded or even anticipated.[9] Yet the profound critical engagement with story Zipes insists on cannot be assumed. The implications of accepting a potential equivalence between adaptation and storytelling go beyond insisting on creative license and defending the legitimacy of changes. For Zipes, an effective manifestation of a story is one in which the appropriated text is required to 'justify [itself] in the present' in ideological terms as well for the artistic opportunities it might seem to invite. By extension, the adaptation eventually realized in performance must feel pertinent in the moment. To argue this does not, of course, mean seeking out texts that endorse a certain ideological stance; it virtually suggests the reverse, since responsibility rests with the new tellers to confront the complexities of their text and what it might seem to 'say' when reiterated in a context of sometimes profoundly altered circumstances, perceptions and values.

Zipes's own writing has always engaged directly with social and political questions. His landmark 1979 study *Breaking the Magic Spell: Radical Theories of Folk and Fairy Tales* approached its material from a Marxist perspective; in it, he urged readers and scholars alike to attend to the critically neglected relationship between storytelling and social class, economics and ideology. The 2002 edition of this work contained, amongst other revisions, a new chapter titled 'The Radical Morality of Rats, Fairies, Wizards and Ogres: Taking Children's Literature Seriously'. In this essay, Zipes underlined the continuing importance of children's books – as well as films and television programmes – in developing complex critical literacies. His personal position on this remained unequivocal:

> If a text does not somehow stimulate a reader/viewer to reflect creatively and critically about his/her surroundings, to question himself or herself and the world, then it has, in my opinion, very little value for the social, moral and psychological development of young people.[10]

Zipes thus strongly emphasizes the ideological function of stories and hence the accountability attached to the telling. As his writings on traditional and contemporary fairy tales have amply demonstrated, this is not for him *all* that a story is or does; rather, his argument is that storytelling is inevitably a form of ideological transaction – whether conservative or actively questioning – and as such, participants in that tradition should intervene with critical awareness, or not at all.

The theories outlined in *Breaking the Magic Spell* continue to be 'radical' in the sense of the case Zipes makes for a story's rootedness in the history of social relations. But in 1979 his argument was radical also in its fierce and explicit critique of the methods and findings of fellow American Bruno Bettelheim. Bettelheim's highly influential work

The Uses of Enchantment: The Meaning and Importance of Fairy Tales, published three years earlier, made a persuasive case, underpinned by Freudian psychoanalytic theory, for the therapeutic role of fairy tales in children's identity formation and the 'moral education' such tales provided, to quote Bettelheim, 'subtly, and by implication only'.[11] Modern versions should not seek to expunge or otherwise sanitize the violent, cruel and grotesque aspects of these stories, Bettelheim argued, since children intuitively comprehend and respond to this darkness and actively need this to help them pass from one stage of life development to the next. Bettelheim's readings of the classic tales proved compelling, and through their impact 'pediatricians [...] restored harsh fairy tales including the Grimms's to children's bookshelves, and endorsed the therapeutic powers of fictional cruelty and horror'.[12] But while the case he made against 'cleaning up' fairy tales has had a lasting effect – reflected in the uncompromising themes and surreal or macabre illustrations now commonly seen in children's literature – the reasoning that supported his argument was not comprehensively or enduringly convincing. Zipes was swift to challenge Bettelheim's view that fairy tales shored up a natural, necessary and apparently universal process of psychological maturation, and other voices – many of them feminist – joined in to express alarm at the implications of an approach that effectively bypassed the contexts in which stories had been shaped and told. Thus, in *From the Beast to the Blonde: On Fairy Tales and Their Tellers*, British writer and mythographer Marina Warner rejected Bettelheim's argument that (in his own words)

> the typical fairytale splitting of the mother into a good (usually dead) mother and an evil stepmother serves the child well. It is not only a means of preserving an internal all-good mother when the real mother is not all-good, but it also permits anger at this bad 'stepmother' without endangering the goodwill of the true mother who is viewed as a different person.[13]

Warner showed how the consequence of such a reading had been to make the bad mother

> an inevitable, even required ingredient in fantasy, and hatred of her a legitimate, applauded stratagem of psychic survival. [It] has contributed to the continuing absence of good mothers from fairy tales in all kinds of media, and to a dangerous degree which itself mirrors current prejudices and reinforces them. His argument, and its tremendous diffusion and widespread acceptance, have effaced from memory the historical reasons for women's cruelty within the home and have made such behaviour seem natural, even intrinsic to the mother-child relationship.[14]

For Bettelheim, the characters of fairy tale were not individualized representations but symbols that, through their interaction, played out the internal drama of the maturing self. However, to apply that interpretive frame in the abstract is disingenuous since symbolic meaning must accrue *from somewhere*; as Francis Spufford has observed, '[e]very story has to be taken literally before it is taken any other way'.[15] Warner's accusation that Bettelheim's archetypal approach problematically 'leeche[d] history out of fairy tale' echoed Zipes's insistence that our comprehension of the durability and vitality of stories is deepened, and not undone, when we disenchant ourselves sufficiently to reconnect narratives to their origins rather than commit them to an ahistorical dreamtime.[16]

American folklorist Maria Tatar likewise took issue with manifestly gendered assumptions in *The Uses of Enchantment* that allowed its author and others after him to read, for instance, a tale like 'Bluebeard' not in the way its narrative action would suggest – in other words, as a story examining extreme violence by men against women – but, perversely, as a warning to women against (sexual) curiosity.[17] Tatar further questioned the validity of a method that approached any tale in isolation; it made little sense to conclude that children would – or should – take from 'Bluebeard' a lesson about the hazards of curiosity when alternative and even closely related tales showed the same trait saving the protagonist's life.[18] Tatar's inclusive vision demonstrates how appreciation of intertextuality both extends understanding and problematizes the perception that any single telling is 'true'. As readers, we too are encouraged – to cite Barthes once more – 'to mix writings, to counter the ones with the others', and moreover to be suspicious of any critic who does 'rest' too weightily on a single narrative; for as Tatar remarks, '[n]o fairy tale was ever meant to be written in granite'.[19] The advice to mix writings adheres in respect of critical perspectives also, and certainly Tatar's own model is more flexible and self-consciously eclectic than the strictly Freudian paradigm that drives *The Uses of Enchantment*. However, Tatar does not dismiss the potential rewards of a psychoanalytic approach to fairy tales. Like Bettelheim, she is fascinated by the ways in which these tales 'speak' to children, to comfort, terrify, excite, stir and change them; unlike him, Tatar has been consistently suspicious of interpretations rooted in an adult perspective that has too tightly harnessed specific narratives to particular and questionable meanings.

The issues explored can be applied and are to an extent already reflected in the context of theatre and adaptation, whether or not the source text is derived from popular tale tradition. Acknowledging the potential radicalism of the storyteller role implies that those stepping into this tradition should above all find the social in their material, through research and by means of creative and critical reflection; in this way, both the making process and eventual production aspire to 'serious entertainment', continuing a history of storytelling as vital community engagement – although not, of course, necessarily taking the form of community theatre. But equally, the same tradition requires that attention to contemporary context be balanced with appreciation of what makes stories (or elements of stories) last, even as they are changed and transformed; and while it is vital to remain alert to the clichés that sometimes accompany a psychoanalytic or therapeutic approach, such analyses can help illuminate why certain story images, symbols and structures have continued to prove resonant. Where an interpretation looks poised to 'set' too hard, the advantages and opportunities of intertextuality become apparent: exposing the ways in which stories of different kinds intersect with one another – old and new, popular and literary, playful and doctrinaire, textual and more broadly cultural – underlines the fictional dimension of all narratives and suggests in turn that the seemingly authoritative might yet be countered and contested. Moreover, the perception of unlimited narrative possibility can be sharpened still further in the context of live performance. Immediacy, creativity, spontaneity, participation in a larger shared event: recognition of all these qualities can be exploited to rouse, however temporarily, something akin to the resistant and utopian spirit that has significantly shaped storytelling tradition.[20]

While storytelling and theatre have many elements in common, they also have noticeable differences. Storytelling as a performance form (as opposed to an everyday act) is typically practised by an individual, not an ensemble; a teller is more likely to follow a story 'map' than a memorized text, and to present rather than represent characters. Further, storytelling performances generally take place in less hierarchical spaces than the traditional theatre building, with any set and costuming kept minimal, in this way working to establish an atmosphere of connectedness between performer and audience in which 'comeback' from the latter is encouraged or at least exists as a genuine possibility. Yet to detail such differences immediately calls attention to exceptions that undermine the clarity of this distinction. Storytelling performances *do* sometimes happen in theatres; they can involve multiple tellers who interact with one another; the practice of some artists involves techniques that would commonly be considered 'acting'. At the same time, theatre regularly incorporates characteristic features of storytelling, and, I suggest, especially so where stage adaptations of literature explicitly refer to the narrative origins of their material. That each art readily appropriates aspects of the other emerges clearly through the body of interviews Michael Wilson has conducted with storytellers in Britain and Ireland. For example Taffy Thomas, who in 2009 became the United Kingdom's first laureate for storytelling, told Wilson that 'storytellers borrow from the world of theatre and performance the things that are useful to us and dispense with the ones that aren't'.[21] As I will show, this largely benign thievery extends both ways.

Andersen/Kneehigh: *The Red Shoes*

The work of UK-based Kneehigh Theatre typifies the kind of socially engaged, lively-yet-serious storytelling theatre I describe. Formed in 1980 originally as a Theatre-in-Education company, Kneehigh built their reputation with colourful, accessible shows influenced by popular performance forms: music, dance, storytelling, puppetry, participation and spectacle have all combined to shape their distinctive aesthetic. But within this mix, storytelling is emphasized most prominently and consistently as a thread running through all their work and tying together a lengthening list of stage adaptations for which the source might be a novel (Carter's *Nights at the Circus*, 2005; Morpurgo's *The Amazing Story of Adolphus Tips*, 2016), classic drama (*The Bacchae*, 2004; *Cymbeline*, 2006), film (*A Matter of Life and Death*, 2007; *Brief Encounter*, 2008), television series (*Steptoe & Son*, 2013) or traditional tale (*The Red Shoes*, 2000; *Rapunzel*, 2006; *The Wild Bride*, 2011). Emma Rice, for many years the company's joint artistic director with Mike Shepherd, unites these very different orders of text by the simple assertion that Kneehigh tell 'stories because they matter'; further, approaching any source as 'a story, not as a text' means that in the devising process, 'the landscape of choices gently alters'.[22] For Rice, theatre-making starts with 'an itch, a need' that leads her to reach 'instinct[ively]' for a story that responds to this.[23] When Rice explains what has guided Kneehigh's selections, it is notable that she cites Bettelheim. Rice's experience of the profound rewards storytelling theatre can have for both audience and creators is implicitly supported by the argument made in *The Uses of Enchantment* that as human beings we turn to stories as a means of explaining our world back to us.[24] Precisely what matters in a chosen story lies somewhere between the itch and the instinct and is discovered, in Kneehigh's case, through a highly physical, knockabout process that opens up the material and enables it, step by step, to 'take on a life of its own'.[25] If Bettelheim's work is offered as a source of unproblematic inspiration, this perhaps suggests that the grounded, embodied practice of theatre-making itself counteracts the risk that context and history will be 'leeched' from the material (the argument of Zipes, Warner and Tatar); certainly Kneehigh's theatre, as I will show, does not aspire to harness the archetypal at the expense of the rootedly social.

The Red Shoes, an award-winning production first directed by Rice in 2000 and remounted successfully at the Battersea Arts Centre a decade later, illustrates how a relatively simple popular narrative can be probed and provoked to bring it vital and kicking into the contemporary moment. The 1845 fairy story by Danish author Hans Christian Andersen describes an orphan girl who longs for a pair of red shoes, which she obtains and then wears to church, to the extreme disapproval of the community. The shoes are confiscated, but the girl steals them back: when she next puts them on, she can neither stop dancing nor remove them. Desperate, she begs an executioner to chop off her feet with his axe. He does so, carving her a substitute wooden pair on which she hobbles to the church only to find her entrance barred and the chopped off feet in red shoes dancing mockingly beside her. The final section of the story tells of the girl's bitter repentance and dedication of the rest of her life to the church; eventually she is shown mercy by an angel, but the joy of this moment causes her heart to burst and she dies, her soul rising to heaven unencumbered. Andersen's tales were advocated by his contemporaries for their educational value and on this level 'The Red Shoes' describes graphically what will happen to those whose actions and attitudes depart from the normative. However, the impact of the story exceeds its didactic purpose: the grotesquely memorable imagery lingers in the mind after the precise nature of the protagonist's 'crime' is forgotten. Perceptions of this tale might equally be influenced by some knowledge of Andersen's life: the son of a cobbler and a washerwoman, he regularly expressed through his fiction a strong degree of sympathy for the underdog or outsider.[26] From this perspective, 'The Red Shoes' could be interpreted as a story about rebelliousness that describes rather than proscribes the harsh penalty exacted. Andersen himself was no rebel, however ('Politics is not for me to dabble in'), and his stated views were distinctly conservative.[27] Nonetheless, he maintained a fundamentally ambivalent attitude towards the powerful classes whose patronage brought him wealth and fame, and something of this equivocation can be traced through the body of his work and in individual tales.

'The Red Shoes' had been dramatized before, most famously in Powell and Pressburger's 1948 film of the same name that stars Moira Shearer as an ambitious ballet dancer. Kneehigh's production likewise seizes on the already theatrical pivotal image of Andersen's tale and from this pair of scarlet-shod dancing feet extracts both the physical energy that drives the performance and a wealth of connotative meaning. Reviewing Kneehigh's remounted 2010 production in the *Guardian*, Elisabeth Mahoney argued that their adaptation could be appreciated on several levels, 'as a folk or fairy story about some magic footwear, as a parable about desire, or a spiky tale about women's lives, or all three together and more'. Mahoney continued:

> There are hints of suffragettes, concentration camps, anarchy, wise witches and kind butchers, and the fable as presented here is a blend of brilliantly simple visual richness and a kaleidoscope of ideas. It's a story about longing, about getting what you want and having to live with that as the delirious, half-crazed passion subsides. Mostly, though, this is intensely charismatic theatre about what it is to be alive and, as the witch says in the epilogue, the fate of 'those who dare to dance a different dance'.[28]

Mahoney's commentary describes a production that self-consciously stitches political and contemporary versions of difference and resistance into traditional story fabric. In part, such themes are conveyed through the aesthetic of the piece: the appearance of the performers – shaved heads, dirty white vests and briefs – itself speaks of a story stripped back in the telling to expose the absolute harshness at its core. At the same time, this visual signing of victimization is offset by a flamboyant spirit that is evident throughout, expressed through music, dance and deliberately fumbled magic tricks, and personified in Lady Lydia, a 'glamorous and glorious' transvestite compère played by Giles King.[29] The performers wear wooden clogs, shiny black and, in the one case, bright red; this choice references folk tradition but also lends the production a certain hard edge, an almost punkish quality intensified by the players' dark-smudged eyes. Where Andersen's 'The Red Shoes' describes the brutal punishment of specifically feminine vanity, Kneehigh's retelling conveys in a more layered and defiantly celebratory way a web of complex sexualities, desires and cross-gender constraints.

Kneehigh's adaptation does not turn 'The Red Shoes' into drama as such: visual, physical and musical as it is, the show is still presented consciously as an act of storytelling. The audience watches individual performers ('Storytellers' in the cast list) selected as if at random to take on the role of the Girl, the Old Lady, or the Shoemaker. This level of alienation – echoed in the use of battered suitcases that are deployed to establish makeshift settings, or from which items of clothing are unpacked – plays with the possibility that characterization is ascribed temporarily, not psychologically identified; parts could be otherwise assigned, we are invited to suppose, on a different night. This is not true in practice, quite the reverse: Rice has noted elsewhere how recasting a role – sometimes unavoidable, at a later stage – 'always rips your heart out.'[30] Nonetheless, the appearance of a ritualized distribution of roles conveys the impression that this ensemble accepts the responsibility to tell this story collectively between them. The act of telling is not limited to the words spoken, as writer Anna-Maria Murphy makes clear:

> Everything in this company's work tells the story: the actors, the set, the music, the costume, the props. A living script grows with Emma and the actors, through devising, improvisation and the poems [authored by Murphy]. Each plays an equal part. I say living, as it's always changing and we all own it.[31]

The claim that any and every aspect of a production has a storytelling function is endorsed by Kneehigh's example in overt ways – for instance, when a song is used to communicate plot development – but it is also more profoundly true of theatre as a form. Zipes's insistence that the responsible, critically alert storyteller must uncover the resonances of a given tale, both for him or herself and in relation to a changed context of reception, can be addressed in the theatre not by rewriting text but – as Brecht knew – through the introduction of music that jars rather than harmonizes with the narrative line, or in the proposition that a visual image implicitly extends. In *The Red Shoes*, the performers' shaven heads invite spectators to expand their interpretive frame well beyond young girls on their way to church, illicitly attired; moreover, the multiple connotations in this particular visual symbol – it evokes no single, simple parallel – keeps spectator engagement open and questioning. The image of the shaved head reverberates historically and in the present: it signals exposure, humiliation and punishment, but also stands for the refusal to conform. Kneehigh's audience spans a wide age range: and while children will not find in this image precisely the same meanings as their accompanying adults, they will register something of these resonances and find them starkly at odds with a story that deals, at least on the surface, with feminine vanity.

In this way, intertextuality is established across the whole fabric of performance rather than being confined to verbal allusion. Even in a mid-nineteenth-century context, Andersen's tale can hardly have been thought to describe straightforwardly 'immoral' behaviour and its well-deserved punishment; his readers and listeners would have had to negotiate for themselves any lingering unease at the nature and severity of retribution meted out, or look perhaps towards editors and illustrators for comment or critique. By contrast, theatre can embed resistance to the problematic assumptions or moral stance of a text within a production, and without necessarily changing the course of the narrative. Consider this sequence, in which the Old Lady (who is blind) quizzes Kneehigh's Storytellers about the new shoes her adopted daughter has chosen:

Old lady Are they smart?

Storytellers Yes.

Old Lady Are they shiny?

Storytellers Oh yes.

Old Lady Are they black?
Pause.

Storytellers … yes.[32]

By that momentary hesitation, spectators understand that the telling has turned against the tale. Brief as it is, the pause opens up a space of questioning: determination, not vacillation, is implied in this little gap. It marks a point at which actors step back from character and narrative; here, as in the staging of those magic tricks that periodically arrest rather than promote the flow of story, the tellers remind us that sometimes you must try to resist the tide.

If everything in theatre tells the story, as Murphy says of Kneehigh, it follows therefore that anything can also, if desired, tell against the story. As explored in Chapter 1, critiques of adaptation in general have regularly emphasized lack: when literature is translated into (especially) visual drama, so much – narrative tone, metaphor, authorial perspective, the rendition of inner states – will, it is claimed, inevitably be lost. Yet to consider adaptation in such terms is to ignore the opportunities the new medium allows. Theatre brings more valuable and complex gifts to a telling than the obvious additions of colour, sound, or physicality. Because it is multidimensional, theatre enables layering, juxtaposition and provocative formal contradiction. Because it is always participatory, at least to some degree, theatre can choose to exploit the live(ly) and unpredictable qualities of audience engagement. Because it simultaneously *presents* and *represents*, the theatrical event is characterized by gaps – between actor and role, place and imagined space, the people and things onstage and what they stand for – and such dislocations can be used productively to disturb, if not altogether overturn, the 'order' of the text. An adaptation may also choose to contest its material in overt as well as subtler ways and Kneehigh do this in their handling of Andersen's conclusion. In the fairy tale, the protagonist, Karen, is finally shown divine mercy but this comes hand in hand with death:

> [B]efore her stood an angel of God in white robes; it was the same one whom she had seen that night at the church-door. He no longer carried the sharp sword, but a beautiful green branch, full of roses; with this he touched the ceiling, which rose up very high, and where he had touched it there shone a golden star. He touched the walls, which opened wide apart, and she saw the organ which was pealing forth; she saw the pictures of the old pastors and their wives, and the congregation sitting

in the polished chairs and singing from their hymn-books. The church itself had come to the poor girl in her narrow room, or the room had gone to the church. [...] The bright warm sunshine streamed through the window into the pew where Karen sat, and her heart became so filled with it, so filled with peace and joy, that it broke. Her soul flew on the sunbeams to Heaven, and no one was there who asked after the *Red Shoes.*[33]

In Kneehigh's version, by contrast, the girl rejects the forgiveness that is so graciously extended:

Angel It's over.
Come with me.
Up into the blue.
Heavenward.

Lydia It's over.
Up into the blue.
He leads her away but she falters. It is as if she has remembered something: herself.
She breaks away.

Angel Now come along, your place is booked.
Salvation is yours.
Come along ... Heaven.
I'm afraid I must insist.
She breaks away again and a vicious fight ensues.
She beats the ANGEL and goes her own way.[34]

Here, not just the manner of telling but the tale itself is redirected towards affirmation rather than condemnation of an independent spirit. Kneehigh's decision to change the ending in this way is instantly comprehensible, given the dated moralism of Andersen's original; and as already argued, the idea that storytellers should make a tale their own is both a right and a responsibility actively embraced by the company in their work. To some extent, the combination of Kneehigh's upbeat energy and the composition of their family audience might seem more or less to enforce some sort of happy ending, yet the sequence I cite is nonetheless not easily celebratory: the 'vicious' character of the struggle makes clear that taking an oppositional stance may be difficult and painful.

However, interventionist or corrective rewriting is not imperative, even with the most troubling of texts, nor will it necessarily satisfy us. At least one reviewer challenged Kneehigh's revision of Andersen, suggesting that the adaptation's more optimistic conclusion – perhaps paradoxically – denied its audience the release that the fairy tale, harsh as it is, nonetheless allows; for Miriam Gillinson, the altered turn made for 'an odd conclusion, which side-steps the threat of comeuppance that glows in the dark underbelly of this story'.[35] Andersen's 'The Red Shoes' remains compelling for contemporary readers and not only as a result of its macabre imagery; it disturbs because of, and not despite, a complacent resolution in which pardon takes the form of 'a final and fatal punishment'.[36] Its author did not write anger and repugnance explicitly into tale's ending, but this does not mean that such reactions are disallowed; in some ways, the fact that they are *not* voiced can stir the reader's desire to challenge the logic of its closure the more strongly. To argue this is not to suggest, conservatively, that Kneehigh should have left well alone, but is rather to invite reflection on the ways in which new tellers choose to represent ideologically problematic stories in a contemporary context. We must also ask whether theatre as a medium *can* close its tellings on so bitter a note, should its creators desire, or whether the very qualities that make performance uniquely suited to popular storytelling – animation, collectivity, spontaneity, participation, connectedness – are also those that make genuinely dark and unsettling conclusions unsustainable.

Pullman/Ludovico: *I Was a Rat!*

In 2012, the British author Philip Pullman published a collection of his retellings of fifty stories by the Brothers Grimm. Pullman had few apprehensions about the project, explaining that he drew confidence in the knowledge that '[w]hen the story is already so strong, you can play with it without fear of damaging it'.[37] Such a view might seem to contradict my commentary on Kneehigh's altering of Andersen's ending, yet there is a distinction between rewriting the Grimms and tackling 'The Red Shoes'. While Andersen inevitably borrowed motifs that can be traced back to earlier and alternative tale traditions, and his works have been reimagined subsequently, they are not in themselves versions of pre-existing narratives. In contrast, Jacob and Wilhelm Grimm, in early nineteenth-century Germany, were collectors as much or more than they were authors. The brothers invited tellers to their home and wrote down the stories as they heard them; these tales, together with others taken from books and journals, were subsequently refined, rendered more or less stylistically and ideologically coherent, and issued in collections that have proved enduringly popular.[38] Moreover, some of the Grimms's most familiar stories – 'Cinderella', 'Little Red Cap' – exist in equally well-known form in earlier variants and have been rewritten since and in terms that have in their own way made as vital an imprint on literary storytelling tradition.[39] This in turn illuminates Pullman's claim in the introduction to his collection that 'a fairy tale is not a text' but an event of narration 'in a perpetual state of becoming and alteration'; and while the Grimms's 'event' may have been more notorious and formative than many others, their intervention did not arrest or control the flow of narrative (re)production. Pullman's aspiration with *Grimm Tales for Young and Old* was not to update, relocate or linguistically reframe the stories but to strip away anything that inhibited their 'running freely' and so 'produce a version [...] as clear as water'.[40] By comparison, *I Was a Rat!* (1999), a novel within Pullman's expanding series of fairy tale rewritings, is less transparent or supposedly 'neutral' and more knowingly subversive. In what follows I examine one adaptation of *I Was a Rat!* but preface this with a discussion of this novel for children, itself already an adaptation of a (very) familiar story and one that interrogates the corruptive as well as generative potential in storytelling.

I Was a Rat! or The Scarlet Slippers opens in archetypal territory with a shoemaker and his wife companionably at home, he finishing a pair of dainty shoes made 'for the love of it'.[41] They are childless, and while this is not represented as a source of sorrow – their life is industrious, not barren – the information establishes a conventional tale motif suggesting a situation soon to be overturned.[42] The cosy stasis is disturbed by a knock at the door: outside, a little boy in a grubby page's uniform explains himself only by repeating, in answer to their questions, 'I was a rat.' He does not know his name or why he is dressed this way; evidently uncivilized, he puts his face directly into a bowl of bread and milk and rips up the sheets Bob and Joan put down for him. The little he can say makes no sense, that he is three weeks old and once lived behind a cheese stall. The couple are further bewildered when he points at a photo in the paper of Lady Aurelia, royal bride-to-be, and identifies her confidently as 'Mary Jane!'[43] The boy is responsive to guidance, quickly acquiring terms and concepts that he applies sometimes correctly ('thank you') but often not (he is permanently confused about pencils, which he misnames and nibbles compulsively). Bob and Joan initially undertake to restore Roger – their intended name for a son, had they had one – to wherever he came from, but, thwarted by the indifference, bureaucracy and/or inhumanity displayed by the City Hall, hospital, orphanage, school and police station, they agree to keep him. Almost immediately he gets lost and here Pullman's novel acquires shades of *Oliver Twist*. Frightened at his treatment by adults disgusted by his rat-like habits, Roger runs, loses his way, and naively falls in with a series of individuals who variously exploit him. The opportunistic showman Mr Tapscrew exhibits him as a freak; the streetwise Billy engineers his escape, recognizing in Roger's skinny frame a valuable 'wriggler' to augment his gang of burglars. At his lowest point, crushed by his failed efforts to be (accepted as) human, Roger scavenges in the sewers: '"Once a rat, always a rat", Billy had told him, and it must be true, because he certainly wasn't any good at being a boy.'[44]

Rumours of the 'monster' spread and Roger is caught, caged and set before a tribunal predisposed to convict (and exterminate) him. In desperation, Bob and Joan appeal to Lady Aurelia, attracting her attention through the gift of the scarlet slippers. She proves surprisingly approachable and, struck by the mention of a 'rat boy' and the name 'Mary Jane', promises to help.[45] In Roger's prison cell, she reassembles their shared history: she was the servant girl transformed into a princess, he the rat/pageboy who – in this version – accidentally got separated from both his mistress and the 'Cinderella' tale. By making a marginal character central, Pullman's adaptation turns the Grimms's 'Cinderella' around: yet at the same time this retelling echoes its model by the motif of a slipper that enables confirmation of identity and by reinforcing the theme that even the littlest and most downtrodden is still the hero of his own story. That is not the same as being in control of it: indeed, realization of the ways in which boy and girl are perceived and constructed – intuited by Roger, conscious in Mary Jane – has produced disillusionment in both. They try in vain to summon the fairy to reverse the transformation: as Aurelia/Mary Jane says, 'Maybe she only comes once and grants you a wish, and then you're stuck with the consequences.'[46] Roger is finally restored to Bob and Joan and the ending describes them gathered as a family around the hearth, with Roger apprenticed to the cobbling trade.

The story of Roger's adventures is conveyed to the reader by Pullman in two principal ways. Prefacing his arrival in Chapter 1 is a page that a reader might overlook: a sheet from Bob's newspaper, the *Daily Scourge*, including a column headed 'LOVE AT THE BALL' that excitedly describes how 'Hunky Prince Richard' danced all night with mysterious Lady Aurelia Ashington (it was 'like something out of a fairy tale', gushes the 'Romance Correspondent'), a photo of the happy couple complete with twee tagline, and pointers to other pages promising a 'fact-file of the playboy prince's previous girlfriends' and exposé of 'the lovely young Princess-to-be'.[47] The page does more than plant a clue to the embedded narrative, the knowledge of which would establish Roger's identity more quickly. In its parody of a genre – the tabloid press – this insertion and others that follow alert the reader to another source of popular tale-telling, different in kind but equally obsessed with fantasy and marvel. The initially playful burlesque ('"I've never seen him so in love", said a close friend of the Prince') becomes more biting as the novel progresses. Roger's adventures are tracked in these 'extracts', both coincidentally – through a feature advocating corporal punishment for wayward schoolchildren, and alarmist accounts of crime rises – and explicitly, with an 'artist's impression of the evil monster in his lair in the sewers'. Observing the tabloid's strategic distortions, and its eventual shameless *volte-face* following the Princess' intervention, the reader can hardly fail to register Pullman's critique.[48] While the *Scourge* betrays its proclaimed by-line of 'Truth' at every entry, it lives up to its name in more ways than one: as a whip or lash, the *Scourge* inflicts punishment where it chooses; as a plague of sorts, the spread of popular, crowd-pleasing narratives is implicitly condemned as a dangerous substitute for direct experience and knowledge.

Pullman's focus on tabloid mythmaking is particularly illuminating considered in the context of the late 1990s. The *Scourge*'s treatment of the royal bride recalls British media obsession with Diana, Princess of Wales and the manipulation of Diana's image in the press up to and following her death in 1997 (the year *I Was a Rat!* was published); Pullman evidently had this in mind at the time.[49] The same year, Pullman expressed concern with how the James Bulger murder case had been reported and, in particular, how the press helped demonize Bulger's ten-year-old killers in the eyes of the public by circulating selected photographs and video clips. 'So many of our most powerful judgements are made because of what things look like', he remarked, adding, 'In this age, we can't escape these visual presences, so we must learn to read them.'[50] The emphasis on media mythmaking in *I Was a Rat!* updates a story that, despite its conventional opening, is subtly disturbed throughout by ruptures of the modern. A world that at first recalls the atemporal or at least preindustrial realm of fairy tale gives way – through the imperative that the 'problem' of Roger be tackled – to a series of encounters with recognizably contemporary bureaucratic structures of educational, legalistic or judicial control. At each point, Pullman invites the reader to see how language functions crucially to organize experience and perception. Thus the doctors are quick to diagnose a case of 'rodent delusion', while for the Philosopher Royal, Roger's claim to know the princess indicates '[f]antasy-identification with figures of glamour', a trait common to the 'lower classes'.[51] The attempt to explain and linguistically contain 'uncivilised' behaviour is repeated in more directly exploitative fashion by Mr Tapscrew, whose poster hyperbolically advertises a now-caged Roger as 'The World's only genuine living!!RAT-BOY!!', 'half-human, half-rodent, altogether ABOMINABLE'. Tapscrew insists the bewildered child dons a rat-suit; the artist Peter Bailey's illustration of this moment neatly conveys a blankness in Roger's expression acutely at odds with both the overwrought language of the billboard and the sharp-featured and calculating show people.[52] In addition, interruptive echoes of another kind of language suggestively contest the imposition of these regulatory discourses, this time drawn from the rudiments of polite speech taught Roger by Bob and Joan. Remembering his manners, the 'savage and ferocious' rat-boy absentmindedly says 'thank you' when a rotten potato is hurled into the enclosure, a mistake a vicious beating ensures he will not repeat; and alone at night, he whispers a mantra ('Bob and Joan – bread and milk – nightshirt – privy – patience') that for him symbolizes a place and time where his blunders met with gentler treatment.

The multiplicity of competing languages and modes of narration in *I Was a Rat!* reflects arguments Pullman has made elsewhere, that a book effectively extends a proposition to its reader that is passed back and forth through the activity of reading in an almost conversational fashion. This is a dialogical process, since for adult and child alike engaging with a book means bringing to that encounter 'our own preconceptions and expectations, our own intellectual qualities, and our limitations, too, our own previous experiences of reading, our own temperament, our own hopes and fears, our own personality'.[53] Unlike a lecture, a book may be picked up and put down at will, its pages read in any order and at the pace we choose; its claims can be checked against other sources and thus 'we can assent, or we can disagree'. Democracies enable interactive reading, distinguishing them, for Pullman, from theocracies in which the authority of particular texts is held to be above dispute. Yet as he acknowledges, democracies can quite easily forget how to read.[54] A former teacher, Pullman has argued for the complex educative role of reading and has been outspoken in his criticisms of government-sponsored literacy schemes whose damaging effects include the introduction of 'barren' phonics-driven texts in schools, or reading only that which is to be tested.[55] Exemplifying these arguments, the layered mechanisms of telling in *I Was a Rat!* shape a reading encounter in which curiosity and pleasure join with scepticism. The reader sees the vulnerability of the outcast's story against ideological 'grand narratives' of inclusion and exclusion, victims and predators, civilized and savage; she understands further that most insidious of all is the boy's suggestibility to their insistent force ('Billy had told him, and it must be true').

I Was a Rat! insists that narrative authority be questioned, not just through representation of the fluctuating and distorting activities of the *Scourge* but in the subtler provocations of the visual image. Bailey's understated black-and-white line drawings extend the interactive relationship between text and reader by setting up a different kind of conceptual task: that which the illustrations do not show prompts use of the imagination 'to [...] "colour" the image in the mind in a similar way to the activity of fleshing out text when reading'.[56] At the same time, Bailey's drawings are eloquent in their very restraint: the delicate, oblique and almost characterless delineation of the 'rat boy' – whether grotesquely costumed, looking up through a sewer grating, or naked in a prison cell – suggest disquietingly Roger's susceptibility to manipulation and, by extension, the vulnerability of all children at the hands of adults. *I Was a Rat!* obliges us to distrust the tales told about this particular child, yet the task of distinguishing fact from saleable or otherwise ideologically convenient fiction is complicated by the book's adherence – amidst all this myth 'debunking' – to the logic of fairy tale, whereby the marvellous is accepted and rendered ordinary. In this territory, feet that dance out of control are chopped off; a poor girl can change into a princess; a rat may turn into a boy. So while in Pullman's novel the 'monster' in the sewers was only ever a frightened child, the larger mystery of his transformation is left intact; despite the contemporaneity of the telling and deconstruction of opportunistic mythmaking, the reader's appetite for the marvellous is still nourished by the magical, the silences in the text that have not been explained away. Such work poses manifest challenges for adaptation, therefore: the illustrative completion that performance seems designed to provide risks filling in those gaps and in the process pre-empting the imaginative – and dialogic – responsibility of the receiving audience.

Teresa Ludovico's 2013 production of *I Was a Rat!,* created in association with Birmingham Repertory Theatre, Nottingham Playhouse and the New Wolsey Theatre, is one of a series of theatrical fairy tale reworkings written and directed by Ludovico since 2000 but the first for which the source was a text by a living author. With Teatro Kismet – the Italian company she joined as an actress in the late 1980s and of which she became artistic director – Ludovico's previous adaptations have included *Beauty and the Beast* (2002), *The Snow Queen* (2006) and *The Mermaid Princess* (2007), the latter two based on tales by Andersen.[57] These shows and *I Was a Rat!* have played largely to family audiences, but while their appeal to the young is evident – and Ludovico pays close attention to that experience, 'testing' material with children during the rehearsal process – it is notable that adult spectators and critics have also found her work deeply engaging.[58] This cross-generational success is explained partly by a directorial aesthetic derived from Ludovico's background in classical theatre (as opposed to theatre intended for children), and partly in the source material: her practice has always drawn on traditional tales, their resonant symbols and structures enabling exploration of the kinds of human journeys and life stages whose significance can be widely understood. Clearly, a symbol will not hold identical meanings for children as for adults (nor mean the same to each child or adult); likewise, what lends potency to a tale on the page may not prove equally productive on the stage. It takes longer to make theatre for children, Ludovico states, as the work carries increased responsibility: with such an audience 'the wrong symbol can hurt'.[59]

This ethos would seem potentially compatible with Pullman's own. Many of the author's books (above all his *Northern Lights* trilogy) have been as popular with adults as younger readers and Pullman has insisted that the only major difference in writing for these audiences is that

> when you're writing for children, you cannot expect them to *know* as much. That's all. You expect them to be just as intelligent, just as curious, just as alive to all the story offers, just as capable of being moved by the same sort of things. But they just don't know as much about the world and about things in general, about human behaviour, so you just explain a little more.[60]

For Ludovico, similarly, 'the difference between a child and a grown up is only a matter of time'.[61] From this shared perception, Pullman and Ludovico produce layered texts of which it cannot be said that certain aspects – magic, or comic silliness – are included for the children, with more 'sophisticated' elements – emotional weight, intellectual reference – for the adults. This is work that respects the mature sensibility within the child, and vice versa: Pullman's fiction and Ludovico's theatre proceed from the assumption that wonder, insight, delight in mystery and an appreciation of darkness as the counter-side of light are shades of human response available at some level to all readers and spectators.

Pullman sought out Ludovico after watching *The Snow Queen;* a 'meeting of minds', in her phrase, informed the decision to adapt *I Was a Rat!* Pullman's fiction has been adapted before, for theatre and for cinema. Nicholas Hytner's ambitious six-hour, two-part *His Dark Materials* for the National Theatre (2003) and Chris Weitz's *The Golden Compass* for New Line Cinema (2007) – both based on the *Northern Lights* trilogy – have attracted most attention, but there have been additional quite different mountings of Nicholas Wright's dramatization, as well as numerous adaptations of other Pullman texts (another novel for children, *The Fireworkmaker's Daughter*, has proved especially popular on the stage).[62] Pullman had some involvement in the National Theatre production – Hytner describes his presence in rehearsals as that of 'a benevolent observer and sometimes very trenchant participant' – but typically distances himself from adaptations.[63] Asked by Kate Kellaway of the *Observer* whether he feared his books would be ruined as a result of selling the film rights, he responded bluntly: 'No. Waste of time. Take the money and forget it. I have no power.'[64] Similarly, in a 2011 Open University lecture, he responded to a question about his attitude to adaptations by saying he would 'go expecting the worst, then [he wouldn't] be too disappointed'. Essentially, he has seemed to regard (especially film) adaptation with little hope but no great alarm: luckily, he remarked to the OU audience, 'there is no law saying that [after adaptation] all the copies of the book should be taken away and burnt'.[65] Thus Pullman avoided rehearsals of *I Was a Rat!*, despite his admiration for Ludovico's earlier work; but on watching the production, he wrote to the director to explain that the tension he felt, seated in the auditorium, was dispelled on realizing that 'his story was in the hands of a real storyteller'.[66]

Where Kneehigh self-consciously emphasize the activity of telling – the performers conveying Andersen's moralistic tale in implied quotation marks throughout – Ludovico's production fully embraces enactment. This show does not 'tell' by means of narration; the spoken text is virtually all dialogue, with no explicit inclusion of the authorial voice. Ludovico's version of Pullman's inside-out Cinderella story is constituted through a heterogeneous mix of discourses including dramatic characterization and dialogue, carnivalesque comedy, mask, puppetry, acrobatics and a score by Frank Moon that clashes together 'East European folk and gypsy music, grotesque circus melodies, wonky fanfares [and] some very noisy drumming.'[67] An ensemble of eight takes on multiple roles as the narrative requires: the one constant characterization is Roger, played throughout by dancer Fox Jackson-Keen. The production employs a range of conventions to represent the different worlds that Roger encounters: Bob and Joan (Lorna Gayle, the one woman in the cast) are relatively 'natural', dressed and lit in earthy shades; the institutional figures wear bird-like half-masks, their mise-en-scène drained towards black and white; Tapscrew's fairground folk are saturated in gaudy reds and purples (in design inspired by the illustrations of Lorenzo Mattotti), with exaggerated silhouettes, garish make-up, false noses and beards that together evoke carnival and the crude humour of the cross-dressed dame. The set is limited to an oversized chair, wheeled on at different moments to provide height and pomposity (the Philosopher Royal) or double as the prison cell in which the supposed 'monster' is later confined. The playing register shifts from the exuberant and comical, to a mood that is very much bleaker and which leaves pantomime villainy decisively behind: Roger is viciously whipped by Tapscrew (that the rope cracks the air makes the scene hardly less shocking); later, hiding in the darkness of the sewers, he howls, 'I want to die…!' His eventual rescue through the princess' intervention has a dreamlike quality, with Mary-Jane/Aurelia created onstage as a puppet who leaves a drift of pink petals in her wake: this moment has a delicate simplicity that contrasts markedly with the rough knockabout and grotesquerie that shapes much of Roger's journey.

What space remains – amidst all this effervescent theatricality – for the dialogic spirit insisted on by Pullman, the sceptical reading the novel cultivates with such care? Ludovico's adaptation introduces no equivalent for the collage-like textual assemblage of the original (although newspaper men do proclaim headlines in between scenes); indeed, far from disrupting the communication of narrative, the stage version of *I Was a Rat!* seems to dissolve between one inventive sequence and the next. The act of storytelling is quite differently interpreted by novel and adaptation, yet nonetheless I suggest that both Pullman and Ludovico recognize and exploit the doubled activity constituted within it. A story, Ross Chambers argues, 'is nothing if it does not digress': the telling must necessarily move the story on but must also, paradoxically, delay its progress to prolong and stimulate pleasure in narration itself.[68] The novel introduces digression on the surface, in the spiralling chaos of Roger's misadventures, and more profoundly through the mock-tabloid insertions: these pages prompt the reader to pause, laugh, subconsciously to attempt separation of truth from lies; they both hold up the narrative and undermine its authoritative claim. The stage adaptation likewise diverges periodically from the story 'proper', but through different and inherently theatrical forms. We can see how such detours function in practice with the examples of acrobatics, slapstick routine and puppetry.

As noted, the part of Roger is played by a dancer (Jackson-Keen trained as a gymnast and for two years had the title role in the dance-led musical *Billy Elliot*). The quality of his physical presence – wiry, barefoot and semi-naked – is unlike that of the other players and draws attention by contrast to the overt artificiality of those characterizations. He is savage to their civilized, perhaps: yet at the same time the distorted features and exaggerated colours of the latter oblige us immediately to question this distinction. While a stripped-back, feral air shapes all Roger's movements, there are scenes where the difference of the freakish rat boy is explicitly dwelt upon. Sometimes this agility loosely serves the story – when extraordinary contortions are worked into a chase sequence – but elsewhere his gymnastics undoubtedly dazzle the audience more than they advance the plot, as when at Tapscrew's command he produces a bravura tumbling act (a scene that is not in the novel). A related kind of theatrical digression is the production's incorporation of slapstick, to some extent referencing the entertaining *lazzi* of *commedia dell'arte*. Notably, the most extended use of this occurs at the story's bleakest point, between actors playing incompetent policemen. Roger surrenders himself for 'extermination', whereupon his captors launch into a comic ritual of truncheons used on each other and misapplied handcuffs, the whole exchange drawn out through improvisation for as long as the spectators continue to delight in it. In both examples, the audience is diverted from the core of Roger's story to pursue pleasure in performance for its own sake. It is easy to regard these sequences as 'excuse' for impressive acrobatics (the first) and 'light relief' (the second). However, the impact of each goes further. Jackson-Keen's gymnastics explosively interrupt narrative progress; although Tapscrew makes him leap and wriggle, what he gives far exceeds the simple needs of the plot. In the production's interval and after it had ended, children from the audience could be observed turning cartwheels and attempting handstands in the foyer; the spirited physicality they had witnessed had, it seemed, worked infectiously to ignite renewed belief in their own momentarily limitless capabilities. This sort of contagion recalls Pullman's own account of imaginative engagement with stories as a child, sometimes 'acting out' narratives with friends but as often playing alone:

> Sometimes I was me, and sometimes I was me pretending to be Davy Crockett. [...] In some ways I was more myself at those times than any other, a stronger and more certain myself, wittier, more clearly defined, a myself of accomplishment and renown, someone Davy Crockett could rely on in a tight spot.[69]

That children felt the impulse to turn a cartwheel or walk on their hands, and many acted on this, however inexpertly, can be read as a sign of their ownership of the work. This is not passive consumption but fierce bodily engagement, shaped by the imaginative possibilities inherent in being (albeit temporarily) both 'me' and 'not me'; both *in* the story with/as Roger, and bringing him *out* of the story and into the world. Within this process, narrative becomes fluid and authorial control passes between the production's creators and its receiving audience.

The pursuit of theatricality in the abstract functions differently at other moments in the show. When Roger is at his lowest – literally so, in the underground sewers – and actively seeking the death that would end his misery, the police embark as described on farcical slapstick in which the two of them, rather than he, are physically abused; the scene carries echoes of the Keystone Cops of early twentieth-century silent film, or the cruel but clumsy guards who struggle to trap Disney's Aladdin. Ludovico explained that for her a sequence in this style deliberately courts 'stupidity', a term that denotes more than the policemen's foolishness. Stupidity produces a kind of numbness (stupor), a suspension of feeling: this effect is physically signalled by the actors' bodily resilience, and translated in the minds of spectators in a way that brings some release from the harshness of Roger's predicament. The stylized antics and performed pain substitute for serious violence and actual pain; the comedians' improbably bendy limbs and impervious scalps are offered in place of the rat boy's exposed and vulnerable flesh.

It is more than coincidence of the plot that, following this apparent digression, the action turns to the meeting of Roger and Aurelia. If the policemen are distinctly rubbery, the princess is still less real: a transitory configuration of sticks, mask, cloth and petals, she is manipulated by visible puppeteers in the manner of the Japanese Bunraku theatre. In this way, the manifest artifice in the slapstick routine eases the transition from a body of flesh and bone to one scarcely more solid than a dream and helps to instil in spectators the shift of vision that can accept this seemingly magical resolution of the crisis. Certainly, Ludovico's interpretation of Aurelia/Mary Jane departs radically from her representation by author and illustrator; Pullman emphasizes that the princess is thoroughly down to earth – a relieved Bob and Joan discover her to be 'just like a real person […] but a thousand times prettier' – and Bailey's drawing shows her coming to the door in jeans and a T-shirt.[70] In the novel Roger's freedom is secured by means of an empathetic human intervention, whereas onstage the same end is brought about through an encounter that is decidedly otherworldly. This reimagining of Aurelia can be variously interpreted. There is a pragmatic aspect to the staging decision; no one in the (predominantly male) cast could credibly portray a character who cannot, for the plot, be yet another grotesque. But beyond this, while Pullman's princess may be 'ordinary' underneath, and with the capacity for feeling that this implies, her present situation is arrived at through magic and her assistance can only be secured now with the help of a semi-magical stratagem: the scarlet slippers. With this in mind, Ludovico's dreamlike projection of the princess reworks in overtly theatrical terms the fantastical qualities already present in Pullman's text. Aurelia on stage is something more than the traditional fairy godmother who intercedes and grants wishes. Kenneth Gross proposes that the figure of the puppet 'reminds us of our powers of animation. It may remind us by contrast of our human tendency to turn ourselves, our thoughts, our memories, and our words into fixed, frozen, inanimate, or mechanical things'.[71] This puppet is animated with great skill: the sequence inspires a sense of wonder at the alien beauty of the figure and in the way the players conjure this. For spectators, child and adult alike, satisfaction is brought about through resolution of the crisis – Roger will not be exterminated after all – but the impression of recuperative possibility is further established by means of a formal choice that inherently expresses the power and persistence of life even in the most 'fixed' and 'frozen' circumstances. Of course, one might argue that to make Aurelia a puppet indicates that she is herself trapped and manipulated, much in the same way as Roger (and these parallels in their respective situations are underlined by Pullman). Yet in performance, these readings can coexist: the princess is controlled by larger forces, but this does not make her a *mere* puppet; recognizing her as a being of sticks and cloth makes her impression the more delicate and poignant. Finally, the pink petals, beautiful in themselves, hint at the coming of spring and so reinforce on a symbolic level the themes of hope and regeneration. Such a range of meanings might seem too wide or complex to be readable in the moment of performance, especially by younger spectators, yet Ludovico argues that this layering is what gives theatre depth and force. A sign of regeneration, the cherry blossom instinctively reassures us: simultaneously, the fragility of the petals might temper this with the recognition – felt, if not conscious – that human lives are vulnerable and precarious.[72] Roger is safe, but never wholly secure: the 'world outside' remains 'a difficult place'.[73]

Pullman's *I Was a Rat!* retells 'Cinderella' and updates *Oliver Twist*; in addition, the novel recasts in story the development of the self. In Francis Spufford's memoir about growing up (through) reading, the author explores the ways in which the consumption of fiction feeds and supports the route into maturity. In words that somewhat recall Bradbury's, Spufford argues that stories, whether told to us by others or read by ourselves, become fused

> not with the ordinary traffic of our existence, but with the accelerated coming-to-be we do in childhood. Story's lucidating way with experience rushes into the primary fashioning of a self, the very first construction of a person out of the materials of environment, and family, and reading silence.[74]

When Pullman's rat boy cowers in the dank of the sewers, having all but abandoned hope of admission to the human world yet still clinging on to the rudiments of language that he has acquired, the narrative directs him back up to the daylight. That twisted maze of underground passages could be an urban version of Bettelheim's forest, considered by the psychologist to symbolize the unconscious; for Bettelheim, the forest is 'the place in which inner darkness is confronted and worked through; where uncertainty is resolved about who one is; and where one begins to understand who one wants to be'.[75] In Ludovico's adaptation, a family of rats finds Roger in the sewers: their presence provides some small comfort but rats are 'other' to the child now and he cannot return to the animal condition. Roger's eventual restoration to Bob and Joan marks a new stage in his maturation; clean, clothed and learning a trade, he 'hardly ever nibbled the leather any more'.[76] Following the unfolding story, and taking in the pleasures of the narrative in its adherence to and divergence from orthodox lines, the reader of the novel – this novel, any novel – silently compares his or her life experience with the experiences of fictional others and through this activity enters a liminal space – what Pullman has called reading's 'borderland' – in which everyday perceptions are relaxed and new perspectives may be acquired. This state of mind is something akin to Keats's notion of negative capability: not an effortful striving for knowledge, nor blankly passive, but a condition of receptivity.[77] In adaptation for the theatre, this engagement with story is not solitary but social; the journey through narrative becomes companionable. The act of telling is registered differently in each case, yet reader, listener and spectator alike are urged to be part of a world made, in Kearney's phrase, newly 'shareable'.

The adaptations discussed in this chapter wrestle with the problems and possibilities of story in observable ways, engaging directly with an established tradition of narrative circulation. This negotiation is particularly clear in *I Was a Rat!*, where the production is built on a literary text that is itself already a sceptical retelling. While Pullman plays games with the reader through his disguised Cinderella story, interlacing this narrative thread with others structured to intrigue and variously provoke, Ludovico's adaptation is more concerned with finding a performance language able to handle the real darkness in the source material, while retaining its humour and spirit. The highly theatrical 'digressions' pursued in this adaptation serve to support the communication of story in complex ways. This is not a unidirectional telling but a shared act in which the story comes to meaning through the relationships established in the auditorium. Kneehigh's *The Red Shoes* also constructs a performance event that can be clearly distinguished from the narrative event; and here, the production and its actors signal discomfort with and distance from the ideological basis of their source material. The blind old lady asks for confirmation that the shoes are black, and the pause that precedes the lie shows resistance to the tale, on the micro level. In performance, *The Red Shoes* holds off the flow of Andersen's original and in so doing reminds its audience that no telling of a story is definitive. While these adaptations participate in a recognizable tradition of tale circulation, the perceptual frame discussed in this chapter may be extended and applied to adaptation practice in the theatre more broadly. The task of the storyteller in preserving yet transforming the source material – inevitably and necessarily – is equally the task of the adapter; re-articulation of a story demands that the teller has the freedom to digress from the established path in his or her own way. By embracing this divergence, adaptation can richly exploit the doubled pleasure that its activity already contains in latent form, by exposing the distance between the story of the story, and the story of the telling. As I have shown, adaptations in the theatre can mine still further the resistant potential in storytelling by replaying narratives critically, collaboratively and communally. For theatre is uniquely able to make its audience part of the telling process too, as Pullman emphasizes:

> That isn't a real room, it's painted canvas, and it looks like it; that isn't a real boy, it's a little wooden puppet. But the limitations leave room for the audience to fill in the gaps. We pretend these things are real, so the story can happen. The very limitations of theatre allow the audience to share in the acting. In fact, they require the audience to pretend. It won't work if they don't. But the result of this imaginative joining-in is that the story becomes more real, in a strange way. It belongs to everyone, instead of only to the performers under the lights. The audience in the dark are makers, too.[78]

4

Layered Space: Adaptation, Immersion and Site

This chapter examines the creation, occupation and operation of space in theatrical adaptation, considering how the explicit geographies of prose literatures are remodelled for a physical stage, and the ways in which adaptations address the complex relationships between those external landscapes and the inner 'worlds' of fictional characters. In particular, my discussion focuses on adaptations created for site-specific, promenade and immersive theatre: such forms experiment directly with spatial reconfigurations, in the process blurring the boundaries that divide actor from spectator and demanding redefinition of dramatic constructs such as character, narrative and *mise-en-scène*. While the contemporary theatre's ever bolder ventures with audience interactivity have their implicit forerunner in the experimental performance practices of the 1960s (especially Allan Kaprow's Happenings, Richard Schechner's Performance Group, and Julian Beck and Judith Malina's Living Theatre) the distinct vogue for participatory theatre events in the twenty-first century is also uniquely shaped by advances in digital technology. Josephine Machon notes that contemporary forms of immersive theatre have developed in a period in which immersive computer gaming has likewise expanded in popularity and sophistication. This relationship – between audience participation in performance environments and the use of interactive technologies to open up virtual 'worlds' – is consciously exploited by some immersive artists (see, for instance, the work of Blast Theory, or Rotozaza), but, as Machon states, may be more sceptically regarded by others who perceive 'certain limitations of digital realms in regards to the sensual involvement of the interactive participant'.[1] The kind of immersion enabled by digital media is not the concern of this book; however, tensions between the virtual and the sensory are directly relevant to an examination of literary versus theatrical environments, and our absorption within both.

Site-specific and immersive theatres offer distinctive and intriguing frameworks for adaptations of prose fiction – as well as for formally inventive, and interactive, productions of play texts – with companies such as Punchdrunk, Grid Iron, Dreamthinkspeak and Wildworks variously testing how locations and literatures might valuably be brought together. At the centre of this chapter's discussion of adaptation's layered spaces is a consideration of two contrasting projects, one by an established company and the second by a group of emergent artists. With *The Masque of the Red Death* at Battersea Arts Centre (2007–08), Punchdrunk staged an immersive experience for spectators, a promenade journey through a 'world' the seams of which were, for the most part, laboriously disguised. I argue that this adaptation usefully exploited the intensity of action and tone characteristic of Poe's stories, not by close attention to or retention of the source material (which became highly fragmented) but in the way that this quality was relocated onto the theatrical encounter. Punchdrunk's production occupied a dedicated arts space, transforming it beyond recognition but at the same time inviting spectators who knew the building to appreciate this wholesale reconfiguration. By contrast, the second project I examine borrowed a sprawl of streets and buildings in inner London. Retz's interactive *The Trial* (2013) is constructed in two parts: in the first, spectator-participants pursue a largely individual journey which begins at Shoreditch Town Hall, in the course of which they, like Kafka's protagonist, find themselves accused of an unspecified crime; in the second, a month later, spectators return – this time, to a faceless office building in Haggerston – for their 'trial', only to discover that sentence has already been passed. As I discuss, Retz's provocative relocation of the novel invites audiences to read Kafka through the site, and the site through Kafka; the two become inextricably interleaved as the fictional world of the performance is disrupted continually by the sights and sounds of city life around and overhead.

The practice of mediating prose literature through immersive or participatory performance allows rich opportunities for creativity but poses just as many questions. How might the experience of physical immersion in an environment compare with the condition of mental immersion – that sense of being 'lost in a book' – that characterizes deep reading? The spaces of fiction can sometimes appear richer, more desirable, hospitable and even in a sense more *real* than the generally mundane realm of ordinary existence; given this, the chance of actual ingress might seem to signal a kind of wish fulfilment. Yet alternatively, and perhaps paradoxically, the ability to enter a fictional world made solid might achieve precisely the opposite effect. In his seminal work of psychoanalytic criticism *The Dynamics of Literary Response*, Norman Holland argues that imaginative absorption in fictional worlds, and the dilemmas of the characters who inhabit them, is facilitated by the bodily passivity that typically accompanies the act of reading; able to concentrate their whole attention on mental engagement, readers 'begin to lose track of the boundaries between themselves and the work of art'.[2] According to this argument, then, book reading encourages relaxation of intellectual or emotional defences precisely because it is understood that fictional conflicts, and our reactions to them, do not have real world consequences. It follows from this that physically traversing or directly intervening in enacted fictions might actually inhibit imaginative acceptance of them: obliged to negotiate two environments simultaneously, a fictional space and a physical one, the risk is that audiences become alienated from both.

Whether site-specific and immersive events visually transform the location of the production, or choose instead to accentuate the unique architectural qualities, histories and associative meanings of a site and consciously incorporate this within the piece itself, the decision to bring audiences inside the performance environment prompts questions of who audiences become when they are no longer 'simply' spectators. Consciously or inadvertently, individually or en masse, audience members are made to some degree part of the fictional realm once inside its demarcated borders. It is possible to conceive of the audience's position in such work on a kind of spectrum: at one end, spectators remain essentially 'themselves' within a site, and watch, rather than directly interact with, the performance presented; at the other, spectators are given an explicit or implicit role in the drama, must negotiate an often challenging environment and are expected to improvise text and action within staged scenarios that overtly solicit their response. I will return to this matter of the qualities and consequences of spectator 'animation', played out in forms both modest and more extreme, in the analysis of shows by Punchdrunk and Retz that forms the second half of this chapter. But that discussion is prefaced by examination of perhaps more fundamental questions about the nature of space and place in literature and in the attempt to adapt literary texts for performance. First, drawing on the theory of Elaine Scarry, I consider the means by which writers 'build' spaces for the reader and how the methods of theatrical adaptation compare; this debate is illustrated by close reading of a sequence from Complicite's *The Master and Margarita*, a stage production, briefly mentioned in Chapter 2, that is non-interactive – at least, in conventional terms – and which serves to illustrate some central distinctions between the composition of written and performed space. Second, I discuss the issue of *reader* animation: who are we and 'where' are we, when we read a book? Making reference to Mary Jacobsen's analysis of literary space, I show how an understanding of the imaginative positions occupied by readers with respect to fiction may illuminate the experience of audiences required to assume (literal) positions and attitudes within immersive adaptations.[3]

Possible impossible scenes – Bulgakov/Complicite: *The Master and Margarita*

The apparent transparency and clarity of the literary medium – just words on a page, or on a screen – is counterbalanced by the freedom of conceptual range and the precision of expression that its mechanisms make possible. In fiction, the laws of time, space and economics cease to apply: a narrative travels wherever its author elects to take it. That combination of agility and expansiveness poses self-evident challenges when books are tackled in dramatic adaptation. Of course, such 'problems' can be a spur to creation; even so, the extraordinary imaginative flights of some authors might well leave actors, directors or playwrights struggling to find a language that could get an adaptation off the ground. A specific example will illustrate this, demonstrating both the complex ways in which fictional places are conjured and the implications of this for artists grappling with theatrical adaptation.

In Mikhail Bulgakov's often bewilderingly surreal novel *The Master and Margarita*, a demon gives Margarita a jar of magic cream: if at nightfall she undresses and rubs it into her skin, he instructs, she will be able to fly. The cream achieves the promised effect: she exits from her window on a broomstick and shoots across Moscow, naked, stopping off to exact violent retribution on her lover's enemies in their homes before joining Satan and his associates for a midnight ball. Such a sequence, in cheerful defiance of natural laws, cannot be translated into theatre through representational realism and remains a formidable challenge in any performance language. The issue is not just the manifest one of staging human flight, whether naked or decorously clothed. More subtly problematic is the communication of a space and movement that is entirely precise, yet still ungraspable. Bulgakov's narrative is built from dislocated swoopings: Margarita flies above crooked streets – 'rivers' from which 'little streams diverged [...] and trickled into the lighted caves of all-night stores' – and zigzags up the façade of apartment blocks.[4] The shifting vista is revealed alternately through wide-angle and zoom lenses: the reader 'looks' down, up, in, across. Bulgakov's text provides a vivid example of how space operates in fiction, constructed less as scenery than as location shaped in action. In this chapter, Margarita does not simply fly through space; she produces space meaningfully by flying. Here, flight matches the nature and the pace of thought. In Heidegger's essay 'Building, Dwelling, Thinking' (1971), the author writes that when we think about a particular thing in its location – in his example, 'the old bridge in Heidelberg' – our 'thinking toward that location is not a mere experience inside the persons present here', but instead 'gets through, persists through, the distance to that location'.[5] Heidegger's proposal, that by imagining (towards) a place, we are, in a sense, already there, helps to convey the fluid character of fictional spaces, as constituted on the page and in the minds of readers. It is this liquidity of movement, rather than fictional locations in the abstract, that is hardest to reproduce in dramatic adaptation. For while play scripts anticipate and to an extent facilitate scenic realization, and the transitions between scenes, prose fiction has no such imperative. Novels in which construction and negotiation of space is far less dizzying than Bulgakov's still employ this quality of mutability and lightness; to use the clunkiest of metaphors, literary space transforms without a pause for furniture to be carried off and on.

However, the metaphor just employed is of course disingenuous since contemporary theatre rarely involves 'scene-shifting' in that old-fashioned sense. Today, the literary sources of adaptation are unlikely to be remoulded dramaturgically according to the number of stage sets a company can afford to mount, or rejected altogether on this basis.[6] Instead, dramatic locations are established in performance instantaneously through word and action, their boundaries marked by lights, or projection; alternatively, abstract and polysemic stage designs readily enable discrete fictional spaces to coexist. Indeed, I opened this chapter with Bulgakov's example not just to introduce the problem of space in dramatic adaptation but because, as Complicite demonstrated in their 2012 staging of the novel, such scenes *are* stageable. In that particular production, Margarita's 'flight' was achieved skilfully, yet with relative simplicity. Her cream-smeared body appearing weirdly blue under the lights, the actress Sinead Matthews writhed face down on the stage floor while her figure was projected against a moving photographic backdrop of the city on the cyclorama. And just as the actor could, by this means, occupy multiple spaces at once, so too could the minds of an audience: seduced by the fiction, while relishing the mechanism of its production; in imaginative flight, but firmly grounded by the material stage.

Complicite's extraordinary adaptations of literature exemplify a level of ambition and transformative creativity that is evident in contemporary theatrical practice more widely. Even the swiftest sampling of adaptation projects across the last decade would indicate that (to paraphrase Berkoff) it is the seeming impossibility of translating fictional worlds to the stage, rather than the ease of accommodation, that drives artistic activity. Whether tackling epic and fantastical journeys, as in Simon Armitage's *The Odyssey: Missing Presumed Dead* (English Touring Theatre, 2015), or Caroline Horton's more intimate reworking of the same story, *Penelope Retold* (Derby Theatre, 2015); finding stage language to articulate the internal patterns of modernist stream of consciousness, in Mitchell's *Waves*, or Olwen Fouéré's *Riverrun*, the latter a one-woman show based on Joyce's *Finnegan's Wake* (Galway International Arts Festival, 2013); representing the world through the eyes of a narrator with Asperger's syndrome, in Stephens's adaptation of Haddon's *The Curious Incident of the Dog in the Night-Time*; or conveying dual narratives, as well as a parallel universe, with Yukio Ninagawa's production of Murakami's *Kafka on the Shore* (Barbican, 2015), it would appear that no literary scene can stump the expressive capacities of the contemporary theatrical imagination.

Nonetheless, adapters do not face only the difficulty of remapping specific fictional places – whether through a broadly realistic or more symbolic approach – in physical terms. As I aim to show by my example of Bulgakov, a scene described in a novel, or short story, is bound up in and, in a meaningful sense, inseparable from its evocation through literary language. I emphasize this not to echo the conservative view that certain novels 'cannot' be adapted, or that adaptations are inevitably inferior to their sources, but to argue that bypassing the ways in which narrative content has been produced linguistically can result in stage worlds that seem shallow – or alternatively, immotile – by comparison. It does not follow that literary scenes are easily and automatically imprinted in the imagination; indeed, as critical theorist

Elaine Scarry observes, for authors to summon qualities of vivacity and vitality requires great skill within a medium 'almost wholly devoid of *actual* sensory content'. In her 1999 study *Dreaming by the Book*, Scarry identifies a series of compositional strategies by which writers enable readers to 'see' fictional spaces vividly in the mind's eye.[7] These strategies include the use of what Scarry terms *radiant ignition*, meaning flashes of light, beams, glints and sparks; *rarity*, indicating a quality of transparency, as in the haziness of veils, shadows, a glance under eyelashes; and *manipulation*, meaning movements in which people or things are made to stretch, tilt and fold. Through multiple examples taken from prose and poetry, Scarry argues that such techniques work to lend elements of movement and gravity to images that would otherwise fail to achieve solidity in the reader's imagination. It is not necessary to pursue Scarry's line of analysis all the way towards what are, at times, some rather idiosyncratic conclusions, to accept the underlying principle set out in *Dreaming by the Book*: that literary composition – a medium infinitely free to show anything, go anywhere and do anything – still depends absolutely upon patient and laborious 'building', through an accumulation of gestures, textures, glimpses, angles and resonances.

We can illustrate how such techniques of construction are made to work in practice by returning again to Bulgakov's scene of the midnight flight. Leaving the city behind, Margarita flies over the forest and moves closer to the trees until she is

> no longer flying over their tops, but between their trunks, silvered on one side by the moonlight. Her faint shadow flitted ahead of her, as the moon was now at her back. Sensing that she was approaching water, Margarita guessed that her goal was near. The fir trees parted and Margarita gently floated through the air towards a chalky hillside. Below it lay a river. A mist was swirling round the bushes growing on the cliff-face, whilst the opposite bank was low and flat. There under a lone clump of trees was the flicker of a camp fire, surrounded by moving figures, and Margarita seemed to hear the insistent beat of music. Beyond, as far as the eye could see, there was not a sign of life.

> Margarita bounded down the hillside to the water, which looked tempting after her chase through the air. Throwing aside the broom, she took a run and dived head-first into the water. Her body, as light as air, plunged in and threw up a column of spray almost to the moon.[8]

Applying Scarry's model to this passage highlights how Bulgakov shapes Margarita's journey in the imagination of the reader. Her flight is made visible to us by means of sparks and glimmers: silvered tree bark, dancing flames, moonbeams. The veiled light, 'chalky' slope and the swirl of the mist above the water, together produce the effect of blurring, or transparency (Scarry's 'rarity'); positioned like a watcher from the ground, the reader 'sees' the impossible flight yet acknowledges it, simultaneously, as potentially a trick of the light. Bulgakov adopts the technique of 'manipulation' in conveying Margarita's physical elasticity, from gossamer-light floating, to sloped descent, and concluding with the abrupt plunging of a *light* body that is still able to throw up a fantastically high jet of water. Thus, I suggest, following Scarry, that the mechanisms Bulgakov employs here – perhaps unsurprisingly prominent in a scene of night-time flying, but notable, as Scarry demonstrates, for their frequency in literary composition in general – function to shape and illuminate Margarita's magical journey in the imagination, giving this just enough weight for an eloquent impression to be made.

If a key challenge of novel writing, then, is that of making language come to life in the minds of readers, in the processes of stage adaptation the theatre might initially seem to have an advantage since the new medium is already fully sensory. Yet as I have already hinted, this does not follow in practice and indeed, the very animation of theatre may produce the inverse problem: the material stage, the flesh and blood bodies of actors, can too easily weigh down and 'deaden' a narrative that leaps and sparkles on the page. The question of how stage performance could convey Margarita's flight thus carries with it complex implications about gravity: the audience's imagination must soar, and this matters more than (and does not depend on) the ability of performers to leave the ground. The imaginative imperative is understood precisely by Complicite, and demonstrated through staging which juxtaposes solidity with translucence, stillness with hurtling movement. Yet it is notable that the techniques of this adaptation, deployed in this moment to overcome the manifest 'problem' of human weight, are strikingly similar to those identified by Scarry in literature's struggle to *add* solidity to the image in the mind of the reader. The staging choice goes beyond merely the use of atmospheric stage lighting (clearly a given); in the sequence described, Complicite trick the eye with light cast over hazy blue ('radiant ignition'), and use layers of film projection ('rarity') and sharply projected angles ('manipulation') to propel Matthews's body, joyously, anywhere it wants to go. That theatre should use similar methods to those detailed by Scarry suggests that techniques of illumination, transparency and a physical 'stretch' and 'tilt' may be ways not just of adding or subtracting imaginative heft, but of crossing the border between literary and theatrical form. In other words, where the literary work endeavours to make its readers infer animation, the theatrical adaptation of the same text strives rather to lighten and soften the excess of solidity brought by fleshy bodies and a hard stage floor.

The analysis I present here risks, paradoxically, appearing almost anti-theatrical – and this despite my praise for Complicite's directorial sleight of hand. The implication of the argument could seem to be that for theatre to 'speak' literature effectively, the former must become less *like itself*: somehow less heavy, messy, loud and alive. Abstracted as a general tenet, such a position would require a performance practice too esoteric to be sustainable; moreover, the widespread evidence of highly creative and critically acclaimed adaptations that manifestly adopt quite other approaches to their source texts would seem to undermine its legitimacy. Nonetheless, the principles set out by Scarry which I have reapplied here remain valid, and valuable, in helping to show how adaptation across media must negotiate the characteristics peculiar to each art form – especially in cases where the adaptation project aims to *retain* certain qualities of 'bookishness'. The discussions of Chapter 2 serve to demonstrate that part of the inherent appeal of literary sources for theatre makers lies in their very unlikeness to scripted drama: and in the effort to preserve that distinction, the use of physical manipulations, touches of reflective transparency and the veiled play of light and shadow combine to enable the antithetical qualities of page and stage temporarily to coexist.

To a degree, the kinds of staging techniques I describe are designed to produce a level of illusion. In the example of Margarita's flying this is clearly the case, even if the mechanisms of the trick are in no way disguised. Founded in the early 1980s as a relatively small, Lecoq-influenced physical theatre ensemble, Complicite have since become a major international company creating high-concept (and high-budget) productions for huge stages and packed audiences. Does their distinctive application of 'radiant ignition', 'rarity' and 'manipulation', borrowing Scarry's terms, depend on a distanced audience perspective for its effect, or at least, does the clear separation of spectators from actors serve to facilitate this? In theatre that operates on a more intimate scale – further, in immersive performance practices which bring audiences into the heart of the 'illusion' – are such devices rendered weakly ineffectual? This chapter's discussion of Punchdrunk's *The Masque of the Red Death* and Retz's *The Trial* will explore the extent to which such methods are employed, and how they fare when their effects are brought up close. Alongside this, I examine what proximity in immersive and interactive adaptations makes possible: my analysis will suggest that altering the distance at which performance is conventionally viewed can work provocatively to unsettle spectator perception of and relationship to site, actors and stage narratives.

Inside the 'play space'

Examining Bulgakov's description of the midnight journey, I sketched in the figure of a nominal reader gazing skywards and catching a fleeting glimpse of Margarita's impossible flight. Yet that image is flawed, for if she is flying downwards, amongst trees, to 'see' her at all that reader cannot be on the ground, but elsewhere: Where? Above her, or flying alongside? Somehow within the body of Margarita herself? Or is the reader not 'inside' the work at all? I have proposed already that reading *does* lead us into the spaces of literature in a meaningful sense. Holland's argument, cited above, which suggests that deep reading relaxes the boundaries between the self and the work, persuasively accounts for characteristic features of the reading experience.[9] When somebody immersed in a book fails to respond when addressed, it could be said that he or she has drifted, figuratively, into fictional territory, correspondingly becoming less powerfully moored both to the physical context of the reading, and the temporal moment at which the (attempted) interruption is made. Likewise, Heidegger's example of the bridge is used by him to show how language enables thoughts to move instantaneously through space to the point where part of our consciousness seems effectively to have arrived at the described destination. Unlike Holland, Heidegger does not specifically deal with reading; the essay I reference here deals rather with spatial boundaries and locations, and our philosophical and physical relationships to them. Nonetheless, his analysis is useful in articulating the tension between mental and material 'spaces' and so may be brought into conjunction with Holland's proposal. Heidegger claims that space as a concept is ungraspable until it is boundaried; space acquires meaning, he argues, as 'that for which room has been made, that which is let into its bounds'. Following on from this, a boundary, he explains, 'is not that at which something stops but [...] is that from which something begins its presencing'.[10] If we accept as a basis Holland's account of the reader's relaxed boundaries, or lowered defences, this proposal by Heidegger implies further that the activity of reading *makes room* for fictional realms. So just as the reading imagination travels to (and into) literary spaces, equally significant is the way that this engagement allows these spaces 'into' the reader. Heidegger's insistence that a boundary represents the marginal point at which something 'begins its presencing' suggests, in turn, that the softened borders of the self in reading can bring the worlds of literary composition peculiarly close: in this way, the presencing of fictional places in the reading process is constituted as intimate and interior.

To accept this argument is to admit a certain blurring, produced by the activity of deep reading, that causes the worlds of text and reading self to overlap. But for the reader, the nature of this liminal, doubled space remains hazy. If we enter the literary work, in what capacity do we do so? Clearly, different kinds of writing may consciously seek to shape the reader's position in this, but it is not as simple as saying that third person narratives locate one as observer, or that a book written in the first person takes one inside the protagonist's head. In Chapter 3, I cited Philip Pullman's account of his own childhood reading: his impression that he did not so much 'become' Davy Crockett – his particular hero – while he read and played, as that he imagined himself alongside him, in the position of Crockett's ideal 'best friend'.[11] It may be significant here that Pullman is describing the experience of reading as a child, since locating oneself within narratives of adventure is an acknowledged stage within the process of self-development. As Spufford puts it,

> the words we take into ourselves help to shape us. They help form the questions we think are worth asking; they shift around the boundaries of the sayable inside us, and the related borders of what's acceptable. [...] They build and stretch and build again the chambers of our imagination.[12]

Yet while childhood reading might predictably produce a strong and formative relationship with fictional spaces, studies of adult reading have likewise shown that this sense of creative participation can still persist.

In her essay 'Looking for Literary Space', Mary Jacobsen argues that the world of a literary work is located not within the printed text, nor in the mind of the reader, but in the 'potential space' (a term she borrows from psychoanalyst D. W. Winnicott) which 'joins and separates the individual and the person or thing he cares about'.[13] Jacobsen draws on a small-scale study she initiated with students in which they were asked to describe and visualize the experience of reading a given short story (privately and outside of class time), in this instance either Ernest Hemingway's 'The Killers' (1927) or Virginia Woolf's 'Kew Gardens'

(1919). On finishing the story, students noted their responses to questions such as 'Where do you feel you are during the reading?' and 'Did you feel alone or in the presence of real or imagined others?'[14] Many recorded their attention shifting between imaginative engagement in the fiction and bodily engagement in the activity of reading, a sense of 'drifting away and coming back': the impression was not of immersion and interruption, but of being poised in a dreamlike inter-space where two worlds overlap. Others felt situated inside the story, with readers of Woolf picturing themselves as 'a drop of rain', or 'in the place of the snail, [...] low on the ground, an observer'; another wrote, 'I am no one, just a spirit in the room, or I am one of the characters.' Students reading Hemingway similarly saw themselves in the fictional space, yet safely peripheral: 'I am sitting in a booth at the diner, hidden slightly by the booth, watching the story unfold without being seen'; 'I felt as if I were right there watching it all happen.'[15] The students' diagrammatic sketches of themselves reading Hemingway, reproduced in Jacobsen's essay, typically positioned them looking at the action through a window, or hovering above, or from around a corner. Reading Woolf proved harder to map visually; even those who imagined being inside the garden expressed a confused instability in that perspective. Both texts appeared to locate these readers marginally within the fiction, but where students reading Hemingway reported a sensation of being powerfully *there*, some who were assigned Woolf noted feeling somewhat alienated, excluded from the significance of the narrative. Jacobsen understood that where reading the first story was typically experienced as play, the second, for many, was closer to effortful work.[16] She concludes that educators should reflect on the qualities of texts and, crucially, the styles of teaching that can inhibit pleasure in reading and limit the ability to 'read creatively and deeply'. The model of 'potential space' – a way of thinking which does not dichotomize reader and text but encompasses both – can, she suggests, helpfully counter students' 'long-standing, habitual (if resentful) view of themselves as passive receivers of the teacher's literary values', encouraging them to recognize and value their role 'in setting up the "stage" on which they evoke literary works'.[17]

Notwithstanding the distinctive effects produced by individual literary genres, the underpinning model of reader liminality can usefully be applied to adaptation and is especially charged when considering the appropriation of prose literature by immersive theatre. Seated in an auditorium, spectators may be able to occupy something akin to the 'drifting' space, described by Jacobsen's students, that makes room for imaginative acceptance of the (stage) fiction as well as for self-conscious awareness of the activity of engagement (listening and watching). The situations of reading and theatre viewing are far from analogous, however. The collective dimension of audience experience, the wide-angle perspective upon the stage action, the recognition of an event's liveness, all work against the possibility of 'losing' oneself in a fictional world. Further, an audience's ability to process any theatre show requires not just negotiation between the activity of spectating and the onstage fiction, but additionally with the means of representation employed by the production. Drawing once more on the example of Bulgakov, it will be evident that while the author does use 'devices' to convey the sensation of Margarita's flight, these are not highlighted for the reader in the moment of reading. By contrast, Complicite's audience instantly understand, and can actively delight in, the means employed to present the same sequence. Dan Rebellato has shown convincingly that the audience's ability to process both levels of signification at once is evidence of theatre's 'metaphorical' operation. Rebellato argues that metaphor asks us to imagine one thing in terms of another (a process that does not necessitate any sort of 'make-believe'); similarly, he proposes, 'when we see a piece of theatre we are invited to think of the fictional world through this particular representation'.[18] Although theatre audiences must handle distinct and sometimes conflicting kinds of signification – Margarita flying, but grounded – their relative passivity (in physical terms) makes this easy to accommodate; in Rebellato's words, it demands simply that we 'lean in, we concentrate'.[19]

Interactive or immersive theatre manifestly turns patterns of audience engagement around. Denied the position of physical passivity – or, put conversely, liberated from this – the moving spectator is necessarily more *self*-aware, since attention must now be paid to bodily activities like exploring, speaking, walking in relative darkness, even running. This kind of direct participation implies more immediate engagement with the theatrical representation, at least on the surface; however, in practice the added labour of this involvement could diminish the opportunity to relax the boundaries between self and artwork, a process which, I have argued, is central to the way we grow absorbed in fictional worlds. It follows from this that in constructing an immersive adaptation of a literary text, the creators must consider carefully decisions about audience positioning, in every sense. The production may allow the spectator to occupy a stance that is, at least superficially, close to that of the 'spirit in the room', so able to observe but (by mutually accepting this convention) 'without being seen'. Alternatively, the show can construct a directly implicated role (or roles) for spectators, correspondingly allowing fewer opportunities for unhurried 'reading'. The two immersive productions discussed next construct both of these extremes for an audience, with many shades of variation in between. Participation in these events leads spectators – specifically, those who also already 'know' the texts behind these adaptations – into peculiarly altered relationships with those works. This practice of (re)association with literature through theatre, by means of adaptation, is most productively understood not hierarchically, but in terms of the complex levels of engagement that such orderings of space allow.

Poe/Punchdrunk: *The Masque of the Red Death*

Since its inception in 2000, the UK-based company Punchdrunk, directed by Felix Barrett together with director and choreographer Maxine Doyle, has established a strong reputation for immersive theatre that is at once sweepingly ambitious (in scale and in structural complexity) and intricately precise. Punchdrunk's theatre is site-specific, with the company's productions taking over disused factories, warehouses and derelict buildings (*The Firebird Ball*, 2005; *Faust*,

2006; *Sleep No More*, 2011 New York revival), an entire office block (*It Felt Like a Kiss*, 2009) or a decommissioned postal sorting office (*The Drowned Man*, 2013). Arriving at a Punchdrunk show, audience members are separated from companions with whom they might have arrived; thus 'alone', and with the degree of anonymity conferred by the mask each is required to wear, the spectator is left free to explore the breadth and depth of the theatrically transformed site. Given the scale on which Punchdrunk's productions are conceived and constructed, that reconnaissance in itself demands a number of hours; yet however long the evening, it could never be long enough for any one spectator to grasp the entirety of the work. The New York City production of *Sleep No More*, for example, was staged in a block of three disused warehouses, in total occupying something like a hundred rooms, over six floors; every room, as well as each transitional space, was dressed in layers of 'naturalistic' detail which audiences could examine up close. Even appropriated buildings which are not in reality quite so vast – such as the Battersea Arts Centre, formerly Battersea Town Hall and the site for *The Masque of the Red Death* – can appear so to audiences, because Punchdrunk's method renders the spatial encounter disorienting; dimmed lighting and black drapery lay a veil over the whole, making the visitor uncertain, in dreamlike fashion, whether this staircase, or that doorway, has been tried before.

Although Punchdrunk's audiences experience unusual freedom, in practice their promenade through the site is tightly managed: spectators may discover their entrance barred from certain rooms at certain times, and everyone will be neatly manoeuvred to congregate in a particular place by a given point in the evening. Nonetheless, the individual route each person takes is not overtly controlled. As a result, it is understood (by artists and audience) that audience members will encounter 'scenes' in different orders, and, since certain sequences are played on a loop, that they may end up seeing part of the action more than once, accidentally or by design. The vast spread of the theatrical event and multiplicity of pathways through it makes it impossible as noted for any spectator to experience everything and likely that some will 'miss' major sections (of the environment and/or the prepared action) altogether. This dispersal of audience attention has manifest consequences for the communication of narrative. Immersive theatre need not base itself upon narrative, certainly; it might instead, for example, in the manner of Kate Bond and Morgan Lloyd's cult show *You Me Bum Bum Train* (devised in 2006, and remounted many times since) lead participants through a series of absorbingly visceral but essentially disconnected scenes/environments. That said, it is notable how regularly large-scale immersive theatre productions have turned to pre-existing texts. For Punchdrunk, this has typically meant a dramatic work, with Shakespeare, Buchner, Goethe, Weiss and Webster all serving as sources. A related strategy is evident in the work of Dreamthinkspeak, directed by Tristan Sharps, a company also well established in immersive theatre: Dreamthinkspeak's first production, *Who Goes There?* (staged across several indoor and outdoor spaces around Crawley's Hawth Theatre complex, in 1999), was a radically deconstructed *Hamlet*, with *Before I Sleep* (mounted in Brighton's former Co-Operative department store, in 2010) revisiting Chekhov's *The Cherry Orchard*. In one way, the potentially disorienting aspects of such productions – the sprawling or labyrinthine environments, and the extent and unpredictability of spectator movement within them – is offset by the relative structure and knowability that classic texts would seem to provide, even if in practice little of the source is straightforwardly presented, and what is retained is filtered through a kaleidoscopic lens. Thus, where traditional or proscenium arch theatre typically presents an unfolding narrative to its audience, in immersive theatre of this kind each spectator shapes their own more loosely associative narrative, based on the individual route taken through the physical space.

The Masque of the Red Death was unusual for Punchdrunk in taking inspiration not from drama but prose fiction. The short stories of the nineteenth-century American writer Edgar Allan Poe provided highly fertile material: Poe's fictional spaces, filled with walled up cellars ('The Black Cat', 'The Cask of Amontillado') and opened tombs ('The Fall of the House of Usher', 'Berenice', 'Ligeia'), would seem natural territory for a theatrical method that similarly sets out a teasing multiplicity of 'clues', weighs the suspenseful journey more heavily than the ultimate disclosure, and strives throughout to shape a mode of encounter that leans towards the Gothic in blending nervous uncertainty with exhilaration. The production drew on other tales of Poe, beyond the above: 'William Wilson', about fatal pursuit by a doppelganger; 'The System of Dr Tarr and Professor Fether', in which it transpires that a mental institution has been taken over by its inmates, who have imprisoned their doctors; and one of Poe's best known stories, 'The Tell Tale Heart', where the grisly relic of a murder appears to pulse and beat vengefully from where it was hidden under the floorboards. The chosen framing story, 'The Masque of the Red Death', describes a period of deadly plague in which the aristocracy attempt to avoid infection by hiding in Prince Prospero's abbey, reveling in a prolonged and grotesquely indulgent masked ball. One mysterious visitor is 'blasphemously' disguised as a plague victim: at the denouement the Prince angrily rips away the guest's disguise, only to find that there is no body beneath the blood-spattered shroud; facing Death after all, he and the nobles meet their inevitable end. All nine stories mined for Punchdrunk's production suggest not just extraordinary environments to experiment with in theatrical terms, but identities, perceptions and attitudes which both performers and audience members could adopt. The immersive promenade style meant that regularly actors in role as Poe's characters were glimpsed only fleetingly, with spectators literally pursuing them to discover who they were and where they were going; when a presented scene – or scene fragment – was chanced upon, the watching audience could not know if what they saw and heard should be believed; left to explore often untenanted spaces, the implied invitation was to open drawers, examine letters, or put an ear to the wall. The beak-like masks Punchdrunk handed out to audience members, which have today come to be associated with Venetian carnival, were originally worn in the seventeenth and eighteenth centuries by medics who believed these would protect them from putrid air: the themes of carnival and infection both tie into the title story, and the fraught mix of gaiety, permissiveness and trepidation fairly describes the experience shaped for spectator-participants.[20]

Punchdrunk's *Masque of the Red Death* did not only aim to revisit Poe but additionally to re-read the physical site playing host to the production. The show was the first of three 'Playground Projects' launched by the BAC, together with architects Haworth Tomkins, with the express intention of finding radical new ways to occupy the space; in so doing, stated the BAC's Artistic Director David Jubb, they hoped to '[create] legacies for the way we use the building in the future'.[21] Jubb's desire to extend the impact and life of the site reached to its past as well as what might lie ahead. Referencing the building's former function (since 1893) as the Town Hall, he acknowledged:

> Sometimes in trying to change the space into an arts centre we have plastered over its magic: like advertising hoardings on street corners, in danger of making everywhere look the same. We want to create a radical performance environment which is a million miles from the sanitised, comfortable, tastefully lit, dead arts spaces that feel more like hotels than somewhere where risk and possibility are alive and kicking.[22]

The BAC's occupation by Punchdrunk – theatrical 'specialists in peeling back the surface and unlocking magic and mystery in architectural space' – would, it was hoped, both expose the fullness of the site and simultaneously produce an accretion of new 'layers of proven theatrical possibility'.[23] Unquestionably, *The Masque of the Red Death* succeeded in doing this: until this point the BAC had presented work in three 'black box' studios, but Punchdrunk's production appropriated corridors, stairwells, cupboards and offices, re-opening some spaces within the building that had been disused for years.[24]

It is especially difficult to convey the content and progression of an event which actively sought to overwhelm and even bewilder its audience, aiming to create (in Barrett's words) something like a 'parallel theatrical universe' in which normal rules no longer seem to apply.[25] As one spectator posted online, immediately after this production: 'Feel like I've been away 3 weeks, can't believe it was 3 hours'.[26] The disorienting twilit gloom, produced by radically lowered lights and careful draping around doors and in passageways, made it impossible for participants to grasp the shape of this 'universe' while travelling through it. Taking up the invitation of the Playground Projects, Punchdrunk's show occupied all three floors of the labyrinthine Victorian building: a succession of corridors led off into rooms meticulously transformed into a library, a morgue, several bedrooms, an apothecary, crypt, wine cellar, opium den and more. The huge marble staircase, down which a wedding couple danced and tumbled, blurred at its foot in the unearthly blue light into a petrified forest with trees reaching up to the first floor gallery; over a balustrade, life-sized statues gazed impassively at the nuptial celebrations below. The smaller rooms, sometimes briefly inhabited but as often 'uncannily' abandoned, were all dense with the signs of implied occupants. A bedroom with fretfully rumpled sheets, lit by flickering candles, vividly suggested a sickroom, with tinctures, powder traces, prescriptions, letters and diary pages scattered on each available surface. In the library, one of the building's long boarded-up fireplaces had been opened for use; entering this room, spectators might have been startled to discover at the fireside a live black cat. In a larger room, a series of hospital beds were pushed together to serve as a table around which a choreographed dinner party, wild and erotic, was conducted by the insane. Elsewhere, spectators could have glimpsed a man trapped in the action of trying to force his way out of a wall; or, on leaving the apothecary, which was filled with shelves upon shelves of tiny glass bottles – remedies, perfumes, poisons? – a visitor might have had crushed herbs pressed into his palm by the seller, accompanied by her whispered promise that the charm could save a soul from damnation. Running on a continuous loop structure, the production had no conventional interval; however, participants lucky enough to locate the bar at any point could remove their masks temporarily, obtain a drink and stay to watch a Victorian-style variety show whose acts included 'Roderick Usher' practising mind-reading on members of the audience, before being forcibly dragged offstage when his telepathic powers seemed to backfire against him. Throughout the evening the clock chimed on the hour, mimicking the 'dull, heavy, monotonous clang' that marks out the diminishing time left to Prospero and the party guests in Poe's tale.[27] For the production's finale, spectators were unobtrusively led to congregate in the main hall, where they watched – and if they chose, joined – a fantastical, flamboyant *danse macabre* performed to a warped classical theme. Dance, or at least, tightly choreographed physical action, was central to the production aesthetic (and is characteristic of Punchdrunk's work more generally): an important aspect of the impact of the show for audiences was that daring, high-energy choreographic sequences are experienced immersively 'up close', rather than appreciated from a distance, as in the conventional theatre auditorium.

Poe's writings have influenced development of a range of literary genres, most notably the detective story, science fiction and horror. The ways in which such genres position the reader – attempting to penetrate a mystery, struggling to reconcile the evidence of their eyes with natural law, filled with anticipatory dread suddenly disrupted by an appalling revelation – have ready affinities with the experience of Punchdrunk's 'immersed' spectator. Yet Poe, an acknowledged master of the short story, also emphasized the need for rigorous control of every aspect of a literary work: the deep intensity of impact he aimed for with his writing required, he believed, a form of readerly immersion that is quite unlike Punchdrunk's interpretation of this idea. In his famous 1846 essay 'The Philosophy of Composition', Poe uses the example of his poem 'The Raven' to illustrate his method of writing. Commencing the composition process not with narrative or plot but with a desired effect, he explains, he employs a combination of incident and tone – often juxtaposing the peculiar with the apparently banal – to shape a steady movement towards the final denouement. For Poe, the climactic ending must remain constantly in view while writing because only then will all that precedes this gain 'its indispensable air of consequence, of causation'.[28] The poem or short story are his preferred artistic forms, the author adds, since these can be 'read at one sitting'; nothing breaks engagement with the text from beginning to end.[29] And while in principle the narrative of a poem or story can 'travel' anywhere, in practice, Poe argues, a 'close *circumscription of space*' (original italics) is essential – in 'The Raven', it is the enclosed chamber of the bereaved lover – in lending 'the force of a frame to a picture'.[30] All these aspects of Poe's compositional process presuppose a reading experience in which an individual work – a poem or story – is allowed to unfold without interruption. For Poe, the reader must submit to the authority of the text, absorbing the gathering intensity of a precisely identified and constructed emotional effect; he or she enters a tightly delineated fictional space and may not emerge until the full shock of the seemingly inevitable conclusion has registered. It is notable too that Poe regularly employs metaphors of the stage to describe the process of writing; although not a playwright himself, he was a regular and sometimes stern theatre critic who considered that the drama of his time needed shaking out of its state of stagnation.[31] His insistence on reading in a 'single sitting', and on the importance of a tightly focused location *within* the fiction, both evoke the theatrical condition; he also borrows the terminology of production mechanics to describe the structure of literary composition, remarking on how the finished text disguises all 'the tackle for scene-shifting – the step-ladders and demon-traps – the cock's feathers, the red paint and the black patches' that underpin the illusion.[32] In this way, Poe implies that literary compositions should impress themselves theatrically upon the reader: or at least, in the way that theatre has the potential to do.

The approach set out in 'The Philosophy of Composition' is highly methodical, so much so that critics have questioned whether Poe genuinely adopted it; indeed, his essay might have been closer to fiction than to the claimed disclosure of the purely 'mathematical' process by which he built a work 'step by step' to its completion.[33] Nonetheless, it is illuminating to contrast the kind of reader engagement Poe insists on here with the very different mode of encounter experienced by the audience of a Punchdrunk production. For the latter, spectators shape their own unique journeys through the event-text, without the controlling hand of an external author, but also without the knowledge that would give them real autonomy in choosing that route (there is no map or 'guidebook'): they come upon abandoned rooms where nothing is 'happening', in the sense of performed action; they witness scenic fragments, disconnected from a framing narrative and in a random order.[34] For *The Masque of the Red Death*, the audience explored a theatrical environment built from multiple stories as opposed to a single work, an intoxicating and exhausting 'world' of Poe, as if his tales were interchangeable rather than the separate, carefully crafted entities from which, that author believed, no element could be detached without damage to the whole.[35] One might infer from this unlikeness that Punchdrunk's production as adaptation is less interested in textual specifics than in borrowing a broadly Poe-esque mood and using this as inspiration to fill in the gaps within an already established performance event structure. Were this description fair, it need not constitute a criticism: adaptation implies a movement between texts and forms, with no imperative for the source text, or texts, to drive the work that results. A reverse influence is equally valid, so while one creative route in adaptation is to build a 'new' performance language inspired by the qualities of a literary source, it is also legitimate to see what results when a vivid style of writing is 'poured' into a pre-formed theatrical mould. However, I argue that Punchdrunk's *The Masque of the Red Death* allows for a more complex and critically productive relationship between adaptation and source than such an interpretation implies. Some of Poe's compositional rules *are* implicitly upheld, I suggest, but are effectively transposed from the individual poem or fiction to the 'text' of the production as a whole. Additionally, I propose that the immersive promenade form creates the opportunity for the reader-spectator – in other words, he or she who experiences Punchdrunk's show as adaptation – subtly to negotiate tensions between the Poe of private imagination and the realized sensory realm of the stage environment.

As we have seen, Poe's advice to writers assumes a reader who is wholly immersed in the text: consumption in one go is crucial, since if 'the affairs of the world interfere' then 'everything like totality is at once destroyed'.[36] While Punchdrunk do not allow anything like so steady an exposure to a self-contained narrative, the company does strive to achieve precisely this impact through the wider operation of the production. Barrett explained to Lyn Gardner that their minute attention to detail across any performance site – with every 'seam' hidden, and every object standing up to audience scrutiny – aims to support and sustain the theatrical illusion: 'we never want anything to happen that breaks the spell. If they suddenly remember they're in London in 2007, then we've failed'.[37] (Arguably, Barrett's ambition here underestimates an audience's ability to read the event in complex ways; visitors already familiar with the BAC as performance venue were fully capable of absorbing the production at the level of theatrical illusion while relishing the new insight it provided on the building.[38]) None of Poe's works, whether poem or story, demand several hours of reading time – but all the same, Punchdrunk's long night of promenade performance fostered in its audience that sense of inescapability bordering on claustrophobia which Poe's readers also experience, according to critic Shoshana Felman: 'What is unique, however, about Poe's influence [...] is the extent to which its action is unaccountably insidious, exceeding the control, the will, and the awareness of those who are subjected to it.'[39] The effect of Punchdrunk's production was analogously overwhelming; whether willingly swept along or frustratingly trapped, audience-participants were subjected to the laws of a world that was unfamiliar to them, yet with which – their own semi-costumed presence suggests – they were already complicit. However, the potent impression Poe sought to create – in the example of 'The Raven', it is the 'elevation of soul' that arises from 'contemplation of the beautiful' – went hand in hand, for the author, with the drive towards the text's closing lines; every poetic effect produced along the way served to 'bring the [reader's] mind into a proper frame for the denouement'.[40] Punchdrunk's adaptation did mount a version of the framing tale's climactic ending, but did not attempt to communicate the narrative that preceded this other than by, for example, strewing books and papers about the library which made references to the plague. Instead, the ultimate gathering together of spectators to witness, collectively, the full-cast dance finale offered *event* fulfilment: in this concluding sequence of the performance, fragments and faces that had been glimpsed throughout the evening were woven into a chaotic patchwork that did not tie up discrete narrative strands, but could satisfy the audience on a structural and sensory level.

For some reader-spectators, Punchdrunk's production might have proved frustrating for reasons already outlined: chiefly, that Poe's tales were 'reduced' to the level of potent impressions dislocated from the narrative structures that gave them meaning (albeit meaning of a twisted, alogical kind). However, and perhaps paradoxically, the company's refusal to deliver more of the source text(s) could instead offer such spectators a degree of liberation. The accounts of reading described by Jacobsen, explored earlier in this chapter, pointed to a liminal space somewhere between, and overlapping, two places: the one physically occupied by the reader, the other imaginatively evoked by the fiction. Inside this 'play space', readers typically envisaged themselves positioned marginally, peering from around a corner or through a window, looking down from above, or up from below. From there, the reader experienced a sense of freedom to watch, listen and dream; because not required to act, he or she could drift in and out of the fictional world unobserved. In Punchdrunk's *The Masque of the Red Death*, the audience are given something akin to this power. The decisive actions of separating visitors from their friends, and conferring anonymity through the mask, combine to make experiencing the performance a peculiarly solitary and intimate affair even in rooms peopled by others. Passing through different spaces in the transformed building, the spectator is persistently rendered a silent and implicitly hidden observer of mysterious encounters and impassioned conflicts; the fact that only fragments of these are witnessed reinforces the impression of being simultaneously inside and outside the fictional world. As noted, those scenic fragments are often conveyed through dance rather than realistic action or spoken word; the use of stylized physicality thus serves similarly to keep the narrative source at a remove, gesturing towards this through the movements of costumed characters but in a language that expresses visceral energies more than literal translation. Throughout the evening, audience members will enter rooms where no one else is present, yet which seem to signal that they are only momentarily vacated: such spaces, far from 'empty', allow profoundly gratifying opportunities for the reader-spectator to dream into the fictional world, to enter a realm between theatre and the book which draws the two imaginatively, even ideally, together.

Punchdrunk's spectators do not only drift and dream. The company's productions have become notorious for including a scattering of 'one-on-one' encounters throughout the evening, miniature 'scenes' which take place between an individual performer and audience member: only a few attendees, chosen randomly in the moment, will experience this. In these fleeting encounters, the spectator's implied invisibility is overturned and their physical mask temporarily removed. One-on-ones allow for a direct and private exchange that plays powerfully on the senses, often seductively: spectator accounts tell of intimate proximity, whispers, hands being held, even a kiss.[41] Although one-on-ones are not part of spectator experience per se, their inclusion within the show structure is judged vital by Punchdrunk both as a counterpoint to the way audience engagement is predominantly constructed – with spectators positioned effectively as anonymous witness – and because these private encounters are considered to represent immersive experience at its most powerful and 'essential'. Barrett has stated, 'A one-on-one, for me, is the purest form of Punchdrunk; it's distilled Punchdrunk.'[42] In *The Masque of the Red Death*, the one-on-ones reportedly included an encounter in which a male character urgently confessed a history of his crimes to a female spectator, who was addressed as his 'long-lost sister Rose' and offered a glass of absinthe.[43] In a second, which took place inside a cupboard, the character spoke of the 'secret love affair' going on between himself and the spectator with whom he was closeted, finally wiping off some of his make up and smearing this gently on the other's face.[44] In a third one-on-one, a less fortunate spectator was locked into a room and made the target for a stream of furious, paranoid abuse.[45] In all cases, such encounters are constructed to produce a highly charged experience, made all the more intense because brief and (in the spectator's case) unpremeditated. Writing about these intimate confrontations in *The Masque of the Red Death* and the company's earlier *Faust*, Rose Biggin has remarked on the tension between spectators' impressions that they are unique and personal (and, it is often assumed, will be as memorable for the actor as for the audience member) and the reality that these illicit and seemingly spontaneous moments are in fact 'tightly scripted [with] the performer [...] in control at all times.'[46] Jan Wozniak observes further that the degree of secrecy and rumour around what goes on in Punchdrunk one-on-ones now leads some spectators almost aggressively to compete for the experience, adopting any tactic – pursuing individual actors, 'brazenly' signalling his or her own availability – that might seem likely to bring about a one-on-one, with its associated thrill.[47]

Wozniak, Biggin and, elsewhere, Adam Alston have discussed critically the operation of one-on-one encounters within Punchdrunk's wider show structure and the complex ethics of this actor-spectator exchange. All three comment on the way in which the palpable sense of risk accompanying one-on-ones is offset by the artists' skilful *management* of this; the frisson the encounters provide thus arguably becomes another selling point readily accommodated within a twenty-first-century 'experience economy'.[48] These entirely justified concerns are perhaps less pertinent to a consideration of Punchdrunk's work as a practice of adaptation than questions about how one-on-ones affect spectators' relationship with the appropriated source material. The imaginative freedom granted to the audience, which, I have argued, results from their marginality in relation to the drama, is radically disrupted by an encounter which first, de-anonymizes, and second, obliges the participant to relate directly to a character from the fictional world. In their very brevity, these private scenes reproduce the impression of transience that colours the whole production, the implication that one must seize the moment before it dissolves. But the kind of 'seizing' fostered by the one-on-one is in sharp contrast to the way in which a drifting spectator may grow increasingly sensitized to the significations of site and action. Abruptly put on the spot, the spectator-participant now occupies a disconcertingly unstable – and thus for many, an exciting – place in which it is difficult to judge how far one's actions carry consequences. In terms of the dramatic representation, testimony suggests that the choices of participants have no discernible impact on the whole; whether someone does or does not respond to a character's appeal for help, for instance, will not alter what happens next in the wider context of the production. Yet clearly, in terms of performance – an engagement between real people, in real time – what is done here necessarily bears responsibility. There is a tension in this for adaptation and, paradoxically, a risk of *dis*empowerment for the reader-spectator, when the invitation to dream into the fiction through relatively gentle immersion is unexpectedly replaced by face-to-face confrontation inside that realm but without one's own character identity, past, or future. Reading literature, as already argued, invites relaxation of the boundaries of self; in a one-on-one, the reader-spectator is implicitly encouraged to lower defences of a different kind and shed the inhibitions that ordinarily regulate behaviour when alone with a stranger. This inversion of the spectator's previous position – from detached observation to effective imprisonment with a single actor-character, without witnesses – is exhilarating in its own terms but at the same time profoundly punctures 'readerly' experience of the work as adaptation.

The content of one-on-ones is necessarily tangential to the textual source, not least because, as explained, Punchdrunk productions do not prioritize conveying narrative exposition. None of the stories directly drawn on for the show include a 'sister Rose' (see my earlier example); an audience member would struggle, therefore, to map this particular one-on-one against any prior familiarity with Poe's work. However, Poe himself had a sister (or as some biographers believe, a half-sister) named Rosalie, from whom he was separated at an early age; if as seems probable this autobiographical material informed the development of the scene, that knowledge would surely be more intelligible to the actor than the spectator-participant.[49] From the perspective of adaptation, then, perhaps these one-on-ones approximate what happens when the contents of a book in which you are engrossed later trouble your sleep: in that liminal state, the dreaming mind authors a perplexing, fragmentary parallel text in which narrative influences detach from their original contexts and disconcertingly intertwine with ordinary life, fragments of knowledge and submerged desire. In this way, even while Punchdrunk cheerfully dispense with so much of the chosen text, and place that which they do retain tantalizingly beyond reach, this immersive *Masque of the Red Death* shapes a mode of audience reception that provocatively echoes the border-crossing effects produced by the very activity of reading. Further, while the dislocating one-on-one encounters might not grapple directly with the textual source, they could instead seem to stage the unstable and sometimes troubling engagement between literature and the reading self.

Kafka/Retz: *The Trial*

Whereas Punchdrunk's show took the form of a vast immersive promenade punctuated by private scenes with a few audience members, *The Trial* by London-based theatre company Retz (later renamed Rift) was shaped almost exclusively around the one-on-one encounter. Retz's production casts the spectator in a role suggestive of Kafka's hapless protagonist, Joseph K, charged with a crime whose nature is never fully disclosed and who is unable to penetrate the judicial system to prove his innocence. This interactive adaptation was constructed as two linked live performances, with audiences booking a ticket for Part One, then receiving notice of a Part Two date only once the first was over.[50] In Part One, each spectator attends a personal appointment at Shoreditch Town Hall, which results in him 'chancing' on a room filled with incriminating documents. The opportunity to examine the material is cut off by a security alarm bell: there follows in swift succession the spectator's 'arrest', a meeting with smoothly unhelpful solicitors, and finally an encounter with K himself in a lonely lock-up, in which Kafka's protagonist appeals to the spectator desperately for help before being silenced by a guard with a syringe. Part Two, scheduled a few weeks later, is ostensibly the occasion of the spectator's trial; however, on arrival at the so-called Department for Digital Privacy, situated in another district of East London, he discovers that he has already been found guilty and faces execution. He is directed from one dingy office to another – fictionally trapped inside a circuitous governmental system, where no one can provide help or illumination – and led finally to a peepshow booth that looks onto a torture chamber, inside which another 'criminal' is being readied for punishment. Drawing on Kafka's story 'In the Penal Colony', this section of the production – more conventionally 'dramatic' than what had preceded it – has the uniformed executioner eventually strap himself to the machine of punishment. By this stage of the event, it is implied that the intended victim, a young woman, has escaped her sentence. Yet just when the performance appears to be over she is dragged roughly away by guards and 'murdered' in the courtyard below: framed, for the spectator-participants, by the building's somewhat grimy windows.

Retz's adaptation of *The Trial* was inspired by the structure of Kafka's novel as much as its themes. Felix Mortimer, then the company's artistic director, had prior experience in immersive theatre, having worked as a designer on Punchdrunk's *Faust* and *The Masque of the Red Death*; he had also explored narrative fragmentation in Retz's own *O Brave New World* (2012), a six-part performance installation adapted from *The Tempest* and staged in a London shop over a six-month period. Mortimer had been considering the possibility of a production shaped around an audience's journey through multiple interconnected locations, with segments of narrative communicated in each. Kafka's novel seemed structurally suited to this idea, since the story is told solely through the protagonist's perspective and the characters K encounters have little interaction with one another. The theatrical form of the one-on-one was adopted with the twin aims of first, making the participant hyper-aware of her own role inside that narrative and second, imparting something of Joseph K's frustration while propelled, more or less passively, from one bewildering encounter to the next.[51] Thematically, too, the novel's articulation of the frailty of the individual against a system of inquisitorial yet incomprehensible bureaucracy seemed newly resonant in a twenty-first-century culture marked by growing unease about digital surveillance. Retz's producer Daisy Cooper explains that the company kept 'seeing news articles about the Big Brother state, about monitoring our internet activity' and so concluded that Kafka's story, already pertinent to contemporary times, 'just needed re-placing into a digital world'.[52] This motif of the power of information was thoroughly woven into the production, as participants were surreptitiously photographed en route, their movements tracked through private Twitter accounts, or subtly induced to provide snippets of personal data early on which were fed back, uncannily and threateningly, into the encounters faced in Part Two ('Would you like us to contact Marcus for you…?').

Kafka's novel is widely known, by repute, if not always through first-hand reading. It has had extraordinary critical impact: the front cover of the Penguin Modern Classics edition cites the *Sunday Times*' designation of *The Trial* as '[o]ne of the greatest philosophical works of the century'; elsewhere, exploring Kafka's wider influence, Allen Thiher concludes that it is above all his 'ambivalent legacy of play and madness that defines the narrative space in which unfold our most contemporary fictions'.[53] Such weight of regard necessarily bears on adaptation to some degree; Cooper's observation that the novel 'just' needed relocating within the context of new technologies might seem to underestimate the task, therefore, since in reception audiences will inevitably assess what a production keeps, discards or transforms of a famous source text in considerably more loaded ways. To recognize what is at stake in adapting Kafka it is important to take account not just of narrative content and formal structure, but of the ways in which *The Trial* acts upon the reader, and the complexity of interpretation that has resulted.

The term 'Kafkaesque' has become a common shorthand to describe frustrating systemic processes whose baroque operations are more self-perpetuating than problem-solving. Kafka trained as a lawyer and worked for a Prague insurance company; he openly loathed what he dismissively termed his *Brotberuf* ('bread job') which sustained him economically while he wrote fiction in his spare time.[54] In common with his famous short story 'The Metamorphosis' (1915), *The Trial* seems to reflect many of Kafka's own frustrations with petty bureaucracy and officialdom, and the vulnerability of the individual under the crushing weight of the totalitarian state. *The Trial*'s protagonist is a bank clerk. Finding himself accused (but of what?) in the book's opening lines, he spends the rest of the novel attempting unsuccessfully to defend his case and clear his name. K engineers meetings with individuals he is initially persuaded can help him – amongst them his uncle, a lawyer, the chief clerk of the court, the court painter Titorelli – but the chain of actions is disjointed and each encounter mountingly bizarre. K makes no progress, rather the reverse; every effort to advance his cause seems to mire him further, diminishing his expectations of success and compounding the recognition that his punishment is both inevitable and even deserved. A further layer of confusion is supplied by a succession of sexually charged encounters with female characters, including K's neighbour Fräulein Bürstner, the wife of the court attendant, and Leni, the lawyer's nurse; the seeming susceptibility of all the women towards K and the fascination he holds for them (and they for him) make these figures more easily readable as the product of masculine fantasy than as plausible individuals in their own right. At several points in the narrative, K seems retrospectively to have missed an opportunity to advance his case because he has been sexually distracted; the female sex is represented collectively as a kind of quagmire that sucks the protagonist down, endlessly thwarting his questing journey. Yet even without the cloying interventions of the women characters, Kafka makes it clear that K's position is hopeless. On the evening before his thirty-first birthday, two men come to K's door, 'pale and fat', looking to him like 'clapped-out old actors'.[55] K puts up no resistance as they lead him away through the dark streets and to a quarry, where he is killed by them – 'like a dog!' – with a butcher's knife.[56]

The philosopher and political theorist Hannah Arendt argued in an influential 1946 essay that *The Trial* explicitly satirized the pre-War Austrian bureaucratic regime. She suggests, however, that at the time Kafka's work was published (1925), bureaucracy was not widely recognized in Europe as a true *evil*, and thus, in that context, the extremes of horror and terror expressed in it seemed excessive and inexplicable; in consequence, critics had been driven to search for 'deeper' meanings in the story, for example, understanding it as a parable of corrupted theology.[57] That critical 'misinterpretation' nevertheless had some narrative basis, Arendt acknowledged, since Kafka was describing 'a society that considers itself the representative of God on earth and […] men who look upon the laws of society as though they were divine laws that cannot be altered by the will of men'.[58] Although Arendt insisted that K's struggle was above all against the 'senseless automatism' of the state, as the novel overtly suggests, her analysis did not forestall a succession of alternative interpretations in the following decades.[59] Thus *The Trial* has been variously understood as offering a metaphor for mental disintegration, in the form of a nervous breakdown or psychotic episode; via Freud, as an expression of the Oedipal conflict, repressed desire and sexual guilt; autobiographically, in terms of Kafka's relationships with family members and with women (especially his then fiancée, Felice Bauer); and sociologically, in prophetic anticipation of the totalitarian regime of Nazi Germany.[60] It is unsurprising that the novel has proved so fruitful a source of interpretive meanings: its very premise of unexplained accusation seems to present itself as a puzzle to be solved; further, Kafka's superficially transparent writing style – a quality aptly termed by Erich Heller 'obscure lucidity' – makes it hard to accept that there are not submerged meanings still more troubling than the surface narrative conveys.[61]

Part of the difficulty in penetrating *The Trial* in critical terms lies precisely in the instabilities of that narrative 'surface'. Throughout, what so troubles protagonist (and the reader) is not just how disturbingly or irrationally individual characters behave, but how the world itself behaves: the *physical* environment of the novel refuses to abide by Enlightenment principles of space and time. From the opening paragraph onwards, K's shock at his arrest is conveyed in terms of spatial disruption. Waking in his lodgings to find himself face-to-face with 'a man he had never before seen in the house', K asks in bewilderment, 'Who are you?' The man 'ignored the question, as if his appearance were to be accepted without query'.[62] As the novel proceeds, people materialize in rooms without warning; or, elsewhere, seemingly anonymous individuals are discovered – when K looks at them a second time – to be fellow officials from the bank: 'How could K have overlooked this fact? He must have been absolutely absorbed in the supervisor and the warders not to recognise these three.'[63] Similarly, rooms that appear in a particular guise on a given day transform themselves wholly on the next. When speaking to Fräulein Bürstner in the lodging house, K is startled to hear loud bangs from the other side of the wall:

> 'Don't be afraid', he whispered, 'I'll see to everything. But who can it be? Here next door there's only the living-room, and nobody sleeps there.' 'Oh yes', Fräulein Bürstner whispered in K's ear, 'since yesterday a nephew of Frau Grubach sleeps there, a captain.'[64]

Here, K's neighbour can give an apparently innocent explanation: 'It just happens no other room is free.' But nothing explains why, when K – eager to see the Fräulein again – opens her door, he finds its furniture reorganized: 'There was nobody in the room. It hardly looked like the room as K remembered it.'[65] Throughout the novel, K's encounters with other characters, and his spiralling descent into the judicial abyss, are conveyed through the unruliness of physical space. The counterpart for this unnerving fluctuation is the resistance of spaces to alteration, when the passage of time *should* make them change. This second behavioural characteristic is manifested starkly in the chapter titled 'The Whipper'. Alarmed to hear gasps from behind the door of an old lumber room in his office building, K discovers that behind it the two warders who first arrested him are being violently flogged because, they explain, he had complained about them to the examining magistrate. Appalled, K slams the door on this dreadful scene and throws open a window, allowing him to explain away the noise to passing clerks as the howl of a dog from the courtyard. Unsurprisingly, he remains haunted by the memory of the flogging and his implied responsibility for its infliction. The next day, passing the lumber room, he opens the door 'as if by habit' to find the action inside continuing exactly as before: 'The printed forms and inkpots just over the threshold, the whipper with his cane, the warders still fully dressed, the candle on the shelf' all replay the previous day, as does the warders' wailing appeal –'Sir!' – and K's own horrified slam of the door.[66] The precise repetition of this scene 'makes sense' only in ways that defy the Western model of orientational space and linear time. Since the punishment cannot have continued without respite for more than twenty-four hours (the candle has not burned down), the alternative explanation is that the scene manifests *when* and *because* K opens the door.

On one level, the irrational spatial and temporal operation described is merely what makes Kafka's novel nightmarish: in that sense, it could be argued that the unfolding action of *The Trial* straightforwardly obeys the 'logic' of the dreaming mind. Yet this is an unsatisfactory reading of those disobedient territories, since to privilege the dreamlike is to insist that *The Trial* is, after all, comfortably explicable in realist terms. Philip Weinstein has offered an alternative interpretation of the novel, demonstrating persuasively how Kafka undoes the realist model. In *Unknowing: The Work of Modernist Fiction*, the author explores how Kafka works to articulate human experience beyond the assumptions that underpin Western knowing. According to Weinstein,

> realism proposes – and this is its master stroke – that the representational field of space and time and others that its protagonist moves through corresponds to the objective world itself. Its stage thus artfully configured to enable the coming resolutions, realism denies that it has stacked the deck (or pre-arranged the cards), insisting instead on its protagonist as a free-standing subject moving within a lawful and indifferent frame.[67]

In contrast, Kafka's modernist work shows space and time misbehaving, and the 'objective' world as dislocating, disordered and (potentially) malign. Further, if realism's assumptions about the world and our human relationship to it are thus contested, it follows that the realist construction of the self is also undermined. Weinstein continues:

> When space becomes uncanny rather than lawful (no longer open to orientation and ownership), when time loses its negotiability (no longer linear/progressive), things become unfamiliar; the subject immersed in them becomes unfamiliar as well.[68]

In *The Trial*, K is increasingly denied the props which would enable confident orientation; as a result, he grows 'lost' in both the physical and psychological sense. Weinstein insists that loss of self should not be understood pessimistically, however, despite the terrifying surface of the narrative: for if modernism rejects realist protocols of knowing, one can infer that the strangeness of *un*knowing is necessary (and thus desirable) to radically relearn the dynamics of self and world.

Reinterpreting *The Trial* as visual drama necessarily means tackling the issue of material environment given its implications for the way in which K's journey is understood. Yet the task of adapting Kafka is already fraught, since representing his work *at all* makes it more concrete than the author wanted it to be. Kafka famously insisted with reference to 'The Metamorphosis' that there should be no illustration of the monstrous insect on the cover of the published edition; any form of visual interpretation, he said, would diminish the potency of the idea behind it.[69] For the same reason, Kafka hated Kurt Wolff's edition of his story 'The Stoker': he complained that the cover image of an early nineteenth-century steamboat, besides being 'too pretty' and insufficiently modern, produced its effect on the reader *before* the story could and so distorted its meanings and impact.[70] *The Trial* is a different case insofar as the narrative can, initially, be roughly mapped against the daily world; but as I have argued, the revealed instability of what its protagonist had believed he knew fundamentally constitutes the novel's power. In this way, *The Trial*, in common with Kafka's fiction more broadly, implicitly urges that adaptation should sustain, rather than contain, that quality of material volatility; it will be inadequate to fashion a dystopia, however ingenious, if this space is ultimately made safe by its very fixity. Orson Welles understood this when he shot his version of *The Trial* (1962), the first substantial attempt to adapt Kafka for cinema. The expressionist aesthetic of the film consciously revisited the style of Welles's earlier work, such as *Citizen Kane* (1941), making use of a series of surreal sets to accentuate the increasing alienation of the protagonist (played by Anthony Perkins). *The Trial* was partly filmed at the Gare d'Orsay, an abandoned Parisian train station, where an already complex network of levels, tunnels and stairways was further augmented to represent a terrifying maze suggestive of the convoluted structures of the legal system. The huge size of the building enabled extreme distortions of perspective, with elongated or foreshortened camera angles conveying K's 'littleness', his insignificance and the gathering momentum of the action against him.

Steven Berkoff's stage adaptation of the novel (1973) employed a more minimalist approach than Welles's film – unsurprisingly given the medium, a far leaner budget and its creator's background in actor-centred 'total theatre' – but likewise tended stylistically towards the expressionist and surreal. Drawing on *The Trial*'s embedded parable of the man seeking admission to the Law ('Before the law stands a door-keeper…'), this adaptation took the image of a doorway and reinterpreted it as a series of steel frames which, together with a rope, formed the entirety of the set:

> Our set of ten screens became the story and as the story could move from moment to moment so could our set – no long waits for a scene change but as a flash with the magician's sleight of hand. […] A room could become a trap, a prison, expand and contract and even spin around the protagonist Joseph K. This enabled us to recreate the environment – both physical and mental – of the book.[71]

As Berkoff suggests, the steel frames had to be moved fluidly; to sustain the quality of dynamism, actors would often begin speaking before the physical 'scene' was in place. In this way the set by its endless mutation both constructed and reflected K's nightmarish journey, able to 'melt in an instant and never represent a real heavy piece of pseudo-reality'.[72] An alternative theatrical solution to the challenge of reproducing *The Trial*'s unsettled spaces was adopted in Richard Jones's 2015 production for London's Young Vic: in Miriam Buether's design, this staging incorporated a travelator on which Rory Kinnear as K walked briskly, and almost continually, perspiring freely beneath the lights and from this labour. The moving floor suggested the relentless momentum of the legal case and the fruitlessness of K's attempts at 'progress'; simultaneously it gave the site itself a sick unsteadiness, so that the audience, ranged on each side as in a courtroom, looked down on K as on a man at sea.[73]

In diverse ways, then, the adaptations of Welles, Berkoff and Jones seem to acknowledge the way in which Kafka's novel forces rethinking of the dynamic interrelationship of self and space. All three versions address that theme by showing the actor-protagonist trapped in a kind of scenic vortex, drawn on relentlessly by the current of the mechanism. The viewer of these adaptations is positioned as observer or witness to this, although – if K is readable as an Everyman – that vulnerability arguably reaches beyond stage or screen to encompass the auditorium. Reinforcing this idea, in a discussion of Welles's film, Stevie Chick describes Perkins as 'an ideal extension of the audience, seeming as helpless and befuddled by his fate as we are, even as he works to find answers, confront his accusers, and actually find out what the charges are'.[74] Retz's immersive interpretation of *The Trial* remakes this opportunity to think oneself into the position of Kafka's protagonist as something concrete. Within minutes of Retz's production beginning, the spectator is actively positioned not as K, but as himself or herself in K's shoes. The sustained one-on-one structure of Part One, and the majority of Part Two, thus establishes the spectator-turned-participant as the protagonist of this story. Throughout, the burden of action/reaction remains with them, even though each segment of the production must also convey information and build narrative and atmosphere through various forms of multisensory engagement; this includes, in Part Two, a chokingly unappetizing last meal and ritual hand massage before the spectator is taken forward to be 'neutralised' on the machine.

Reviewing Retz's *The Trial*, arts journalist Miriam Gillinson admired the company's innovative use of the immersive form yet challenged the premise on which the production appeared to rest:

> Can a show convince you that you're going to die within the next half hour or so? Of course it bleeding can't. It seems an utterly bonkers position in which to put a theatre-goer. The brain just doesn't bend that way. Yet much of Retz' immersive take on Kafka's *The Trial* hinges on us believing in our imminent death. We don't.[75]

Holding the threat of execution over the heads of a theatre audience, Gillinson considers, is 'ridiculous' since it is impossible to feel persuaded that this end awaits us (and quite another thing to recognize it as the inevitable fate of Joseph K). She is right in this, as in suggesting that the seeming absurdity could undermine and distract from the broader experience the production seeks to construct. However, while accepting that this disjunction between fictional claim and real world context could prove a stumbling block for some, I argue that Retz's interactive, peripatetic adaptation frames a much richer opportunity for participants than is implied by narrative immersion alone. Central to this is the show's manipulation of space. The audience is obliged to 'read' Kafka through the frame of the site and, conversely, to perceive the site through the lens of Kafka; by this means, *The Trial* in performance effectively echoes and enacts the 'undoing' of realism pursued within the novel. I illustrate this argument with a more detailed examination of the opening and final sequences of the production, in part drawing on direct experience as spectator-participant.[76]

As described, Retz's production begins when the audience member arrives at Shoreditch Town Hall, in East London, for an individual timed appointment. A handful of people are standing on the steps, unsure what to do or where to go. No information is displayed about the performance; no one speaks to anyone else, since it is not obvious who is there for the show. After some minutes, a young woman comes out and checks off names from a clipboard, face expressionless; eventually, the four or five audience-participants are led into the foyer where they are told to sit and wait. The chairs face a reception desk and computer; the woman returns to the desk and whatever work it is she is doing. Attending to the gathered participants does not seem to be a priority for her; this is a waiting room, and there is thus ample time to study the mid-Victorian architecture of this municipal building, its echoing height and faded grandeur oddly jarring with the humdrum business that seems to continue across and around the performance event. Eventually, slowly, the participants are summoned to the desk one by one. A short exchange confirms some personal details; the opportunity to fictionalize is there from the beginning, but at this stage there is no obvious motive *not* to tell the truth. Another wait, then the participant is directed along a corridor and down to a lower floor of the building: there, an open doorway leads into an unoccupied room littered with a mass of papers, files and tiny scraps of information about 'Joseph K' – evidently the subject of a major investigation – and at the same time, a monitor runs a film of K himself issuing a gabbled plea for help to whoever watches it. Giving each participant time alone to explore the contents of a constructed space is now a well-established, even ubiquitous trope of immersive theatre; as noted previously, this is a central element of Punchdrunk's productions which is realized with extraordinary care. But in *The Trial*, it seems as if the familiar deluge of signification has been executed with a studied crudeness; the overload of displayed 'information' makes its sum manifestly unfathomable, and closer examination of individual papers reveals merely the accounts, faxes and order forms of routine officialdom. In any case, there is *too little* time given to penetrate any of it, as the shriek of an alarm, forceful ejection and arrest all proceed very quickly. Out on the street, in the custody of a uniformed guard and in full view of the general public, the participant is searched, interrogated (what were they doing alone in the basement of the building, with government records?), then frog-marched down the street towards the police station.

It is at this point in the event that the focus shifts powerfully onto the spectator-protagonist; yet curiously, this is also the point from which alienation grows alongside the dramatic 'game'. The stony-faced interrogation might induce the urge to giggle, while the demand for answers invites creative lies as well as protestations of innocence.[77] The arrest, although transparently a fiction, remains subtly shaming – still more so, as one is 'walked' forcibly along the pavement. The participant can hardly be fooled into believing that the threat is actual, but might sense, first, that being arrested might feel something like this; and second, that this will be what passers-by understand is happening, since the scene is not outwardly signalled as theatrical. Suddenly, at this point, the guard is told by radio that the suspect is being 'fast-tracked'; he hands over a business card, points to the telephone number and departs. This moment heralds a new kind of alienation as, released from custody, the participant must try to find 'Huld Lawyers' at 297 Hoxton Street, a ten-minute walk away, accompanied only by an impersonal voicemail. This solitary journey takes place along Hackney streets that are busy with the onward flow and buzz of ordinary life, the rush of traffic and blast of a siren, and, punctuating this, the languorous gaze of those in no hurry to go anywhere. What, in this urban scene, is part of the performance? Perhaps little of it, in the sense of deliberately 'planted' action; but in the intensity of the moment, all of it is fictionalized. The curious estrangement fostered by the production takes this beyond surface uncertainties about who is acting, and who 'real'. The street itself splits, or doubles, as one walks along it: the space is daily and dramatized at the same time. Describing her experience of the event as spectator-participant, Mélanie Binette notes, 'I was quite tempted to run away, but this feeling was distant, like observing myself in a dream not in the real action of attempting to escape from a threatening danger'; another audience member, interviewed by Binette, commented similarly: 'I felt as if I was walking through a film. I felt almost as if I could observe myself walking along the street.'[78] Such accounts suggest that Retz's manipulation of space gave London, temporarily, a Kafkaesque layer; the spectator passes through the city, not in the shoes of K, but some steps behind. The journey to the (supposed) lawyers' office is not truly purposeful, however, both because the participant, like K, is not going there by choice and because the alienation of the environment calls purpose and progress into question. The London street is 'no longer open to orientation and ownership', to echo Weinstein; it turns uncanny, at once familiar and alienated.

Thus, where Punchdrunk strive explicitly to build a theatrical illusion with no visible 'chink', for the majority of *The Trial* the opposite effect is produced: Retz's Kafka is laid thinly over urban London with no attempt to staunch the bleed between the two. This studied confusion of layering is further exacerbated in the production's violent conclusion. Part Two of the event is organized differently, without the solitary forays down streets and alleys that characterized the first stage. For the second part, the company took over the Rose Lipman Community Centre in de Beauvoir, Haggerston, transforming that brutalist building, originally a 1970s council estate facility, into the fictional Department for Digital Privacy. From the moment of checking in at reception, sitting – ignored – in a waiting area, then being directed from room to room inside its warren-like structure, spectators may see fellow audience in the vicinity but are largely denied the chance to speak with them. Only later, when four or five spectators – numbered, not named – are gathered in a corridor, lined up against a wall and brusquely interrogated, is there an opportunity for fleeting, collective camaraderie: their mutual awareness draws attention to the action's status as *game*, individually interpreted but nevertheless played together. Yet immediately the production slices through that safety net, when the guard abruptly plucks 'Number Three' for execution, as if at random. Recalling Gillinson's criticism of the adaptation's premise, it is true that one would have to be extraordinarily gullible to fail to recognize the victim as an audience plant. The final stage of the event thus turns curiously anticlimactic, rather than the reverse: for while one of 'us' is led forward for punishment, it appears that the others are off the hook. That impression is reiterated by use of peepshow booths – disturbing as their connotations are – since the perspective these construct on the action refuse immersion, stripping from participants their former (relative) autonomy and effectively reinstating a traditional, explicitly voyeuristic, actor-audience relationship. At this stage, the production invites a quite different mode of engagement from that which preceded it, a position arguably difficult to assume *after* being asked to imagine that one's life is hanging in the balance; and this might indeed produce the edge of absurdity Gillinson remarks upon. Further, once the audience has seen the supposed spectator strapped down, then released and replaced by the officer, the represented fiction is separated still further from its 'readers'. The scene concludes with the character's death-by-machine, after which the audience drifts or is manoeuvred into a community hall space. There is no opportunity for applause and no explicit indication of an ending. The supposed victim of the machine now moves amongst the participants, laughing about her 'narrow escape'. In no sense do spectators need to have believed in the show's fictional premise to desire decompression, given that each one, 'true' or planted, has for the last hour – in a sense, for the last month – supported a sustained and at times discomforting pretence.

It is at this moment, when the overarching fabric(ation) of Retz's show seems finally to have come undone, that the planted spectator/victim is forcibly pulled from the audience's midst, to be 'beaten up and killed' in the courtyard outside. This twist is startling, perhaps even shocking: but it might seem to be so in the manner of a horror movie, whereby an assumed ending is exposed as illusory, to be replaced by an alternate and, temporarily, less comfortable one. Regarded in that light, an audience should be able to accommodate this coda with relative ease: we thought it was over; it wasn't; it is now. However, I argue that this unexpected, second ending retains the power to disturb: not because spectators fail to realize that the scene is staged, but because *what* is shown – a young woman being forcibly repressed by armed officers – acquires shades of reality by virtue of its enactment in the street, in plain view. The 'killing' is difficult to watch, first, for the harsh colours in which it paints the world; second, because we, the spectators, are doing nothing to prevent it. The participatory role ascribed to the audience throughout implies an ethical responsibility on us to protest against, or directly intervene within, this fictional action; but the watchers' vantage point, from inside the building, refuses this possibility even as it shields us from the violence outside.

The sequence described was enacted on a patch of ground outside a small convenience store, open for business at that time. On the date I attended, the scene was accidentally witnessed by a young man who was leaving the shop (indeed, the location would make such encounters a common occurrence). On this occasion, the presence of this passer-by produced a distinctly uneasy comedy for the knowing audience: from two storeys above, spectators were effectively spying on an innocent 'reader' chancing on a fictional scene that masqueraded, convincingly, as real. The actors departed quickly, carrying their victim; the bystander was left hesitating in the courtyard, visibly unsure what had occurred and how to respond. This incident demonstrates the show's construction of a multi-layered space in which distinctions between real and pretended, material and imaginary, contemporary and Kafka(esque) are thoroughly disturbed. On finally leaving the Rose Lipman Building that day, a few spectators encountered a police officer in the street who had been directed to the area, he said, following a call from a worried civilian. So the pretended assault was taken for real, or at least, real enough to produce ripples within and beyond the conceptual and physical spaces of the performance. This 'misreading' of the scene by an outsider – an eventuality predisposed to occur in some form, thus implicitly courted by the production – highlights the ability of adaptation to cross boundary lines, or perhaps more accurately to occupy the space on either side of the 'line' at the same time. Echoing Heidegger's claim that when we think towards a place we are, in a sense, already there, the coda to Retz's *The Trial* served as a theatrical 'thinking towards' a demonstration of repressive power which, through representative embodiment, virtually conjured the reality into being. Moreover, the traces of that action were not fully erased: while the officer was disabused, accepting the proffered explanation equably enough, the witness by then had long gone.

Retz's adaptation of *The Trial* does not, then, enact Kafka's novel in performance; neither does the immersive encounter it constructs straightforwardly place the audience in role as Joseph K. Instead, the production allows multiple routes for participation: the spectator can choose to support the fiction and – implicitly cast, not as K, but as (let us say) B – bow to the accusation levelled against her, or attempt to prove her innocence. Alternatively, she can choose to press down on the *form* of the event, testing what improvisatory freedoms are possible within the boundaries of the audience-performer contract. Or again, she might assume the participant position but observing action more than trying to shape its direction. Or indeed, she might move between any or all of these states, in the process becoming reader, writer, protagonist and interchangeable 'extra'. The gap that is opened up within the production for the spectator is not tied to the content of Kafka's novel, but rooted in the interpretive space *around* it: a space which, as noted, may be experienced more as disorientation than enlightenment. In this way, Retz's adaptation echoes the view of Kafka offered by critic Susan Sontag in her short essay 'The Unseen Alphabet'. Here, Sontag argues that as readers we experience Kafka's 'invisible world' as deeply alien, yet still recognizably our own; his works, she suggests, convey an unsettling sense of inversion at the deepest level, as if he were using a new language, or had unearthed a hidden alphabet. Sontag's 1983 essay formed part of *Kafka Unorthodox*, a gathering held that year – the centennial of his birth – of more than thirty artists at New York City's Cooper Union, curated by art critic Dore Ashton (the latter a champion of New York School abstract expressionism). Sontag devotes much of her essay to a work exhibited at this event by Swedish artist Carl Frederik Reuterswärd. 'Interletters', a sculpture series cast in bronze, resembles an attempt to write but in an unreadable language. Starting from the principle that to 'illustrate' Kafka's fiction directly was impossible, Reuterswärd instead brought form to the squat, silent spaces *between* letters, in so doing positing an alternate alphabet. His 'Interletters', some shapes awkwardly top-heavy, others pot-bellied, had nothing like the relative legibility of the mirror image, but constituted, for Sontag, a vocabulary 'on the *edge* of recognition'. Quoting the words of poet Paul Éluard – 'There is another world, but it is inside this one' – Sontag continues:

> Inside thought is a language. Inside a language are sentences. Inside sentences are words. Inside words are letters.
>
> And inter-letters.[79]

Reuterswärd's sculptures, articulating the invisible, enabling spaces between and behind the controlled verticals, diagonals and curves of the Roman alphabet, were for Sontag an ideal visualization of Kafka's writing, which itself carved out 'a new, terrible relation to space'.[80] Retz's immersive adaptation of *The Trial*, by employing a fictional frame superimposed on urban London, created a form of participant engagement that was not contained within Kafka's narrative, nor grounded in the contemporary sphere of the city, but found in the interpretive, uncanny spaces between both.

This chapter has examined the function of space in adaptation, seeking to tease apart the many levels at which this shapes signification, interpretation and experience. As we have seen, theatrically animating the geographies of literary fiction requires something more than – perhaps, quite other than – illustrative representation, even if that were in any sense achievable: first, because literary landscapes are not backdrops, but inseparable from a text's construction of character, action, mood and narrative; second, because presenting the settings of literature to an audience as if these were pictures fails to take account of the ways we understand and engage with those worlds as readers. This complex appreciation of what and how space 'means' can valuably illuminate the choices made in any adaptation and the extent to which an audience find the realization of these satisfying, or problematic, in performance.

Imagining the word made flesh and form might be thought challenge enough. The example of Complicite's response to Bulgakov is used in this chapter to show one way in which an 'impossible' world can be redrawn, visually and aurally, across the relatively blank canvas of the stage. But the shows of Punchdrunk and Retz attempt something different, choosing instead to relocate texts in alternative sites which insistently throw up narratives of their own, meanings which can complement or conflict with those generated by the literary source. In neither case were locations appropriated for their illustrative qualities, or at least, not simply so. The BAC was, for Punchdrunk, a building whose scale, architecture and warren-like structure did not represent but could help to communicate the perplexing, clandestine spaces of Poe's fiction; additionally, as noted, *The Masque of the Red Death* also aimed to talk back to the BAC about the nature of the site and how its potential might be more fully exploited. Punchdrunk's adaptation dressed the site at a miniaturized level, offering not an illustration of Poe's writing but a fantasy of it in a richly detailed veneer which the bones of the building occasionally poked through. Retz's handling of Kafka effected no such transformation. Instead, the company laid one 'world' sparsely upon another. Even with its indoor spaces, *The Trial*'s representation of locale seemed deliberately partial; outdoors, no attempt was made (nor could it be) to erase the non-fictional scene. This meant that Retz seemed to ask something wholly unachievable from their audience: how could spectators possibly believe in the show's imaginative world, while remaining so solidly in this one? But the production poses that question consciously: *how can* spectators inhabit that imaginative place, while remaining, undisguisedly, in the daily world? My reading of this event has proposed that space was utilized less to locate its audience, than to dislocate us; further, that at times bizarre and troubling obligation to occupy multiple positions at once effectively echoes the disorientation enacted by Kafka's novel.

Taking theatre outside of theatre buildings does not automatically translate into promenade or immersive productions, although making that move will in itself unseat assumptions about an audience's position within the event. However, for many artists a strong attraction of site-specificity is the opportunity to experiment with actor-audience relationship and by extension to propose a more interactive, implicated role for the spectator. This chapter has considered the excitement attached to that possibility, as well as the discomforts that come with relinquishing the safety of distance. Norman Holland argued that, as readers, submission to the laws of a fictional world is made possible through a state of passivity in which it is understood that fantasized engagement, as in dreams, does not carry consequences in daily life. With immersive adaptations, such as those of Punchdrunk and Retz, this process immediately becomes problematized. The invitation to enter the materialized text tantalizingly suggests the chance to be physically 'lost in a book'; at the same time, the interactive form inhibits this possibility, since the anticipation and codes of participation may prompt an audience to put up, rather than relax, their defences. *The Masque of the Red Death* and *The Trial* both enter difficult territory when it transpires that fictional action and our reactions to this have real life consequences: the one-on-ones, the attack in the street. Neither production allays this potential anxiety; indeed, each might be said to court that tension, if for different reasons.

Turning prose literature into performance demands a movement across worlds. Elaine Scarry explores the leap from words on a page into an imagined solidity: in her analysis this change is effected by glints and gleams, shifts of perspective, and a writerly sleight of hand whereby subjects are alternately exposed and concealed. The translation of texts into physical life carries different problems and possibilities, so is not smoothly analogous; nonetheless, where Scarry's model helps is in drawing attention to the liminality of adaptation, its continuing negotiation between implicitly competing realms. The somewhat intangible qualities of 'radiant ignition', 'stretch/tilt' and 'rarity' are not proposed as uniquely applicable to adaptation; indeed, it might be difficult to conceive of a theatrical show which did *not* employ such devices. However, the identification of those elements helps us understand more fully the importance of the gap between art forms, and between concept and materialization. My analysis has shown that this gap should not necessarily be regarded as a chasm that adaptation must overcome. Instead, what is not shown, not told and not completed may offer precisely the opening the reader-audience needs.

5

Resisting Adaptation

It is common, in discussions of theatre and screen adaptations, to encounter the trope of 'impossibility': of the literary text deemed unstageable, or unfilmable. Such assertions may be judged representative of the wider rhetoric that would find dramatic adaptations inevitably wanting beside their prose counterparts. Yet beyond this, insisting on a book's unstageability stands as a defiant claim for, and celebration of, literature's medium specificity. It implies that by content, structure and scale, or linguistic character, certain works actively *resist* adaptation: they will not submit to the pressures imposed by dramatic form. Several of the adaptations considered in this book have been described in such terms, whether by reviewers, playwrights and directors, or by the original author: *The Waves*, *The Curious Incident of the Dog in the Night-Time*, *The Street of Crocodiles* and *The Master and Margarita* have all been declared 'unstageable'. Yet in practice, the concept of unstageability is invoked as frequently to mark the overturning of that presupposition as to uphold it: thus while Mark Haddon had been 'absolutely convinced' that *The Curious Incident of the Dog in the Night-Time* could not be filmed or dramatized, 'Simon [Stephens]'s genius' brought the realisation 'that [Haddon] was completely and utterly wrong.'[1] The proof of the practice in each of these instances did not come in the form of some kind of ideal capturing of the literary work through drama, but by the creation of a new, live, embodied 'text' that could speak back meaningfully to the source, reframing it freshly in a theatrical context. As I have shown, adaptation, in all these examples, required accommodation on both sides of the textual encounter, with literature not so much bowing to the assumed imperatives of drama, as theatre admitting and even actively embracing the difficulties of the written source. In certain cases, perhaps most directly Mitchell's *Waves*, the adaptation did not attempt to recast literary 'narrative' in dramatic form but instead produced something closer to a parallel or analogous experience in a new artistic medium. Such an approach in itself problematizes the idea of unstageability, since to claim this presupposes that adaptation's goal is to mimic the text it appropriates. However, as we have seen, if adaptation is regarded as a process of making fit, this need not mean ruthlessly fit *into*. Instead, the category of 'fitness' is made subject to interrogation: the fitness of the text for the times; the fitness of theatre to articulate this relation.

Nonetheless, while performance is always able to respond laterally to the provocations of literary prose, shaping productions with their own integrity and artistic coherence, to leave it at this neatly sidesteps the question of whether some literature *might* 'resist' adaptation – or more importantly, what the implications would be for theatre if one accepted this were so. For where books are judged unlikely or even hopeless projects for adaptation, this is, as I have said, typically because they appear to conflict, structurally or stylistically, with the fundamental requirements and conditions of the dramatic. A labyrinthine structure, multiple or clashing linguistic registers, meandering narratives or virtual plotlessness, emphasis on interior experience rather than objective occurrence, self-conscious opacity, sheer number of words: such characteristics of a prose text are regularly identified as markers of its inflexibility in adaptation terms. The consequence of this position would be to suppose that the theatre cannot easily tolerate such qualities: in other words, that the nature of drama and the event structures of performance require a graspable structure, lucid speech, discernible shape and purpose to the narrative, dynamic action, focused clarity, and a running time that conforms to the predominant social and economic expectations of theatre-going. Yet while these requirements still broadly pertain within the mainstream, avant-garde creative practice from at least the 1960s onwards has forcefully interrogated or contradicted them by example. In 2006, Hans-Thies Lehmann compellingly described a landscape of millennial 'postdramatic' performance, founded upon earlier experimentation within environmental theatre, the happenings and performance art; by the composers, dancers and poets of the New York School; by writers, like Samuel Beckett, Heiner Müller and Elfriede Jelinek; by directors and choreographers, such as Tadeusz Kantor, Richard Schechner, Robert Wilson, Jan Lauwers, Pina Bausch and Richard Maxwell; and continuing in the example of contemporary companies, including the Wooster Group, Station House Opera, La Fura dels Baus, Forced Entertainment, Socìetas Raffaello Sanzio, Gob Squad and tg STAN.[2] As Lehmann's study showed:

> The demarcation of a new theatre continent with other criteria, values and processes has created the necessity to reveal a number of 'un-thought' implications of that which even nowadays shapes the common understanding of theatre. Apart from this critique of a series of – on closer inspection rather questionable – self-evident notions in the theory of theatre, it is necessary to postulate postdramatic theatre energetically as a concept contradictory to these seemingly self-evident concepts.[3]

Lehmann's analysis of this new theatrical continent exposed profound contestation of precisely the assumptions – or 'seemingly self-evident concepts' – I set out previously. By turning attention onto the material situation of performance, deconstructing and complicating the concept of dramatic representation, and highlighting the role and responsibility of the audience in the process of meaning-making, the postdramatic paradigm has suggested and supported the emergence of theatrical languages which, I shall argue, are able to rework 'resistant' literatures in performance terms.

In this chapter, I examine theatrical treatments of three novels which, on the surface, would seem unpromising sources for adaptation: in chronological order, Denis Diderot's *Jacques the Fatalist* (first published in 1796, although written some years earlier); Marcel Proust's *In Search of Lost Time* (its seven volumes emerging between 1913 and 1927); and David Foster Wallace's *Infinite Jest* (1996). *Jacques the Fatalist* recounts the seemingly directionless journeying of a servant and his master who fill their days and alleviate boredom by sharing bawdy stories which are continually interrupted, or simply abandoned. The book's author is himself the chief disturber of narrative progress, intervening regularly to undermine the account he has just given, to poke fun at other novelists and literary genres, and to chastise the reader for laziness or, alternatively, for asking too many questions. While Diderot's novel – which 'the author' insists is 'obvious[ly]' *not* a novel, since he is 'not doing what a novelist would not fail to do' – is both highly playful and at many points structured in the form of dialogue, its deeply digressive structure and obscurity of purpose would seem antithetical to dramatic (as opposed to postdramatic) representation.[4] Moreover, some of the novel's games are inherently literary: not least, Diderot's incorporation of passages openly 'plagiarised' from Sterne's *Tristram Shandy*, a feature which led the majority of critics in his time, up until the early twentieth century, to dismiss the book as weakly derivative or at best an insignificant 'hoax'.[5] By contrast, Proust's mammoth work, although initially rejected by publishers, was quickly acclaimed as a masterpiece and is, for some critics, the 'greatest novel of the twentieth century and perhaps of all time'.[6] Simultaneously, the author's name remains a byword for literary difficulty: a 2007 cartoon in the *New Yorker* depicts an angry-looking man sitting on a couch with a book, while another beamingly tells his wife, 'That's the guy I hired to read Proust for me.'[7] Aside from the high cultural status and sheer scale of this work, Proust's style, too, is daunting in being persistently excursive (although in a quite different manner from Diderot) and temporally slippery: individual sentences and whole paragraphs effect shifts of tense and perspective that produce, in Roger Shattuck's words, the impression of a 'motionless plot' and, consequently, a disorientating and, for some, frustrating reading experience.[8] Finally, Wallace's millennial *Infinite Jest* rivals Proust's as a book almost certainly more talked about than read in full. With more than 1,000 pages of dense prose, studded throughout with 388 endnotes (some of which come with additional sub-footnotes), with multiple narrative threads, a non-chronological structure and postmodern juxtaposition of textual forms, *Infinite Jest* has been characterized as an 'encyclopedic' novel which directly manifests the experience of data overload that it also explores thematically.[9] Within the fiction, *Infinite Jest* is the name of an 'après-gardist' film allegedly so entertaining that it fatally incapacitates anyone who watches it; Wallace's novel likewise threatens to overwhelm readers who may well, in common with one reviewer, give up part way through to raise 'a limp white flag'.[10]

Despite a publication time-span of 200 years and considerable diversity in scope and scale, these novels make for 'difficult' reading in significantly corresponding ways. Most noticeably, all three confound expectations of narrative momentum: linearity is rejected in favour of circling or spiralling, or, in Wallace's case, a fractal pattern that mimics the structure of a Sierpinski Gasket (a triangle or pyramid containing an infinite number of smaller shapes, in Wallace's words a 'pyramid on acid').[11] Each novel is digressive, or seems to be so, by its author's refusal to adhere to an onward path: and, in the examples of Diderot and Wallace at least, interruptions to this may be openly advertised as irrelevant or misleading. And while the narratives shift backwards, forwards and sideways in time, in and out of cul-de-sacs, each simultaneously undermines the knowability of the spatial terrain too. Proust's narrator walks as a child through countryside – in the process acquiring 'the deep layers of [his] mental soil' – that seems already to foreshadow its own erosion, in consequence instilling in him from the outset the knowledge of its loss.[12] Diderot denies his reader any guiding compass in the opening paragraph: 'Where were they coming from? From the nearest place. Where were they going? Does anyone really know where they're going?'[13] In *Infinite Jest*, the map has already been redrawn such that part of the northeastern United States and southeastern Canada has become a huge toxic landfill competitively termed either the 'Great Concavity' or the 'Great Convexity', depending on the geographical position or political affiliation of the speaker.[14] In this way the territorial foundation of all three novels appears unstable, with narrative movement across this radically disturbed, or else 'aimlessly' drifting.

In 'Forms of Time and of the Chronotope in the Novel' (1937–38), Mikhail Bakhtin proposes the concept of the chronotope as a tool to unpick the ways in which time, space and character are interwoven in fiction and articulated in history. 'Chronotope' literally means 'time-space', indicating the axes which formally constitute the text and which are always inseparable and interdependent. According to Bakhtin:

> In the literary artistic chronotope, spatial and temporal indicators are fused into one carefully thought-out, concrete whole. Time, as it were, thickens, takes on flesh, becomes artistically visible; likewise, space becomes charged and responsive to the movements of time, plot and history.[15]

The chronotope operates analytically as a way to assess how literary time-space represents and reflects history; how time-space functions inside the fictional frame; how a text intersects temporally and spatially with other texts; and how these dimensions influentially frame the interactions of authors, texts and readers. A chronotopic analysis thus aims to expose the fullness and dynamism within literary works, at the same time ensuring these are seen not as 'closed books' but open structures that are perpetually renewed and changed. In Bakhtin's account, the development of the modern novel was necessarily accompanied by a fundamental transformation of the literary artistic chronotope from a structure that was communal, open and exteriorized, to one that was private, domestic and hidden: broadly, a movement from 'the popular chronotope of the public square' to that of the 'salons and parlours [in which] the webs of intrigue are spun'.[16] My analysis of these three novels as adaptation sources for performance will draw on Bakhtin's proposal, using the chronotope of the road and figure of the rogue to discuss Diderot, and the interplay between the (auto) biographical and the 'viscous and sticky' literary time-space of bourgeois society to consider Proust.[17] Bakhtin does not apply the concept of the chronotope to the postmodern novel, for obvious reasons; nonetheless, his reflections on a time-space that conveys 'simultaneous coexistence' (referring to the elaborate internal structure of Dante's *Divine Comedy*) usefully illuminate the ways in which Wallace's novel is composed and received.[18]

As Sue Vice identifies, the transmutation of the literary chronotope over time is viewed by Bakhtin with regret and 'nostalgia' for earlier forms of chronotope and correspondingly for 'the more communal kinds of society these chronotopes refract', even while he celebrates increased sophistication in modern narrative technique.[19] This recognition has significant implications when literary texts are appropriated for adaptation in the theatre, since that process relocates those works – albeit in radically altered form – within a context which, in part, restores the 'lost' communal frame. At the same time, Bakhtin's very description of time become 'flesh' and space turned 'charged' seems to anticipate and invite application of the chronotope with the additional dimensions brought by human actors, lived-out shared time and a physical stage. So while the novels considered in this chapter exhibit, as I have indicated, orders of time-space that are especially unruly, the concept of the chronotope can also be used to reflect on the languages contemporary theatre might draw on to rearticulate those orders, and to what ends. In what follows, I explore how postdramatic, intermedial and durational performance structures have been employed less to 'dramatise' the novels than to relocate and reproduce their unsettling effects. I treat these projects not in the chronological order of the literary sources but according to the decreasing physical space occupied by the adaptations, a 'shrinking' also accompanied by increasingly austere minimalism of form. I therefore begin with Matthias Lilienthal's *Infinite Jest: 24 Hours through the Utopian West* for the Hebbel am Ufer (2012), a million-euro 'theatrical marathon' made up of multiple performances, created by twelve international companies and artists, and staged over a 24-hour period in locations across Berlin; within this, my analysis will focus more narrowly on one piece, Gob Squad's *The Conversationalist*, staged at the Rot-Weiss Tennis Club in the Steffi Graf Stadium.[20] I consider next *Where the World is Going, That's Where We are Going*, a postdramatic two-hander by the young Belgian theatre company Hof van Eede, inspired by Diderot's novel (2012). Finally, I discuss Canadian poet Peter Jaeger's *A Field Guide to Lost Things* (2015), a conceptual, text-based reframing of Proust's

Swann's Way which Jaeger also presents as a performatively unadorned live reading of between three and four hours. As I show, contemporary practices of performance framed by self-doubt and scepticism – about the possibility of originality and authority, transparent communication, or reliable representation – lend themselves richly to adaptation of prose texts preoccupied by the same uncertainties.

Wallace/Hebbel am Ufer: *Infinite Jest – 24 Hours through the Utopian West*

In one sense, consideration of the 'time-space' of *Infinite Jest* has an obvious place to begin: with the sheer size of the book, and the corresponding length of time it takes to read it. One journalist relates cutting her copy into thirds, a literal grappling with the reading task.[21] Yet taking the book apart, physically or metaphorically, is not truly possible according to Dave Eggers, who describes *Infinite Jest* as something like

> a spaceship with no recognizable components, no rivets or bolts, no entry points [...]. It is very shiny, and it has no discernible flaws. If you could somehow smash it into smaller pieces, there would certainly be no way to put it back together again.[22]

Eggers's observation is pertinent at the material level, since sawing up the book severs the main text from its endnotes (unless these too are segmented and stapled on): and while one could opt to treat those pages as a text in their own right, Wallace intended that the notes should operate as a persistent irritant that forced the reader repeatedly to 'stop, hold his or her place in the text, go down, [...] read the interpolation and then return'.[23] Thematically and narratively, the novel is so tightly interwoven that separating its strands is unfeasible, while seeming mockingly to anticipate such attempts, asking, 'are you just looking for some kind of Cliff-Note summary so you can incorporate the impression of depth into some new panty-removal campaign?'[24]

The book's overwhelming density and extensive incorporation of specialist and technical information from diverse knowledge fields have led it to be labelled by some as an 'encyclopedic novel', an inherently unsettling descriptor which fuses fictional invention with what professes to be dependable factual reference. Yet such labelling is further complicated, as David Letzler observes, by recognition that while many of Wallace's instructive endnotes do operate in quasi-scholarly mode, others are used as parody, to *mis*inform, or simply to spin yet further story threads.[25]

The novel powerfully resists summation, therefore, but identifying a few narrative threads helps convey its terrain. One plotline focuses on the Incandenza family, centrally Hal, a brilliant but disturbed and drug-dependent young student at the elite Enfield Tennis Academy in Massachusetts, and his late father James Incandenza, a scientist, former tennis player and filmmaker responsible for creating the lethal movie *Infinite Jest*. In a separate narrative, the master copy of the Entertainment (as it is known) is urgently sought by both US agents and the Wheelchair Assassins, a Québécois separatist group planning to weaponize the film by turning it against the entertainment-obsessed American public. Additionally, down the hill from the Academy is Ennet House, a drug and alcohol rehabilitation centre: some of its residents, chief amongst them the former burglar and recovering addict Don Gately, turn out to be linked to the Academy and/or the plot to steal the Entertainment; the Ennet House establishment also crystallizes symbolically the theme of addiction, which links multiple plot strands and pervades the novel.

Published in 1996, *Infinite Jest* is set 'futuristically' in the early twenty-first century. The world it depicts is characterized by a ceaseless flow of entertainment and information; sophisticated yet ultimately debilitating technology; and commercialism exacerbated to the point where calendar years have become purchasable commodities. The narrative timeline is difficult to follow not least because chapters are headed according to the year of subsidized (or product sponsorship) time in which the action takes place, such as the Year of the Depend Adult Undergarment, or the Year of the Whisper-Quiet Maytag

Dishmaster. This kind of reference within the novel conveys deep scepticism, a typically postmodern irony. But Wallace said repeatedly that he wanted to go beyond the lazy cynicism of an 'ironic' authorial position:

> If the contemporary condition is hopelessly shitty, insipid, materialistic, emotionally retarded, sadomasochistic and stupid, then I (or any writer) can get away with slapping together stories with characters who are stupid, vapid, emotionally retarded [...]. With descriptions that are simply lists of brand-name consumer products.

By contrast, Wallace insisted, '[r]eally good fiction could have as dark a worldview as it wished, but it'd find a way both to depict this dark world *and* to illuminate the possibilities for being alive and human within it'.[26] In *Infinite Jest*, the reality of data overload and the theme of self-destructive pursuit of pleasure find a counterpoint in the profound alienation of individual characters and poignant attempts to articulate and overcome this. In the opening chapter, the teenage Hal is interviewed at the University of Arizona but what he thinks and utters is not what the panel members hear: 'Try to listen', I say very slowly, muffled by the floor. 'What in God's name are those...', one Dean cries shrilly, '...those *sounds*?'[27] Hal seems to anticipate his own collapse a year before this (but 700-odd pages later) when telling his brother that he feels a 'hole' spreading inside him that's 'going to get a little bigger every day until I fly apart in different directions'.[28] His words reflect what Wallace calls 'a stomach-level sadness', 'a kind of lostness'; it was a sensation the author knew intimately and thought characteristic of, if not unique to, his generation.[29]

Discussing Dante's *Divine Comedy*, Bakhtin described its nine circles of Hell, seven of Purgatory and ten of Paradise as a literary architecture which uniquely communicated temporal simultaneity: 'Everything that on earth is divided by time, here, in this verticality, coalesces into eternity, into pure simultaneous coexistence'.[30] What made that time-space so powerfully fraught for Bakhtin was the recognition that many of its human population had been drawn by the author from history; implicitly, Virgil, Thomas Aquinas or Beatrice seemed to strain against their textual entrapment, desiring 'to set out along the historically productive horizontal'.[31] In the postmodern context, *Infinite Jest* conveys a comparable impression of synchronicity not only by persistent disruption of narrative 'order' but because the disorienting, border-collapsing effects of addiction are *mirrored* by the novel, as well as explored thematically. Further, the readerly sensation of movement with little progress – back and forward between text and endnotes, following circuitous or unproductive information threads – seems to mimic the at times frustrating experience of networked culture; as Nicola Johnson and Helen Keane have argued, digital technologies have challenged previously accepted binaries of real and virtual, work and leisure, production and consumption, presence and absence, thereby producing 'new forms of temporality characterised by collapsed boundaries between spheres of activity'.[32] In this way, *Infinite Jest* exploits the opportunities of this altered time-space but suggests that inability to achieve meaningful orientation within it brings a kind of drowning. A small measure of hope is personified by Gately, who pursues the Alcoholics Anonymous recovery programme but breaks down the tenet 'One Step At a Time' still further by '[t]aking it a second at a time. Drawing the time in around him real tight. [...] Living in the Present between pulses.'[33] Gately's terms imply that movement along the 'productive horizontal' might yet be possible, if only on the micro-level.

The decision of German director Matthias Lilienthal to adapt *Infinite Jest* for promenade performance was perceived in many quarters as 'almost unimaginably ambitious'.[34] Lilienthal was then Artistic Director – or to use the German term, Intendant – of the avant-garde theatre amalgamation Hebbel am Ufer; *Infinite Jest* (*Unendlicher Spaß*) was chosen by him as a show to mark the end of his tenure in 2012. At the Hebbel am Ufer and before that, as head dramaturg at the Volksbühne, Lilienthal had established a reputation for developing experimental theatre, supporting groups including the mixed-media collective Rimini Protokoll, and individuals including 'underground' filmmaker and performance artist Christof Schlingensief. While the practices Lilienthal has championed regularly create hybrid aesthetics and incorporate digital technologies, he has also repeatedly emphasized the importance of confronting 'the transformation of ethics' that technological transformation has produced: according to Lilienthal, the art world must 'forget the fights of yesterday, examine where the conflicts of this new society are and consider how art should deal with it'.[35] This ambition also manifested itself in Lilienthal's *X-Apartments* (2002–), an art project first mounted in Berlin and since recreated in several international cities including Athens, Beirut, São Paulo, Warsaw and Johannesburg. In *X-Apartments*, artists create installations or micro-performances inside real apartments, inspired by the stories of inhabitants and often incorporating these 'non-actors' within the work; audiences attend in groups of two, inside the house, perched on the steps or peering through a window, witnessing scenes that convey the hidden realities of the city. It is not always apparent what is authentic to the apartment and what 'fake', a blurring which supports Lilienthal's intention to produce, in the course of an audience journey of two or more hours, the sensation of becoming 'a foreigner in one's own city'.[36] The *X-Apartments* template contains elements also important to his conception of *Infinite Jest*: crucially, a defamiliarized encounter with the city by means of theatre, and the use of polymorphic aesthetic vocabularies whose multiplicity would reflect the heterogeneity of experimental performance, new technology and the urban landscape itself.

Infinite Jest: 24 Hours through the Utopian West was thus conceived in a way that part-mirrored *X-Apartments*, with twelve international artists or companies each invited to create a separate performance – here corresponding to a section or narrative element in Wallace's novel – that would be combined as a 24-hour live event requiring its audience to visit multiple locations across Berlin. The artists – amongst them Richard Maxwell, Gob Squad, SheShePop, Jan Klata and Anna-Sophie Mahler – had considerable aesthetic freedom, meaning that the production itself was internally highly eclectic. Event continuity of a sort was provided by an overarching structure which included buses to transport spectators from site to site, periodic doses of 'stimulants' to keep them going (chocolate, energy drinks, sachets of glucose powder, caffeine) and a different Wallace expert at each performance, who contributed via Skype to a conference held halfway through the day at the 'David Foster Wallace Centre' (a reconfiguration of Berlin's Campus Benjamin Franklin). Before and after the conference, the production's event map led the audience on an architectural tour of former West Berlin, with individual performances situated in a series of grandiose late-Modernist buildings which in themselves epitomize the optimistic but impractical aspirations of the city in the 1960s and 1970s. That period saw an exceptionally high level of construction, with plenty of bombed-out space following the Second World War in which to build, and fierce competition between East and West 'to out develop and out design' the other.[37] *Infinite Jest*'s promenade took in once-radical architectural creations of concrete, grid and glass, including the towering Reinickendorf Finanzamt, appropriated here as the 'US Office of Unspecified Services', and the Vivantes clinic in Neukölln, whose corridors and cell-like rooms posed as the recovery centre Ennet House. A quite differently evocative locale was the Teufelsberg or 'Devil's Mountain', a man-made hill shaped out of the rubble from hundreds of thousands of bombed houses and the remains of a Nazi military training college, on top of which is an abandoned Cold War US spy station complete with radar domes; in the performance, the Teufelsberg was used as the site for a secret meeting between the novel's cross-dressing spy Hugh/Helen Steeply and Québécois separatist Rémy Marathe. In this manner, Lilienthal's production, an imaginative relocation of *Infinite Jest* over Berlin, effected a three-way journey: into Wallace's novel, into the aesthetic territories of contemporary performance and finally into the city's historically charged urban topography and quotidian action.

However, the first three performances that made up *Infinite Jest*, which occupied the morning period from the event's 10.00 am start, were all located at the 'Ennet Tennis Academy', in actuality the Rot-Weiss Lawn Tennis Club. Tennis is a central theme in the novel: like

Hal, Wallace played competitive tennis as a teenager and wrote several essays examining this mathematically elegant sport positioned amidst 'vectors, lines and lines athwart lines, grids'.[38] In *Infinite Jest*, novel and adaptation both, tennis feeds into the themes of addiction, of expectations loaded on children by their parents and of the alienation and fragmentation of identity. The third performance of the event, Gob Squad's hour-long *The Conversationalist*, was staged inside the Steffi Graf stadium; the audience gathered in the stands at one end, witness to the fact that across from them, on other courts, real-life obsessions, anxieties and pressures were simultaneously being played out. On the opposing stands, the seats were empty bar several that were occupied by life-sized flat black figures, resembling shooting targets, each emblazoned with the word 'FATHER'. Gob Squad's performance was chiefly inspired by a section of the novel where James Incandenza disguises himself as a 'professional conversationalist' in a belated attempt to connect with his son, but the company also absorbed other elements from the source, including the interview during which Hal struggles vainly to be understood by the admissions panel. *The Conversationalist* is constructed as a tennis match, and is performed by five actors, one as the umpire and four more as players. All five are identified on their shirts as 'MYSELF', meaning that the piece presents an internal and self-regulated conflict, enacted before a symbolically represented parent. The performers wear tennis whites, with the incongruous addition of striped public school ties; all actors have mics, and their speeches, sequences of music and periodic sound effects – recurrently, words are rendered inaudible by an angry buzzing, like a swarm of insects – are transmitted through speakers.

The Conversationalist begins with the arrival of the umpire, who takes up position at the side of the net. The audience hears her thoughts, which seem to pick up on Hal's interview experience: 'I am in here. I compose what I project will be seen as a smile. 62.5% of the faces in the room are directed my way, pleasantly expectant. I open my mouth. Something is going to come out.'[39] Once the four players are on court, the rule-based system of the performance becomes clear. The piece adopts the structure and scoring of a tennis match, with each opposing pair responding to a subject set by the umpire by means of improvised verbal sparring. The players have no rackets or balls, only their words and the peculiar, dance-like movements that each performs on their side of the court. The conversation topics range from the banal 'Really, I mean it', to the more probing 'The pain I feel inside me' and 'Things we can't talk about', to the overtly (self?-)confrontational: 'Who do you think you are?' To comic effect, the expressionless umpire will declare points lost for example for 'too much repetition of the word "nightmare"' (when debating 'My problem with reality'), or because 'You don't have a clue what you are talking about' (on the topic 'I am a better conversationalist than you, even though I don't know the meaning of "hyperreal"'). Points are equally arbitrarily judged won, as when a female player's improvised discourse on Irigaray – a deconstruction of the activity/passivity binary – on the topic 'Philosophers I studied who deal with concepts of reality' is scored as an 'Ace!'. The witty and highly formal framing of the conversational encounter presents human speech as something vulnerable and untrustworthy, a characteristic attitude for Gob Squad as a bi-national English-German company who have never taken transparency of communication as a given:

> The one who speaks is not necessarily the one who the text belongs to, or the person who wants to give the text a particular reading. Speaker and author do not correspond. In this way, the speech is devoid of any kind of emotion or intention and its woody, constructed nature is laid bare. The words sound as if they have been borrowed, imposed; as if said aloud for the first time. The headphones act like a build-in filter, a go-between, establishing a distance and alienation to what is said.[40]

Alienation grows as *The Conversationalist* continues, marked by increased distance and technological distortion. Garbled mediation of one player's address to the umpire provokes the latter to observe blankly: 'Sorry, I can't understand you. I can't understand Myself. Can you say that again?'; the player takes a drink, and the amplified 'dry sticky salivaless sounds which', says Wallace, 'can be death to a good conversation' mix with greedy, inhuman gulping noises ('SHULGSPAHHH').[41]

Gob Squad's practice, sometimes described by the group as 'Life Art' (originally a misprint for Live Art, but which they actively embraced), has always combined a postdramatic scepticism towards language with sharpened focus on the materiality of performance and the implications of site. Their work has predominantly been made outside theatre buildings, exploiting the layered meanings and sometimes fraught juxtapositions that alternative locations bring. That ethos, here articulated by the group in 2006, chimed well with Lilienthal's adaptation project:

> We have been born into this world, these cities and non-spaces, whether in Britain or Germany. [...] The characteristics that can be found in almost every arbitrary metropolis apply to this city too: flexibility, anonymity, ignorance, brutality, loneliness, chaos, fleetingness and disorientation. This is also exactly where we want to search for the individual rather than the general, the precise and untranslatable.[42]

In *The Conversationalist*, disorientation and isolation are articulated through the sporting game structure in which players and umpire represent the fragmented self. As words are symbolically hurled back and forward across the net, the ritualistic body language of the players simultaneously drives them up and down the lines of the court, or causes them to roll and squirm effortfully on the ground, in the process, staining their sporting whites with reddish brown and leaving imprints of their movement on the surface clay dust; of this performance one could say, as Lehmann observes of Bausch's choreography, that the court site becomes 'an autonomous co-player' which visibly acquires and displays the traces of performance action over time.[43] On the formal level, the actors' cool and even hostile text delivery, the abstract physicality and the unhurried pace of the whole piece, all seem to jar with the severity of mental collapse which the performance explores. There is little momentum to the production of the kind one would expect within a traditional dramatic structure; instead, the audience watch encounters monotonously played out point by point, in 'matches' which draw no excitement, since MYSELF is pitted against MYSELF.

As a treatment of Wallace's novel, *The Conversationalist* absorbs and reframes the dogged, ball-thudding, disciplined labour of the Academy's 'hopefuls' along with the surreal sensation of alienation and looming failure that persistently haunts them. When the players and umpire finally leave the stadium, all that remains are the marks on the clay and the many FATHERS, flapping lightly, hollowly, in the wind.

Lilienthal's production is promenade as opposed to immersive performance, given the sense in which the latter term is usually applied. For while the boundaries of the event are highly fluid, the audience travel and watch the performances as a group, with little direct participation. Sometimes spectators are loosely placed in role, as when, about twenty hours into the event, they must wearily climb several floors up to the roof of the Finanzamt and take an oath as terrorist activists, before sitting in ranked wheelchairs, a yellow 'smiley' bandana rendering each face anonymous. The final segment of the production, in the early morning, involved the last thirty pages of the novel being read aloud to the audience from the stage, to the accompaniment of 'somnolent' bass guitar and slowly rolling tennis balls: as one reviewer remarked, 'If there was anybody who was not struggling to stay awake at this stage, he was a hero.'[44] Other commentators, describing the show on different dates (the event was presented eight times in all), suggest that the majority of spectators – of those who had not dropped out some hours previously – fell asleep at this stage, 'collapsed' or 'incapacitated' by this seemingly 'unending' and 'exhausting' show.[45] The German title of book and performance, *Unendlicher Spaß*, can be literally translated as 'unending fun', a phrase which perhaps more directly than 'infinite jest' reflects ironically back upon the staged event. The 24-hour performance period advertises entertainment on a massive scale, but in practice the show clearly does not deliver 'endless fun', instead requiring from its audience a genuine effort of endurance. For aside from the unusually extended timescale of the production, and despite many moments of wit, beauty or absurdity, the individual performance pieces largely retained a cerebral 'coolness', exacerbated by the distancing impact of technological mediation and the use of different languages (English, German, Spanish) which inhibited comprehension for different spectators at different points. For some reviewers this constituted a frustrating and unnecessary exclusivity, so drew criticism; yet evidently this aesthetic tendency, throughout the event, also manifested a deliberate questioning of the spectacle's legibility.[46] In this way, the production reenacts the preoccupations of Wallace's novel, which references the 'ultimate' Entertainment within a culture desperate to satisfy that appetite; yet the book both critiques that desire, and challenges it directly by adopting a form that anticipates and even courts the frustration of readers.

However, neither book nor production aims to shape a *dull* experience, clearly; rather, both structure questionable 'entertainment' that makes boredom palpable. Wallace wanted to write something 'long and difficult that was also fun', that would 'seduce [the reader] into doing a certain amount of work', obliging them to 'pay attention to some of the strategies that commercial entertainment uses' and having those formulaic expectations 'fucked with'.[47] Likewise, Lilienthal's defiantly anti-consumerist and in capitalist terms 'staggeringly inefficient' production offered hard-won rewards for spectators willing to take the exasperating and wearying along with the absorbing, and who were prepared to stay the distance.[48] For Michael Earley, the event was 'as exhilarating as it is exhausting', hinting that the one sensation is predicated on the other; Urška Brodar describes a similar elation, a 'sweet' tiredness of body and spirit, for audience and actors alike, that 'joined us into a community which we almost forgot could exist in theatre'.[49] To an extent the described state of mind echoes Wallace's aspiration for writer-reader engagement beyond game-playing irony, something 'more like a late-night conversation with really good friends, when the bullshit stops and the masks come off'.[50] The experience of weariness, frustration and boredom along the way, for reader or spectator, derives less from any one section of text or sequence of action than from nagging awareness of the daunting scale of the whole: all that time passed, but so much still left to run. In other words, boredom implies the struggle to focus attention on the present moment; and since the performance, unlike the book, cannot be sawn into manageable chunks then perhaps the only way out of that durational numbness is to try, as Gately does, to take the experience a second at a time.

As an adaptation of *Infinite Jest*, Lilienthal's production was, for some reviewers, unsuccessful. One critic suggests that since the live show was inevitably unable to convey the novel in its fullness, it would disappoint Wallace devotees; at the same time, for the 'uninitiated', the event would be simply 'an impenetrable nightmare'.[51] But if the production cannot capture the novel for its audience, nor does Wallace easily deliver that content to his readers. As I have shown, the matter of the book deliberately exceeds and resists ready comprehension. Instead, the informational overspill and temporal intractability of the text find a parallel of sorts in the time-space of the production. In particular, situating 'framed theatre' amidst '"unframed" everyday reality' confuses the distinction between the two and in so doing infinitely extends the boundaries of the staged event.[52] Similarly, the temporal borders of the show are permeable, since the physical imprints on performance sites, the histories embedded in those architectures and their projected futures, all overrun the 24-hour term. Any work of theatre may be regarded in this light, as spatially and temporally soft-edged: here, however, the topographical and durational seepage becomes deeply pronounced through a production that consciously stakes out big space and time in which to reflect on Wallace's dystopian novel, on cities and their inhabitants, on Germany and America, on art and difficulty, and finally on the capacities of theatre to represent all these, and facilitate encounters between them.

Diderot/Hof van Eede: *Where the World is Going, That's Where We are Going*

Against 1,000-plus pages of Wallace and a full day and night of performance spread across a capital city, an adaptation of 200-odd pages of Diderot over an hour and a half in a studio theatre seems a much more straightforward proposition. Moreover, the inclusion of Diderot's

Jacques the Fatalist within a discussion of literary 'resistance' to dramatic transformation is itself contestable: the novel was dramatized to acclaim by Milan Kundera in 1971; additionally, one of the numerous anecdotes within Diderot's work – about an elaborate 'bed trick' that misfires – was used as the plot for two films, Fritz Wendhausen's *Madame de La Pommeraye's Intrigues* (1922) and Robert Bresson's *Les dames du Bois de Boulogne* (1945).[53] However, I argue that the novel poses challenges which are circumvented rather than met by these adaptations. By extracting an individual story from the whole, those filmmakers reframe the source material in a way that renders it more coherent and conventional than it originally appeared: for while *Jacques the Fatalist* is undeniably full of 'bawdy' tales – one of the reasons why the book attracted significant disapprobation in the eighteenth and nineteenth centuries – no individual narrative is exempt, in Diderot's telling, from the interruptions, criticisms and digressions which distinguish the novel's method overall. Kundera's approach to the material is quite different, not least in that he treats the whole novel; he also enthusiastically embraces the metafictional, digressive qualities of the source and incorporates these in his play. As soon as Jacques and his Master enter Kundera's stage, they show their awareness of the theatrical frame:

> **Jacques** (*Confidentially*) Sir… (*Pointing out the audience to his* MASTER) What are they up to, looking at us like that?
>
> **His Master** (*Giving a start and adjusting his clothing, as if he were frightened of attracting attention by sloppy dressing*) Behave as if no one were there.[54]

Similarly, a few scenes later, the Master suddenly notices that, unlike in the novel, the two of them are not on horseback. Jacques reminds him:

> **Jacques** You're forgetting we're on stage. How could we have horses?
>
> **Master** Thanks to some ridiculous play, I have to go on foot!
> Even though the master who invented us allotted us horses.
>
> **Jacques** That's the danger of being invented by too many masters.[55]

Kundera thus makes the stage itself and the performance condition of the characters the focus of their bantering dialogue, whilst also mocking himself – and by extension, all adapters – for foolish and inept transposition of the source. In doing so, he mimics in theatrical terms the self-reflexive commentary of the novel, for example when Diderot's narration requires master and servant to separate and the author cheerfully admits to the reader: 'I'm damned if I know which of them I want to stick with.'[56] Kundera revels in the luxury of using stage time and space for digressive games of this kind. *Jacques and His Master* exhibits a sense of open-ended play that its author significantly identifies with Diderot's era: Kundera's first novel in French, *La Lenteur* (Slowness), published in 1995, reworked the plot of Vivant Dellon's libertine novella *No Tomorrow* (1777) to present an unfavourable comparison between the speed-driven compulsions of contemporary living and the relative 'slowness' of eighteenth-century literature and life.[57] Kundera praises *Jacques the Fatalist*'s 'masterly disorder', intending that his own 'homage to Diderot' should reflect the original's formal liberty and ludic spirit; advocating a position of ironic, questioning playfulness seemed especially urgent at a point in Czechoslovakian history, following the 1968 Soviet invasion, when as Kundera put it 'the noblest national sentiments are used to justify the worst horrors; and, breasts swollen with lyrical feelings, man commits the foulest acts in the sacred name of love'.[58] However, and despite the fact that Kundera criticizes the medium of drama as typically 'rigid and rule-bound', his own version is far from anarchic; indeed, he is at pains to establish its internal coherence.[59] *Jacques and His Master* adopts a three-act structure, with the intertwined love stories of servant and master conveyed primarily through Acts 1 and 3 and the Madame de La Pommeraye episode contained in Act 2. For Kundera, this dramaturgical shape effects a kind of 'polyphony', whereby the content of the second act intermingles with, and so disturbs, the wider narrative line. Yet, as an intended echo of Diderot's digressive technique, Kundera's strategy is (certainly by twenty-first-century standards) notably modest; the insertion of what is effectively a complete story halfway through the play stops well short of the persistent interruptions and *habitual* dropping of narrative threads evident in the original. In this manner, Kundera's game-playing, metatheatrical references and explicitly anti-illusionist *mise-en-scène* do playfully represent disorder, but coherently and palatably for his audience; in consequence, it becomes possible to enjoy and be entertained by carnivalesque rule-breaking without that transgression fundamentally unsettling the dominant dramatic order.

Certainly, Kundera's adaptation – or variation, as he terms it, since for him the word 'adaptation' is interpreted to mean a dogged summary and 'negation of [a] novel's originality' – is under no obligation to follow *Jacques the Fatalist*'s path to its absurd conclusion: or more accurately its conclusions plural, since the novel provides three, of which the second, '*the Editor writes*', is 'obviously an interpolation' from *Tristram Shandy*.[60] Moreover, for his play to depart from Diderot with (implicit) disobedience is, one might say, entirely in Diderot's spirit. Nonetheless, while *Jacques and His Master* retains the original's playfulness, *Jacques the Fatalist* is marked by a deeper internal anarchy that does not find its way into Kundera's 'variation'; in effect, the play irons out frustrations that the novel designedly enacts upon the reader. Characteristically, Diderot satirically declares his book's failings: the author interrupts a dialogue between master and servant to compare *Jacques the Fatalist* unfavourably with *La Pucelle* (1755), a mock-epic about Joan of Arc by Voltaire which in its original form was distinctly lewd and anti-clerical, qualities its author later toned down (but not sufficiently to prevent its being subject to a legal obscenity case a century and a half later).[61] *La Pucelle* is a masterpiece, says Diderot's author; his own *Jacques*, by contrast, is 'a tasteless mishmash of things that happen, some of them true, others made up, written without style and served up like a dog's breakfast'.[62] That self-criticism is comic, but in large part accurately describes a novel that is cheerfully 'offensive', with its coarse anecdotes and mockery of the clergy (evidently, attitudes that also informed *La Pucelle*); that refers regularly to real world events and people, yet as readily falsifies facts and dates; and that shifts stylistic registers in seemingly haphazard fashion, all the while casually and with lively disrespect for the reader. As the author disarmingly remarks at one point: 'It just seems obvious to me that with a little imagination and style there's nothing easier than churning out a novel.'[63] All this means that *Jacques the Fatalist* is no mere 'folly' but persistent provocation, a deliberate jolting that disturbs and complicates the reading experience.[64]

If *Jacques the Fatalist* is, or at least presents, a 'mishmash', this eclecticism reflects the heterogeneous interests and knowledges of its author. Diderot was a philosopher, art critic and scientist as well as a writer; he was also strongly attracted to the theatre, although his two plays were relatively conventional and certainly less influential than his essay 'The Paradox of the Actor' (1773) and his arguments for a dramatic '*genre sérieux*' that would present a more realistic, less elevated image of the world.[65] Playwrights including Jean-Michel Sedaine, Louis-Sébastien Mercier and Pierre Beaumarchais experimented with the *genre sérieux* and *drame bourgeois* in practice, in an effort to break with classical conventions and dissolve hierarchies of theatrical genre; however, as Peter Brooks has argued, this intervention, 'though largely predictive of the future, seems to have had little immediate impact or influence'.[66] In the 'Paradox of the Actor', Diderot argued that great actors were 'disinterested onlooker[s]' who used observation and technique to convey emotion, not feeling; this theory seemed to anticipate Brecht, yet is also – again, paradoxically – not wholly alien to Stanislavsky's 'System'.[67] But Diderot remains most famous as chief editor of the *Encyclopédie*, the great project of the French Enlightenment, published in 28 folio volumes between 1750 and 1772. The *Encyclopédie*, originally conceived as a mere translation of Chambers' *Cyclopedia*, steadily expanded in scope with the ambition to include every branch of human knowledge. The democratic assumptions that underpinned the project – belief in freedom of thought, religious tolerance, that the needs of common people should be the foremost concern of government – made it fiercely controversial; the process was beset by attempts to suppress it, and hindered by the strategic withdrawals of many contributors.

Diderot was briefly imprisoned in 1749 following the publication of his *Letter on the Blind for the Benefit of Those Who See*, a short book ostensibly describing how the world might appear to someone who had been born blind, but recognized by the authorities as a thinly disguised sceptical assault on the concept of a creator-God whose existence could not be positively verified and thus had to be accepted as an article of faith. Diderot's supporters eventually secured his release, winning the case on the pragmatic grounds that the project of the *Encyclopédie* risked being lost to another nation, and with it a great many French jobs.[68] Once freed from prison, and required to sign a letter undertaking never to write or publish anything blasphemous again, Diderot felt obliged to become, in David Coward's words, more of a 'closet rebel'.[69] Nonetheless, the contents of the *Encyclopédie* were regarded in many quarters as profoundly shocking, internationally so; the 1801 supplement to the *Encyclopedia Brittanica* stated, in its dedication to George III, the British intent to counteract the influence of a 'pestiferous' French work said to have 'disseminated, far and wide, the seeds of Anarchy and Atheism'.[70]

While the *Encyclopédie* was condemned for seeming to attack the deepest foundations of religion, it was also mocked for the quantities of seemingly unremarkable matter that had been included: a commentator in the *Monthly Review* in the mid-1760s ridiculed its illustrations of 'common tools' such as 'files, hammers, and shears', reproduced in the *Encyclopédie* as if 'that grand work was cautiously prepared against some expected general desolation'.[71] But as an instructional reference work systematically covering the 'Sciences, Arts, and Crafts', the *Encyclopédie* was implicitly non-hierarchical: an everyday utensil was in that sense as much a part of human life as theological or philosophical theory. That quality of inclusivity is reflected in *Jacques the Fatalist*, which references the non-fictional world (notable personae, battles, politics, agriculture), treats profound subjects like religion and fatalism (albeit often satirically), but also frequently includes what look like inconsequential banalities – as in this example, configured in the novel in the mode of dramatic dialogue:

Landlady Did you like the wine?

Master It was very good.

Landlady Was the supper alright?

Master Excellent. The spinach was slightly over-salted.

Landlady I'm a bit heavy-handed sometimes.[72]

The littleness of such an exchange echoes qualities Diderot admired in Richardson's *Clarissa*, with its emphasis 'on the many petty details of a petty existence'.[73] For although Diderot does parody fatalistic thinking in his own novel, his intellectual studies would have convinced him that human action is affected by matters apparently trivial; if not necessarily in thrall to a higher power, we did not command our fates either.[74] Kundera, likewise, remarked how the 'insignificant gestures' of human beings 'often form a noose around our necks'.[75] But as we have seen, the inclusion of realistic detail of this kind does not work to present what Whitney Mannies terms the 'reliable and predictable reality that many of his contemporaries assumed', but something much more chaotic and uncertain.[76] *Jacques the Fatalist's* 'mish-mash', meanderings and authorial self-criticisms by implication disavow the capacity of 'purposeful' linear narration and conventionally 'dramatic' matter effectively to represent the world. This scepticism is nowhere more apparent than in the novel's formulation of space and time.

As a story of travelling companions, *Jacques the Fatalist* employs the familiar literary chronotope of the road: a form in which, says Bakhtin, '[t]ime, as it were, fuses together with space and flows in it'.[77] In literature the road may also convey, metaphorically, the course of life; in this way, the physical journey and specific encounters *en route* may be less important, finally, than the maturation of self. Diderot's novel appropriates this literary time-space but also caricatures it (in a style to an extent inherited from Cervantes): the journey is unending and purposeless, the direction arbitrary and the travellers seemingly unaltered by their adventures. In his eponymous hero, Diderot also makes use of a character type who, for Bakhtin, proved crucial in expanding narrative time-space: the rogue, a figure '[o]pposed to convention and functioning as a force for exposing it' and who also facilitated the 'positioning of the author himself within the novel'. Bakhtin argues that the rogue, clown and fool are all 'masks' that bring with them certain rights:

> They grant the right *not* to understand, the right to confuse, to tease, to hyperbolise life; the right to parody others while talking, the right to not be taken literally, not 'to be oneself'; the right to live a life in the chronotope of the entr'acte, the chronotope of theatrical space, the right to act life as a comedy and to treat others as actors.[78]

This is one of the few occasions in this essay when Bakhtin connects the concept of the chronotope to the context of theatre. His reference to the entr'acte is particularly suggestive when thinking about time-space in Diderot's novel as well as in terms of potential stage adaptation. In theatre history, the entr'acte was a brief performance, usually of music or dance, played without props and in front of closed curtains, while scenery was changed. The entr'acte functioned outside the dramatic plot, its purpose to occupy otherwise 'dead' time and space; in this sense it was purely playful. As Blake Stevens observes, Bakhtin's conception of the entr'acte appears to mirror his analysis of the carnivalesque, by representing 'a ludic opening or liberating pause in the drama of social relations'.[79] At the same time, because the entr'acte marked a gap in the play 'proper', it was often interpreted by spectators as a point of freedom in which they could choose to watch or not watch, to talk if they wished, to go out and return.[80] In *Jacques the Fatalist*, the motifs of the road, the rogue and the peculiar conditions of the entr'acte thus combine to create a literary/theatrical time-space of playful action unrestricted by dramatic ordering, meandering dialogues that are sometimes baffling or banal, and a more or less explicit provocation to the reader/audience to be in Diderot's words '[h]uman and curious', or even 'a damned nuisance'.[81]

In 2012 the Belgian theatre company Hof van Eede (Garden of Eden), founded by sisters Ans and Louise Van den Eede, presented *Where the*

World is Going, That's Where We are Going, a treatment of Diderot's novel and the company's first production. Perhaps unusually for artists statedly working within a postdramatic aesthetic, not only this show but their first three productions have engaged strongly with prose literature. *Thirsty* (2013) critically juxtaposes characters drawn from Balzac and the Dutch author Nescio; *The Weiss Effect* (2014) treats an invented writer, Edgard Weiss, an influence on Beckett whose supposedly discovered diary proved 'a source of immense joy to three young actors in need of a hero'.[82] Hof van Eede arrived at Diderot through their enthusiasm for Kundera and for the metafictional strategies employed by both writers. They did not want to stage the novel, as Kundera had effectively done, but originally intended to use only the ideas *Jacques the Fatalist* discusses as the basis of a new performance that would not directly mention the book at all. The adaptation project was also informed by Philipp Blom's *A Wicked Company* (2010), a historical study of the salons of the French Enlightenment; the company sought to draw on the impression of animated conversation perpetually changing direction or contradicting itself, the collective savouring of words and ideas. However, as Ans van Eede observes, paraphrasing Diderot: 'You can have as many plans as you want, life always has other plans for you.'[83] In practice, the aim to pursue and rework Diderot's themes led them round in circles, following thread after thread, generating quantities of material but becoming 'totally lost'. The digressive and almost self-cancelling strategies of the novel did not liberate the artists, but seemingly mired them in it more deeply. Ultimately, and contrary to their original intentions, the performance Hof van Eede created lingered explicitly and obsessively on the 'stuckness' which afflicted the adaptation process.

Where the World is Going, That's Where We are Going is performed by Ans Van den Eede and Greg Timmermans. The show, which premiered in Antwerp in 2012, is a studio piece that quickly establishes an intimate, almost conversational relationship with its audience. While not quite played in a bare space, the *mise-en-scène* is minimal: easy chairs, a small table, pile of books and standard lamp create something resembling a backstage 'green room', the effect functional rather than theatrical. At no point do Van den Eede and Timmermans represent dramatic characters; they appear as if not acting, as 'themselves', yet their heightened energy and subtle competitiveness simultaneously display 'not acting' as a calculated pose. In contrast with this lightly hostile, patronizing manner to one another, the performers' address to the audience is warm, friendly and a touch apologetic. The show begins with Van den Eede's smiling admission that they have somewhat failed with this project:

> **She** We'll have to start with an apology.
> You see, we're having a bit of a problem.
> We really wanted to tell you the story
> of Jacques the Fatalist and his Master
> by the French writer Denis Diderot.
> When we first read the book,
> We thought: this is it.
> This is the story we have to tell
> This story deserves not to be forgotten.
>
> **He** Many people have forgotten
> That Diderot himself was once forgotten
> He was more than just an encyclopaedist.
> First and foremost, he was a novelist
> And one of the prominent leaders in the age of Enlightenment
> There's a great book about this,
> by Philipp Blom
> A very good read actually
> It's called 'The Wicked Company'.
>
> **She** Jacques the fatalist and his master.
> It is *so* good.
> It's about *so* many things,
> It's so many things at once.
> It's grandiose,
> And yet it deals with the smallest of things,
> you see,
> Everything is in there.

He Well, not literally 'everything'.

She No, no
In a manner of speaking, of course.[84]

This passage embeds within the first few minutes of performance the principles on which the show is founded. *Where the World is Going, That's Where We are Going* does not dramatize *Jacques the Fatalist* in any direct sense, but stages, in a 'preamble' that occupies the duration, a rambling and often internally disputed account of why adaptation proved to be impossible. The performers – He and She, as they are identified in the script – use ordinary language, but their lines are organized with just discernible rhythms such that the text is lifted beyond 'artless' everyday speech.[85] Their sparring is already evident ('Well, not literally "everything"'), at first benign and later barbed: now and throughout the show, language itself is the subject at stake. They nitpick terms, adopt expressions of puzzlement or polite incredulity when the other is speaking, or chip in to explain to the audience what he or she believes the other 'meant'. Van den Eede makes bold claims about the novel – 'a radical journey through the spirit of its time' – but immediately disassociates herself, casually, from the words spoken: 'I read that somewhere'. The performers' shared account of the novel's brilliance is suspiciously vague, close enough to bluffing – 'It is *so* good. It's about *so* many things' – that the audience might start to wonder if they have indeed read it. Much of their speech is banal or outright absurd, as when Van den Eede enthuses of the book: 'As I read, I could actually smell the stables/It made me want to get right on up there, in the saddle.'[86] So while the dialogue is about the impossibility of capturing Diderot's words in performance, their exchanges simultaneously display the failures of language and communication on a more immediate level; every address to one another or to the audience brings with it contradictions and qualifications. The exposed inadequacies of language are accompanied by the unreliability of interpretation: the insistence of Diderot's Jacques that 'life is a series of misunderstandings' seems borne out by Van den Eede and Timmermans, who cannot establish the most basic consensus about the characters and concerns of the novel.[87] Nor can they even keep the narrative of adaptation 'failure' on track; repeatedly, they allow their explanation to be interrupted by anecdotes and reminiscences whose relevance is unclear; their dialogue seems formless, circling around its object but getting, if anything, ever further away.

In the novel, master and servant are on a journey of unknown origin, duration and destination ('… for God's sake Reader, does any of us know where we're going?'); they encounter other figures along the way, yet since those meetings are jumbled up amongst stories told, 'live' characters become more or less indistinguishable from those narrated.[88] In effect, this means that the apparently aimless movement that is narrated serves as the pretext for a different journey: the teasing, metafictional route pursued by the narration itself. Similarly, in *Where the World is Going, That's Where We are Going*, Timmermans and Van den Eede play out two journeys: the first, relating to the progress, or non-progress, of their adaptation; the second, that of the performance that frames this. If He and She are not precisely rogues, clowns or fools, they nevertheless strongly recall the terms Bakhtin uses to depict those 'masks': they do not understand; and they do confuse, tease, hyperbolize life and parody one another. Further, Hof van Eede's production is well described by the form of the entr'acte. *Where the World is Going, That's Where We are Going* deliberately claims an in-between space; the show presents itself as a postdramatic pause, with 'meaningful' dramatic action either side. Timmermans and Van den Eede gesture to the endlessly fertile terrain of the text that informed the rehearsal process, but from which they have allegedly made 'nothing'; simultaneously, the very studio time in which they convey this laborious apology is put under pressure:

She And then there's another problem.
We'll have to rush off after the show.
We've somewhere else we need to be.

He An unfortunate coincidence. Unavoidable.
We don't normally have to rush off.
It's just tonight. Sorry.

She It's Diderot's curse, I'd say.
So if we start talking faster,
It's because we've somewhere else we need to be.[89]

In this way, the production identifies a potent text before the performance and a purposeful destination beyond it. In between the two, the here and now of theatrical time-space becomes curiously suspended. Even had an adaptation of Diderot been possible, Van den Eede remarks, a performance is insufficient time to share it: 'We no longer live in a world/where you can tell a story as if you have all the time in the world.' The repetitive, loitering pattern of deviations and bickering from He and She both deny and confirm this: presumably, sustained attention to the task in hand would generate the minutes and hours they need, yet in our 'time-poor', multi-tracked networked culture, the show suggests, such focus is unachievable; however, this position too is contradicted by what is ultimately a *rigorous* pursuit of circuity. As a performance strategy, deliberate cultivation of hesitation and digression brings with it certain risks; while a show of this length could hardly be termed durational, it nonetheless tests the patience of its audience. One reviewer who admired the cerebral game played by the company, nonetheless remarks: 'Going nowhere slowly may be what Diderot would have wanted, but it's really boring.' However, the same reviewer describes *Where the World is Going, That's Where We are Going* as a show that 'deepens in the memory'.[90] This acknowledgement implicitly lends weight to an apparently throwaway line spoken by Timmermans to the audience: that wherever they happen to be headed *after* the show, 'at least you'll be able to talk about having been here'.[91]

Van den Eede's assertion in performance that in the twenty-first-century context it is impossible 'simply' to tell a story is expanded by her into a larger claim: 'We no longer live in the age of the novel, the age of fiction.'[92] If the novel is regarded as a time-space in which narratives, individual or interwoven, are allowed to unfold slowly, this condition of telling has grown harder to sustain and equally to receive. From such a perspective, adaptation becomes a doomed enterprise: indeed, He and She admit that they anticipated failure from the outset, while acknowledging shamefacedly that 'to begin with the belief that something will not succeed/is against the very spirit of Enlightenment'. Therefore, unable to (re)tell Diderot's story, Timmermans and Van den Eede fall back on their respective propensities (of which each accuses the other) for 'drift' and 'erasure'. She defends herself, to him and to the audience: 'Look,/Writing is rewriting./And rewriting requires erasing.'[93] By implication, therefore, theatre is always a form of adaptation, which, in the process, overwrites other texts. Yet this practice does not ultimately disappear prior writings; rather, different threads accumulate, web-like, with authorship and ownership ever more entangled:

He What is true, is that we're drifting off again.
'Jacques the Fatalist and his Master'
Diderot
His story

She Their story

He Our story actually.

She No, we're telling it.[94]

Presenting something that skirts around the idea of dramatic adaptation, Hof van Eede declare the impossibility of conveying *Jacques the Fatalist* in the theatre. However, in so doing, they mimic Diderot's method (not least by parodying their own inadequacies, as does the author) and simultaneously extend the opportunity to 'own' the text, by establishing a time-space in which others can read/write themselves into it. According to Herbert Josephs, this is also precisely the import of Diderot's narratorial provocations:

> his digressive manner and his tendency to disperse what was traditionally wished or conceived as whole constituted an invitation, limitlessly renewable, to the spectacle of ironic activity that undermines (narrative) authority while it shakes from its moorings the complacency of (a reader's) passive, inevitably prejudiced habits.[95]

If this account fairly describes the novel and likewise Hof van Eede's production, it remains necessary to ask – recalling the concerns expressed by David Foster Wallace – what this spectacle of ironic activity achieves. If that were only a satirical shrugging off of the possibility of 'meaning', the enterprise would be empty indeed. *Jacques the Fatalist* determinedly puts certainties in doubt; human beings can be confident of nothing, Jacques argues, beyond the fact of their own ignorance and ultimate helplessness. However, this stated predicament is contradicted by the book's inherent fluidity and playfulness; by the demonstration that servant is no more in thrall to master than the other way around; and by manifestly courting the readerly spirit of curiosity which the author pretends to condemn.

I argue that the rewards of *Where the World is Going, That's Where We are Going* can be drawn by spectators – not always easily – from the ludic time-space of the performance 'entr'acte'. When Timmermans and Van den Eede finally depart the stage, coats on, several minutes of film are projected on the back screen, showing the couple walking away together through the darkening streets. No conversation is audible, but they seem, still, to disagree: one pauses to study a map; after a moment, both retrace their steps. The sole use of film in the show, this closing sequence teases out further the impression of stasis created by the piece overall: at last, the two are going somewhere; but even without their apparent uncertainty, the camera frame ties down the journey strictly in one place. It is an ambiguity also hinted at in Hof van Eede's show title: perhaps She and He are simply continuing to drift aimlessly, swept up in the tide of the city and its many narratives; alternatively, their aura of hesitation may be read as a positive space in which choices are open and independence is possible. The postdramatic situation acknowledges the pull of both positions: the recognition that performance is a time-space powerfully overlaid by tradition and expectation, but also one in which these may be forcefully contested. It is an 'incoherent' position to occupy, admittedly, but one reflective of Diderot's Jacques – loudly convinced that humans are powerless since our fate is already 'written up there', but implicitly contradicted by a narrative frame that repeatedly prods the reader into thinking for herself – and likewise Diderot's Enlightenment, in which the spirit of curious enquiry conveys limitless possibility but at the same time sows sceptical uncertainty into that very enterprise.[96]

Finally, the words of Maupassant roll across the screen, overlaying the continuing footage, taken from the author's summation of what he had learned from his mentor, Gustave Flaubert. Paradoxically, given the production's meanderings and embrace of cliché, the quoted passage centres on Flaubert's claim that 'Style is infinite specificity': that 'Whatever you want to say, there is only one word that will express it, one verb to make it move, one adjective to qualify it.'[97] This evocation of control and precision might seem to jar with the inept attitude assumed by the performance. Yet in practice, those words suggest that the *search* for specificity is what produces writerly style. Similarly, the doubts, dissections and fumbling failures of She and He in Hof van Eede's adaptation enact, albeit back-handedly, an appreciation and celebration of linguistic, postdramatic possibility.

Proust/Jaeger: *A Field Guide to Lost Things*

The perception of style as 'infinite specificity' surely describes no writer more aptly than Marcel Proust. The narrative method of *In Search of Lost Time* (1913–27) conveys the painstaking attempt to identify *precisely* the qualities of any moment, sight or sensation that distinguish it, in the perceiver's consciousness, from all others. Proust's lengthy sentences manifest this insistence; almost any line conveys less an impression of insight acquired and articulated, than of the effort towards truer expression. For example, in 'Combray', the first of the three parts which make up Vol. 1: *The Way by Swann's*, the narrator recalls (in a short sentence, by Proust's standards) an occasion from childhood when he was reading in his bedroom:

> This dim coolness of my room was to the full sun of the street what a shadow is to a ray of light, that is to say, it was just as luminous and offered my imagination the full spectacle of summer, which my senses, had I been out walking, could have enjoyed only piecemeal;

> and so it was quite in harmony with my repose, which (because of the stirring adventures narrated in my books) sustained, like the repose of an unmoving hand in the midst of a stream of water, the shock and animation of a torrent of activity.[98]

The subordinate clauses, qualifications and expansions together communicate the labour involved in articulation: the very difficulty of this, not only in describing experience for the reader, but in grasping its uniqueness for the speaker. The question of how far the unnamed 'I' of the novels should be interpreted as Proust himself has been the subject of much debate; the author's indication (made towards the end of the series) that the narrator could be thought of as 'Marcel' is made, as Roger Shattuck notes, only 'skittishly'.[99] Broadly, however, *In Search of Lost Time* has been regarded as a fictional or creative autobiography, in which the narrator-protagonist's passage through the years, towards increased self-awareness and the recognition of his vocation as a writer, has implicit parallel with Proust's own authorial journey.[100]

But if Proust's narrative style is known for its explanatory precision, it is equally notorious for the opposite: for the impression of frustrating obfuscation brought by a deluge of words and perpetually shifting time frames; for Barthes, the novel series was 'like a galaxy open to infinite exploration because the particles move about and change places'.[101] *In Search of Lost Time* is not readily categorized, but it is sometimes labelled a *roman-fleuve*. This term describes a novel series bound together by connecting characters and conveying a whole family, society or epoch; but its literal translation, 'river-novel', goes further to express the unexpected currents of Proust's language and the reader's awareness of the possibility of drowning. Analysing 'the Proustian sentence', Jacqueline Rose implicitly extended this metaphor: 'You cannot read Proust unless you're willing to really let go. […] It's like jumping into the pool, you have to let it carry you.'[102] Very similar terms are adopted by Shattuck, referring to the plot of what he simply calls 'the *Search*':

> Proust's story does not emerge steadily from his prose like news on ticker tape. The narrative current is highly intermittent. Incidents

> collect in great pools […]. These pools engulf the landscape and give the impression of near motionlessness while we plumb the depths. Then, usually with little transition, we are carried to another wide basin of incident.[103]

Shattuck's description of the ways in which narrative and incident are played out in Proust suggestively intersects with Bakhtin's analysis of literary time-space, even though Bakhtin does not discuss Proust in 'Forms of Time and of the Chronotope in the Novel' (the author's name features in one half-sentence, with reference to the servant character Françoise). Thus, Proust's depictions in Volume 1:i, of daily activity in the French countryside of Combray, and second, in 1:ii, 'A Love of Swann's', the snobbish circles of Parisian society, both significantly resemble the chronotope of provincial life which according to Bakhtin shapes numerous nineteenth-century novels like *Madame Bovary*:

> Here there are no events, only 'doings' that constantly repeat themselves. Time here has no advancing historical movement; it moves rather in narrow circles: the circle of the day, of the week, of the month, of a person's entire life. […] Time here is without event and therefore almost seems to stand still.[104]

This kind of novelistic time, since it is notably 'viscous and sticky', cannot drive the narrative; for this reason, Bakhtin argues, it typically exists as 'ancillary time' interwoven with another temporality that is charged with greater energy. In Proust, not just the 'doings' of the narrator's family and acquaintances, but the language in which these are described, produces that impression of 'near motionlessness'. Laid over this slow pooling of narrative incident is the biographical trajectory of the narrator: nor does this time unfold chronologically through the novels, but is filled in discontinuously and in fragments. Bakhtin observes of auto/biography that, regularly, a 'man's entire youth is treated as nothing but a preliminary to his maturity'.[105] *In Search of Lost Time* conveys almost the reverse, by adopting a movement of retrospective perception that ultimately finds adult experience already rooted in childhood consciousness.[106] Both temporalities, of stagnant social time and biographical time, are interrupted by the processes of involuntary memory, famously exemplified in the taste of a madeleine. Perhaps contrary to expectation, these interjections from deep within the mind do not disrupt an otherwise coherent perceptual flow; rather, they momentarily suspend *incoherent* apprehension, allowing fleeting access to an order of time 'that, common both to the past and to the present, is much more essential than either of them'.[107]

This brief description of the distinctive time-space and narrative method cultivated by *In Search of Lost Time* already indicates the difficulties implicit in any project of adaptation; this is to leave aside the more tedious 'problem' of the work's high literary status, which, as Geraghty shows, has influenced reception of Proust on screen.[108] How might narrative that appears 'motionless' be physically embodied or conveyed? If perception is embedded simultaneously in past and present, does one temporality dominate, or should this duality somehow always be sustained in performance? Equally, adaptation which seeks to adhere closely to the source must establish where narrative meaning is most powerfully located: as I have shown, in Proust this would seem to be far less in plot than in perception; but in terms of dramatic representation, however, it is difficult to articulate character perception other than by means of plot and action. Very easily, one could find oneself tangled in the confusion of Hof van Eede's She: 'Is it not fate that knots the plot?' and He: 'Yes, but how do we unknot the allotted plots?'[109] Equally characteristic of Proust's work is its stream of contemplated/remembered images, often from the natural world: the hawthorn bushes, chestnut trees and cattleyas. But while these are central to the altering consciousness of the narrator, how far could they be evoked or made visible for an audience, given how absolutely these phenomena are constructed by individual observation? For as *The Way by Swann's* concludes:

> The places we have known do not belong solely to the world of space in which we situate them for our greater convenience. They were only a thin slice among contiguous impressions that formed our life at that time; the memory of a certain image is only regret for a certain moment; and houses, roads, avenues are as fleeting, alas, as the years.[110]

The narrator understands that he cannot return to the places and sights that impressed themselves so strongly upon him as a child: 'I was not able to discover the pleasures I desired. [...] I wanted to find them again as I remembered them.'[111] The title of the first English translation of the work, 'Remembrance of Things Past', separates past 'things' from present remembering, at the same time casting that relation in an implicitly nostalgic haze (the title was disliked by Proust for these reasons).[112] The later retranslation, 'In Search of Lost Time', now widely adopted, conveys the attempted reconnection as something active; nonetheless, *lost* time suggests both time past and time spent in vain. Both these titles could be taken as a warning against adaptation: what could rewriting achieve, if the central object of Proust's quest effectively evades the novel itself?

A Field Guide to Lost Things (2015), by Canadian poet and text-based artist Peter Jaeger, reframes Proust on the page and through a live performance reading. Jaeger's creative practice is shaped not by dramatic tradition, but by cross-disciplinary experimentation rooted in the 'Objectivist' poetics of writers including Louis Zukofsky and George Oppen, and developed mid-century by poets, composers and artists at North Carolina's Black Mountain College. In common with John Cage, whose work Jaeger made the subject of a critical study, Jaeger creates art which pursues method rather than 'meaning'. The application of strict compositional rules serves to inhibit, if not wholly block, the subjective impulses of the artist. A rule-based framework also aims to undermine conventional systems of value: similarly to the way in which Cage's compositions regard every kind of noise as valid musical sound, Jaeger's use of textual hybrid, appropriation and relocation – in pieces such as *Rapid Eye Movement* (2009), *The Persons* (2011) and *Martyrologies* (2015) – strives to unsettle 'normative views about what constitutes "good writing"'.[113] Jaeger came to Proust in part through his interest in Walter Benjamin's *Passagen-Werk*, or *Arcades Project*, Benjamin's enormous and unfinished study of nineteenth-century Paris, constructed as a collage of texts drawn from Proust, Joyce, Isherwood and others.[114] As J. M. Coetzee notes, the *Arcades Project* was conceived by Benjamin not as his own authorial creation but something more like a 'magic encyclopedia' which used text fragments almost cinematically, in order to re-view a past which could not be fully known or regained.[115] Of Proust, whose writing is extensively incorporated into the *Arcades Project*, Benjamin said: 'With a passion unknown to any writer before him, Proust took as his subject the fidelity of things that have crossed our path in life. Fidelity to an afternoon, to a tree, a spot of sun on the carpet.'[116] This quotation prefaces *A Field Guide to Lost Things* and is the only explicit indication in the published text (bar the hint in 'Lost') that Jaeger's work is referencing Proust's at all.

Beginning from the principle that the larger themes and meanings in Proust are rooted in this 'fidelity' towards 'things', Jaeger established the procedural rule that *A Field Guide to Lost Things* would reconfigure every single image of a natural object encountered by the characters in *Swann's Way*, the first volume of the novel series. Using the 1922 translation by C. K. Scott Moncrieff, Jaeger's text includes images of nature identified in rural and urban surroundings, and those perceived in the bodies of other characters. The concept of a field guide to Proust seems anticipated by his critics and commentators: Shattuck remarks that reading the author 'bears many resemblances to visiting a zoo'; Patrick Alexander likens his work to a 'beautiful garden, filled with delights but hidden behind a forbidding wall'; Philip Spalding allegorizes the Proustian world as both 'jungle' and 'ocean'.[117] Spalding's 1952 *A Reader's Handbook to Proust: An Index Guide to Remembrance of Things Past* represented a concerted effort to guide the reader 'through the Proustian labyrinth' by providing indices to the novel's characters and subjects, aiming thereby to reduce the risk of missing 'some brief but highly relevant allusion'.[118] Spalding's project of mapping is notably echoed in the Pléiade edition (1987–89), whose fourth volume includes indices to persons, places, and literary and artistic works referenced in Proust's novel. Such efforts strive to counter and contain a text whose 'excessive' dimensions inhibit the possibility of perceiving it in its entirety, from beginning to end.

Like the indices of Spalding and the Pléiade Proust, *A Field Guide to Lost Things* promises on the surface to render the terrain of the novel more familiar and comprehensible; but unlike those earlier models, Jaeger's work severs every element it lists from its point of location within the original, in consequence producing a 'guide' that in practice is perpetually disorienting. In this way, the *Field Guide* radically extends a strategy already characteristic of Proust's writing, described by Thomas Baldwin as a 'developing tendency to represent objects and scenes ekphrastically', resulting in curiously flat 'pictures' that produce a marked 'distancing effect'.[119] Jaeger's method was to identify images first on the page, then use an electronic search facility to establish their reoccurrence in the digitized version. As each image was appropriated for the *Field Guide*, he deleted references to it from his hard copy, visibly disappearing matter as it surfaced, changed, in the new writing context. *A Field Guide* is organized alphabetically, meaning that the entries under A, for example, are listed – methodically, yet eclectically – as follows: Acacias; Afternoon Sky; Agate Marble; Air; All Manner of Birds; Almonds; American Eye; Ampelopsis; Ancient Trees; Animal; Animal's Consciousness; Animals; Ankle; Ant Hill; Apple Trees; Apricots; Aquatic Gardening; Arm; Arms; Asparagus; Astral Body; Atmosphere; Atmospheric Disturbances; Atmospheric Variation; Atom; Autumn; Avalanche. Each entry includes the references to the object in the text, in whole or part sentence, with these also given alphabetically. The system is thus consistent, but the effect produced, incoherent:

> **Air** Her hand, at the same
> time, sketched in the air an
> indelicate gesture. 'Now,
> don't stay here all day; you
> can go up to your room if
> you are too hot outside, but
> get a little fresh air first;
> don't start reading
> immediately after your
> food.' The fresh air made
> one hungry. Then after

> patterning everywhere the
> violet velvet of the evening
> air, abruptly soothed, they
> would return and be
> absorbed in the tower.
> 'You'll come away more "up
> in the air" than I am!'[120]

As the 'A' list would suggest, Jaeger's work contains hundreds of entries; in all, the appropriated words fill 173 two-columned pages. The strict principles used for text selection and inclusion expose something of Proust's idiosyncratic language patterns, or at least, those identified by Moncrieff's translation; thus the 'Z' list exhibits a curious repetition, with entries for Zone of Evaporation; Zone of Heat; Zone of Melancholy; Zone of Pure Air; and Zone of Sunlight. Between A and Z there are many points where the random process generates humour: as when the entry for Codfish is simply 'Codfish!'[121] The elegiac qualities of the source are evoked also by a structure which directly privileges the fragment: thus, the text collage collated under Chestnuts describes

> a double row of orange-red chestnuts [which] seemed, as in a picture just begun, to be the only thing painted, so far, by an artist who had not yet laid any colour on the rest, and to be offering their cloister, in full daylight, for the casual exercise of the human figures that would be added to the picture later on.[122]

In adaptation's repetition, the 'human figures' are never added in; yet as the narrator's words make clear, were they 'later on' to be included in the picture, the chestnuts themselves would have changed.

The field guide appealed to Jaeger both as a reference text structure (as opposed to a fiction form) and from his interest in long-distance walking, trails and maps. Walking is vitally important in Proust's novel: 'the way by Swann's' and 'the Guermantes way' describe two routes alternately taken by the family on their Sunday constitutional, each invested with great significance by the narrator; only much later in life does he learn that these apparently divergent paths intersect.

As a textual form, the field guide carries with it certain expectations, however, which are only partly borne out by Jaeger's work. The modern field guide dates back to the late nineteenth century, to books like *How to Know the Wild Flowers* (1895), and was designed to help non-experts identify flora and fauna, to distinguish between phenomena that might appear similar and to improve the wider state of knowledge by making specialist information accessible to amateurs.[123] This aptly describes Jaeger's treatment of Proust, by pulling out for scrutiny that which the reader is likely to 'encounter' when moving through the novel; by using Proust's own words to insist on, for example, the difference between Lilies, Lilies in their Hands and an individual Lily; and by implication, suggesting that a work perceived as intellectually daunting and inscrutable *is* mappable and knowable. However, the great majority of field guides contain illustrations, whether photographs or drawings: frequently, such books are more illustration than text. By contrast, *A Field Guide to Lost Things* is a guide without pictures, one that does not pin images visually on the page like butterflies, but evokes them 'ekphrastically' in words. This strategy avoids reducing the potential complexity of written images by the specifics of representation, but at the same time it reinforces and reenacts their status as 'lost'. Jaeger's field guide thus becomes a useful map to a world contained in a book – one that will help us locate and comprehend the 'things' within *In Search of Lost Time* – but also a useless one that provides the coordinates of things which are no longer there to be found.

As an adaptation on the page, *A Field Guide to Lost Things* draws selectively but substantially from its source; by the time the *Guide* had been generated, much of Jaeger's hard copy had been blacked out.[124] The format used by the adapted text does not communicate narrative, other than in tiny fragments; yet in practice, this could be interpreted as a heightened version of the original's molecular, non-linear narrative release. Jaeger's compositional method undoubtedly creates a radically altered textual map, but this is not, to recall Diderot's words, a mish-mash: in fact, the reader is precisely oriented through it by the alphabetical structure, again, guided at least as clearly as by the novel.

In terms of content, *A Field Guide to Lost Things* is explicitly unoriginal: none of the text is 'authored' by Jaeger. But rather than playing into old prejudices about the derivative nature of adaptation, this approach can be positively received as a self-conscious practice of conceptual writing that does not seek to bring still more 'new' text into an already overwhelmingly text-dense culture, but rather to explore the potential in 'moving' language from one context to another. Echoing the conceptual art practice of Duchamp or Warhol, conceptual writing deliberately appropriates and recycles; so where work that strives for originality may turn out – arguably, will inevitably turn out – as derivative and formulaic, 'uncreative' art displays its quality and distinctiveness by the manner of its assemblage.[125] From this perspective, *A Field Guide to Lost Things* is not Jaeger attempting to introduce a new authorial attitude; in fact, his text strives *not* to do this. Instead, in the manner of the *Arcades Project*, Jaeger uses passages 'extracted from their original context like collectibles', which are effectively 'set up to communicate among themselves'.[126]

Jaeger has often performed his poetry live but had grown dissatisfied with the predictability of the twenty- to forty-minute reading format.[127] Already interested in pushing these boundaries further, Jaeger used *A Field Guide to Lost Things* to consolidate this impulse, at the very least reflecting, through the eventual non-stop reading duration of three or four hours, the reality that Proust demands a more than averagely long time to read. Jaeger delivered the text live in 2015 at London's Hardy Tree Gallery and at Bury's Text Festival, thus in neither case framed by 'theatre' but within a context of text/art interdisciplinary experimentation. Inherent in durational art practice is the intent to heighten and expose temporality, making the passing of time palpable and even painful; as Adrian Heathfield has noted in his analysis of 'lifeworks' by the artist Tehching Hsieh, the term durational carries within it the notion of endurance, of something undergone by the creator and to a certain extent by their audience.[128] Jaeger's durational reading might be modest indeed, when compared with Hsieh's yearlong artworks, or even with a theatrical event like ERS' *Gatz* (see Chapter 2).

Nonetheless, the extreme simplicity but relentless structure of his text and performance makes considerable demands on speaker and listeners alike. Reading aloud at such length took a toll on voice and body: Jaeger describes a growing hoarseness, his awareness of physical deterioration as the event progressed; compelled to keep going, he could not always keep his mind on the words, meaning that text delivery continued as if by auto-pilot. The boredom that Jaeger suggests always haunts live poetry reading, for speakers and listeners, was greatly exacerbated in a performance context which deliberately courted fatigue. This quality mirrors the notorious difficulties of reading Proust; yet listening to Jaeger, as in reading the source, it is possible for the audience to embrace and profit from an impulse to drift already embedded in the material.

Jaeger's listening audience are given access to a rich text but little else: there is nothing to look at or attend to apart from the man on the chair. But, somewhat as in a work like Cage's *4′33″*, whatever else makes its presence felt within the performance time frame – incidental noise, movements, wandering thoughts – become part of this experience, here interweaving with the textual map. The audience members were free to come and go for this event, and very few remained for the duration. Frequently, Jaeger found himself speaking to an empty room; on another occasion, he became aware of reading for just one listener, a fellow poet. For neither performance, in Bury or London, did Jaeger reach the end of his text; after three or four hours, he was simply too weary to continue. Accepting that the event can stop when such a point is reached suggests a profound rejection of, or disinterest in, the dramatic. ERS' *Gatz* is structured by a reading of Fitzgerald's novel in its entirety, with the performance of all the cast, although most obviously Shepherd, regularly couched by reviewers as attaining the 'bravura'. By contrast, Jaeger's *A Field Guide to Lost Things* has no heroic ambition, on the page or in the live reading. Its alphabetical ordering is non-hierarchical, with X, Y, Z no more summative or resolved than A, B, C; in performance, the conclusion to the event is marked simply by the point at which its activity stops. The decision to end is Jaeger's, clearly; yet to tax himself to reach the final entry at all costs would restore 'dramatic' tension of a kind that the adaptation deliberately resists. The live reading is, therefore, as simple and neutral as Jaeger can make it, emulating the near-objectivity exhibited by the clean lines of text on the printed page. In its own way, Jaeger's text and, especially, his performance, mirror Barthes's perception that Proust's novel is critically inexhaustible. The fluidity of the material, Barthes argued, made it infinitely generative: 'all [Proust] leaves us to do is *rewrite him*, which is the exact contrary of exhausting him'.[129] Indeed, in this re-reading Jaeger, not Proust, is the one exhausted.

A Field Guide to Lost Things is not theatre, but it acquires an additional and distinctive order of life through performance which places Proust's central theme of time, and his 'fidelity' towards 'things', in charged relation. Considered as an adaptation, it is unlike any other project considered in this book: generated with imagination yet dispassionately, *A Field Guide* displays what becomes of a literary source when 'processed' in a particular and systematic way. Its example suggests provocative new answers to well-worn questions about what adaptation brings to its appropriated texts: rather than qualities like originality, commitment and reinterpretation being self-consciously manifested in the contributions of new authors, Jaeger's project demonstrates that all these can be evidenced by artistic method, which in turn allows new textual meanings to be released. Jaeger's one-man gallery event could hardly be further from the Hebbel am Ufer's vast staging of Wallace; and yet, as my discussion has shown, both projects, likewise Hof van Eede's treatment of Diderot, address related preoccupations with the construction of time and space, and with the challenges that all three books present for the reader. *Infinite Jest: 24 Hours through the Utopian West* recreates Wallace in highly visual, spatial, technological and temporally overwhelming terms. By contrast, *Where the World is Going, That's Where We are Going* enthusiastically invokes the novel's 'visual feast' but the company cannot or will not manifest this performatively for an audience. Finally, *A Field Guide to Lost Things*, consciously 'plain' as text and as live reading, uses extreme formal restraint to frame rich verbal language. Audience time spent in these events ranges from the theatre average of two hours, to an effortful three or four hours, through to an intentionally 'excessive' full day and night. Across those structures, the experience of temporality is not comparable: most obviously, in *A Field Guide*, only the performer is obliged to stay for the whole. But regardless of these different time scales, all three adaptations explore the potential of durational performance form: even the shortest, by Hof van Eede, adopts a dramaturgy that makes time *feel* long; moving in small, repetitive circles, *Where the World is going, That's Where We are Going* stages something akin to the impression of 'near motionlessness'.

The explicit problematizing of time, representation and communication that, especially, postdramatic theatre consciously pursues, can result, as Lehmann acknowledges, in events that some audiences will find 'provocative, incomprehensible or boring'; conceptual writing, likewise, withholds familiar and anticipated pleasures and in consequence can sometimes be experienced as frustratingly impermeable.[130] Yet formal strategies of the kinds employed by these artists are not grounded in the desire to perplex but in the position that *only* by these means might such concepts be articulated, performed and understood. Further, the self-questioning, at times potentially alienating languages used by the adaptations discussed in this chapter function to reenact expressive uncertainties that already distinguish the texts they reframe. Literatures from late eighteenth- and early twentieth-century France, and from late twentieth-century America, can be in no sense 'the same': nonetheless, in historically and culturally distinct ways, each of these novels appears at times to undo itself almost in the writing, whether by means of 'infinite', self-qualifying footnotes; an author who questions the value of his own work; or by a perpetual shifting back and forward, inwards and outwards, such that by the end of many thousands of pages we seem to have travelled no further than the beginning. Such irresolution within the text is translated – lightly or relentlessly, but in each case necessarily – onto the experience of the reader. In his introduction to Wallace, Dave Eggers notes that

> there are those who feel that fiction can be challenging, generally and thematically, and even on a sentence-by-sentence basis – that it's okay if a person needs to work a bit while reading, for the rewards can be that much greater when one's mind has been exercised and thus (presumably) expanded.[131]

That 'presumably' should not, perhaps, be brushed over: investment and effort may bring deeper satisfaction, but struggle is not in itself a guarantor of reward. Nevertheless, Eggers's words well describe the import of provocations issued, sentence-by-sentence, by all these literatures. The same can be said of their adaptations, which each stage difficult entertainment, teasing and tasking their audiences, moment-by-moment.

Conclusion

I began this book by asking why the long-standing, pervasive and manifestly thriving practice of prose adaptation in the theatre has not been more positively regarded. I suggested that on the one hand, historic prejudice against dramatization of literature still surfaces in contemporary debates and operates subtly to devalue this work; and on the other, that theatre's intrinsic reliance on modes of repetition and reproduction, and the diversity of forms in which that 'recreativity' is exhibited, has somewhat disguised both the specificity and the richness of its appropriations of prose. A fundamental aim of this book has therefore been to establish beyond question that theatre's practices of adaptation are artistically innovative, critically complex, conceptually ambitious, formally various and fully vital. To demonstrate this, I have examined adaptations that radically disturb expectations about dramatic content, modes of representation and conditions of reception; adaptations that oblige actors and audiences alike to adjust to the rhythms and scale of the material reconfigured; adaptations that position spectators as active 'readers' able to enter the fiction and negotiate its terms; adaptations that perform their own struggle with, or resistance to, the source text, as well as projects in which the apparent impossibility of adaptation is translated into wholly possible, self-critical performance; adaptations in which books have been swallowed whole, alongside others for which forgetting text is expected, accepted and enjoyed; adaptations presented without actors; and adaptations even, periodically, without audience. Throughout, I have explored the ways in which challenges posed by non-dramatic literature on a thematic, stylistic and structural level have spurred creativity, taking artists in unanticipated directions and resulting in boldly experimental theatricalities. Additionally, I have shown how frequently the physical book has featured in performance, with actors drawing inspiration from its material and sensual dimensions, as well as from content and symbolic significance.

While I have emphasized the ways in which adaptation of prose enriches performance, I have also argued that this engagement speaks back productively to literature too. Individual projects provide novel 'readings' of familiar and less familiar texts, situating narratives in charged, sometimes deliberately jarring contexts which oblige us to assess their meanings and relevance in new ways; adaptations structure interpretation by exposing, through performance, the gaps between past period and present moment, and between the potentiality of written words and the quite different opportunities and constraints of the *mise-en-scène*. This strategy of appropriation gives value back to literature well beyond the critical or imaginative insights offered on individual sources. The practice of adaptation in the theatre positively destabilizes prose literature, making immediate and graspable the sense in which the latter is not fixed, final and authoritative but malleable, contingent and contestable. Thomas Leitch has critiqued the traditionalist position that sees adaptations as 'intertexts' but their precursors simply as 'texts'. He argues that from this viewpoint, an adaptation 'is assumed to be a window into a text on which it depends for its authority, and the business of viewers and analysts is to look through the window for signs of the original text'; literary sources, by contrast, 'are assumed to be not windows but paintings that invite readers to look at or into them rather than through them'.[1] Seemingly, it requires special effort, still, in adaptation studies to acknowledge that source texts are not exemplary backdrops but provisional and permeable structures which can be looked at *and* through from all angles. However, this book has shown that performance is particularly well able to ensure that the precarity of literature, as well as that of any re-reading, remains foregrounded. Since the nature of theatrical representation does not support naturalistic verisimilitude but exposes its means of construction, and very rarely induces audiences to forget where they are, what time it is or their sense of how much longer is left to go, the texts that the theatre treats are held at one remove: not lifted up in reverence, but framed with the distance of difficulty.

Adaptations *do* serve as windows on their precursor texts *and* the latter are themselves unsettled by this process. But as well as this, prose literatures provide distinctive ways of looking at and understanding the theatre, as well as the contemporary world in which performance plays a part. In other words, if theatre audiences always remain somewhat conscious of the conditions of production, representation and reception, in adaptation the source text that is treated functions powerfully to structure that awareness. So audiences experience and may be dis/affected by postdramatic aesthetics by means of Wallace's *Infinite Jest*; they look through the frame of his novel at a city's architectural dreams and all those ambitions imply. Schulz's surreally dissolving descriptions of person and place illuminate the fluid, metamorphic qualities of Complicite's stage language. Individual volumes and a whole library space are harnessed to turn attention minutely to sensual impressions in the moment and to enable an expansive awareness of our social and historic relations with the book. While it is clearly possible to reflect on the capacities and limits of performance in relation to any theatrical production, adaptation encourages this speculative consideration precisely because audiences recognize that they are witnessing unlike constructs being brought together. When a cast of actors announce that they are going to convey the whole of *The Great Gatsby* and will not stop until this is done, or when a lone reader settles down to map out Proust for whoever chooses to listen, we are immediately put on our mettle; likewise, being accused of a nameless crime and led inexorably towards punishment cannot dissolve the fictional frame but does force consideration of one's power and responsibilities within it. In this way, the richly complex languages of contemporary theatre function diversely to re-present literary texts in adaptation; simultaneously, those very languages are interrogated and tested through the activated 'voices' of non-dramatic prose.

While theatrical practice is regularly acknowledged by adaptation studies, I have suggested that, to date, live performance has not crucially shaped the development of this inter-discipline. I hope that this book has conveyed that a more extensive consideration of theatre would enrich adaptation theory, not just on the level of individual interpretive projects but more fundamentally. For example, debates about the extent to which adaptations 'should' alter the meanings of their source texts – and whether they could avoid doing so, even if they wished – would be enhanced by an analysis of storytelling performance, a form which recognizes that narrative preservation goes hand in hand with transformation: further, one which understands that adopting *and also* changing narrative are integral to the telling tradition. In that discussion, I also drew attention to the art of digression, a strategy which certainly works differently on the page from in performance, but which in both contexts shows how seeming 'irrelevance' is in fact formally indispensable; as a celebration of expressive power and a way of undermining narrative authority, digression offers a rich analogy for the adaptation process, across multiple art forms. A second example of how theatrical practice could benefit adaptation studies would be in considering how performance 'time-space' negotiates the chronotopic conditions of precursor texts. Contemporary performance has profoundly stretched and complicated the temporal and spatial frameworks of artistic production: the result is not that theatre is able, or that it seeks, to mimic either literary time-space or the particular pace and situation of book reading, but the theatre's experiments in extended duration, intimate proximity, participatory encounters and site-specific staging together convey a sophisticated and nuanced creative apparatus able to tackle qualities which have often been considered beyond the scope of dramatic representation. Thirdly, the self-conscious 'uncreativity' of conceptual writing (discussed in Chapter 5) already intersects compellingly with, especially, postdramatic theatre practice and could valuably be applied further in the context of adaptation studies. Conceptual writing, like conceptual art, resituates and reassembles material by means of processes rigorously governed on the formal level. Moving language and image suggest one way to sidestep circuitous wrangling about originality and authorship and to instead embrace citation and textual 'theft'. At the same time, what might seem unappealingly cool in this rule-driven approach to artistic construction is offset by the different sense in which 'moving' can be understood; for as Kenneth Goldsmith has emphasized, 'moving information' signals both the activity of pushing this around and the capacity of being emotionally stirred by that process and its results.[2] Seen in this light, conceptual (un)creativity challenges textual authority and stability but its habits of reassemblage and reconstitution do not disallow meaning or affect; rather, these offer unexpectedly 'non-invasive' ways to reexamine familiar material and find new significance both in and through it.

I end this study with one further 'adaptation' of a particularly expansive kind. In 2012, the artist Fiona Banner joined with architect David Kohn to create 'A Room for London', a boat-like structure, which, as I write, is still perched startlingly on top of Queen Elizabeth Hall at London's Southbank Centre. 'A Room for London' was centrally inspired by Joseph Conrad's *Heart of Darkness* (1899), a novella about a voyage up the Congo into the 'dark heart' of Africa; Conrad's narrator, Marlowe, relates the tale to friends while they are on a boat anchored upon the River Thames. As a complex and controversial representation of colonialism, *Heart of Darkness* raises difficult and unresolved questions about cultural 'parallels' and the rights of a people to speak on behalf of another. As the inspiration for a new architectural construct, Conrad's novella suggested to these new creators the situation of a boat, poised for movement yet temporarily aground, as well as a defamiliarized perspective on a river central to London's tourist industry and still a major transport route while also being symbolically evocative of other waterways and the capital city's past. Banner and Kohn won funding for their proposal of this one-room boat – moored on a rooftop, the ultimate architectural folly – that would accommodate a succession of artists working in different media, as well as some 'non artists' fortunate enough to secure a stay. The artist occupants – who have included Jeremy Deller, Tim Etchells, Caryl Phillips, Imogen Heap, Luc Tuymans, David Byrne, Naomi Alderman and many others – stayed in the boat-space and were invited to use this place and time to create something new.[3] The little cabin, with its porthole and top deck views across London, is imaginatively capacious on the inside too, containing its own library of cross-genre literature directly and indirectly connected with the city and with Conrad. This library echoes in miniature the famous model used by architect Sir John Soane in his Picture Gallery, meaning that its walls fold out like cupboard doors, allowing it to hold around three times the number of texts a space of the size would normally be able to accommodate. 'A Room for London' is thus a building mimicking a boat, inspired by a book; it is a place to look out from, dream and create in; it unfolds to include far more inwards than you would suppose; and it opens outwards onto the world in any direction you choose. So far, it has produced (at least) digital and print publications, musical scores, videos, essays and a short story, a film and a sound composition, a slideshow and audio track, a painting, a song and an illustrated and interactive online map. Eccentric and esoteric, it is not and cannot be for everyone; as a metaphor for adaptation, however, it vividly conveys the abundant potential of every text and celebrates the infinite possibilities for reconsideration and renewal.

Notes

Introduction

1 C.S. Lewis, *The Magician's Nephew* (Harmondsworth: Penguin, 1963), 38.

Chapter 1

1 Colin MacCabe, 'Bazinian Adaptation: *The Butcher Boy as Example*'. In MacCabe, Kathleen Murray and Rick Warner, eds., *True to the Spirit: Film Adaptation and the Question of Fidelity* (Oxford & New York: Oxford University Press, 2011), 3–25 (3).

2 Susie Mee, 'Chekhov's *Three Sisters* and the Wooster Group's *Brace Up!*', *TDR* 36: 4 (1992), 143–153 (147).

3 Marvin Carlson, Review of Lyubimov's *Three Sisters* at the Taganka Theatre, Moscow. *Journal of Dramatic Theory and Criticism*, Fall (1989), 177–181.

4 Marvin Carlson, *The Haunted Stage: The Theatre as Memory Machine* (Ann Arbor: University of Michigan Press, 2003), 15.

5 Margherita Laera, ed., *Theatre and Adaptation: Return, Rewrite, Repeat* (London & New York: Bloomsbury, 2014), 3.

6 Laera, *Theatre and Adaptation*, 6.

7 The play was Richard Brinsley Sheridan's *Presumption; or The Fate of Frankenstein* (1823). Mary Shelley, letter to Leigh Hunt, 9 September 1823. Florence Marshall, ed., *The Life and Letters of Mary Wollstonecraft Shelley*, Vol. 2 (Project Gutenberg, E Book, 2011), 94. http://www.gutenberg.org/files/37956/37956-h/37956-h.htm#CHAPTER_XIX

8 Philip Bolton, ed., *Dickens Dramatised* (Boston: G.K. Hall, 1987), 3.

9 Charles Dickens, *Nicholas Nickleby* (1839). Ed. Michael Slater (Harmondsworth: Penguin, 1978), 726.

10 See Francesca Saggini, *The Gothic Novel and the Stage* (London & New York: Routledge, 2015); Bolton, ed., *Dickens Dramatised, Scott Dramatised* (London & New York: Mansell, 1992) and *Women Writers*

Dramatised (London & New York: Mansell, 1999); Philip Cox, *Reading Adaptations: Novels and Verse Narratives on the Stage, 1790–1840* (Manchester & New York: Manchester University Press, 2000); John Glavin, *After Dickens: Reading, Adaptation and Performance* (Cambridge: Cambridge University Press, 1999); Patsy Stoneman, ed., *Jane Eyre on Stage, 1848–1898* (London & New York: Routledge 2007). See also Harry Ludlam, *A Biography of Bram Stoker, Creator of Dracula* (London: New English Library, 1977), 123–127.

11 See, for example, Benjamin Poore, *Heritage, Nostalgia and Modern British Theatre: Staging the Victorians* (Basingstoke: Palgrave Macmillan, 2011); John Bradley, ed., *Henry James on Stage and Screen* (Basingstoke: Palgrave Macmillan, 2000); Patsy Stoneman, *Brontë Transformations: Cultural Dissemination of 'Jane Eyre' and 'Wuthering Heights'* (London & New York: Prentice Hall & Harvester Wheatsheaf, 1995); Gina MacDonald and Andrew MacDonald, eds., *Jane Austen on Screen* (Cambridge & New York: Cambridge University Press, 2003).

12 MacCabe, 'Bazinian Adaptation', 4.

13 Allardyce Nicoll, 'The Reasons of Decline'. Nicoll, *A History of English Drama 1660–1900*, Vol. 4 (Cambridge: Cambridge University Press, 2009), 70–78 (77).

14 Sally Ledger and Holly Furneaux, *Charles Dickens in Context* (Cambridge & New York: Cambridge University Press), 130.

15 For more on the influence of the dramatic on James's prose, see Alan Ackerman, *The Portable Theater: American Literature and the Nineteenth-Century Stage* (Baltimore, MD: Johns Hopkins University Press, 1999), 181–220.

16 'Academicus', 'On the Absurdities of the Modern Stage' (1800). In E. J. Clery and Robert Miles, eds., *Gothic Documents: A Sourcebook, 1700–1820* (Manchester & New York: Manchester University Press, 2000), 199–201 (200).

17 See Willard Thorp, 'The Stage Adventures of Some Gothic Novels', *PMLA* 43: 2 (1928), 476–486.

18 See Frances Babbage, 'Staging Angela Carter'. In Eds. Kelly Jones, Benjamin Poore and Robert Dean, eds., *Contemporary Gothic Drama* (Basingstoke: Palgrave Macmillan, forthcoming 2018).

19 Bruce Elder, '"Doing the Inexpressible Uncommonly Well": The Theatre of Steven Berkoff', *Theatre Quarterly* 31 (Autumn 1978), 37–43 (40).

20 Christine Geraghty, *Now A Major Motion Picture: Film Adaptations of Literature and Drama* (Lanham, MD: Rowman & Littlefield, 2008), 51–54.

21 Christopher Innes, 'Adapting Dickens to the Modern Eye: *Nicholas Nickleby* and *Little Dorrit*'. In Peter Reynolds, ed., *Novel Images: Literature in Performance* (London & New York: Routledge, 1993), 64–79 (78).

22 Stephen Lacey, 'British Theatre and Commerce, 1979–2000'. In Baz Kershaw, ed., *The Cambridge History of British Theatre,* Vol. 3 (Cambridge: Cambridge University Press, 2004), 435–436.

23 Linda Hutcheon consciously broadens the range of adaptation referents in *A Theory of Adaptation* to include '[v]ideogames, theme park rides, Web sites, graphic novels, song covers, operas, musicals, ballets, and radio and stage plays', alongside the usual focus on films and novels (although in fact theatre is hardly discussed). Hutcheon, *A Theory of Adaptation* (London & New York: Routledge, 2006), xiv.

24 Broader studies of adaptation that are not rooted in film have made some effort to include the theatre, but the art remains distinctly marginal in these analyses. Hutcheon predominantly deals with opera; Julie Sanders refers to Timberlake Wertenbaker's *Our Country's Good* (adapted from Keneally's novel), as an example from contemporary theatre, but aside from this drama is largely considered by her in relation to adaptations of Shakespeare's plays. Hutcheon, *A Theory of Adaptation.* Julie Sanders, *Adaptation and Appropriation* (Abingdon & New York: Routledge, 2006).

25 See Andre Bazin, *What Is Cinema?* Vol.1, trans. Hugh Gray (Berkeley: University of California Press, 1967); George Bluestone, *Novels into Film* (Berkeley: University of California Press, 1957); Geoffrey Wagner, *The Novel and the Cinema* (Rutherford, NJ: Fairleigh Dickinson University Press, 1975); Morris Beja, *Film and Literature* (New York: Longman, 1979); Dudley Andrew, *Concepts in Film Theory* (Oxford: Oxford University Press, 1984); David Bordwell, *Narration in the Fiction Film* (London: Methuen, 1985); Brian McFarlane, *Novel to Film* (Oxford: Clarendon Press, 1996); Deborah Cartmell and Imelda Whelehan, eds., *Adaptations: From Text to Screen, Screen to Text* (London: Routledge, 1999); Sarah Cardwell, *Adaptation Revisited: Television and the Classic Novel* (Manchester & New York: Manchester University Press, 2002); James Naremore, ed., *Film Adaptation* (New Brunswick,

NJ: Rutgers University Press, 2000); Robert Stam and Alessandra Raego, eds., *Literature and Film: A Guide to the Theory and Practice of Film Adaptation* (Oxford: Blackwell, 2004); Kamilla Elliott, *Rethinking the Novel/Film Debate* (Cambridge: Cambridge University Press, 2003); Thomas Leitch, *Film Adaptation and Its Discontents* (Baltimore, MD: Johns Hopkins University Press, 2007); Geraghty, *Now a Major Motion Picture*; Colin McCabe, Kathleen Murray and Rick Warner, eds., *True to the Spirit: Film Adaptation and the Question of Fidelity* (Oxford & New York: Oxford University Press, 2011).

26 David Bordwell and Kristin Thompson, *Film Art: An Introduction* (New York: McGraw-Hill, 2001), 400–402.

27 For instance, film's narrative capabilities were powerfully represented in an influential 1944 essay by Sergei Eisenstein, who argued that the film montage techniques used by D. W. Griffith closely mirrored the narratalogical patterns of Dickens's fiction. Eisenstein, 'Dickens, Griffith and the Film Today', in Eisenstein, *Film Form: Essays in Film Theory*, ed. and trans. Jay Leyda (Orlando, Florida: Harcourt Brace, 1969), 195–255. For a discussion about the distinctive and competing traditions of 'art cinema' and 'narrative cinema', see also Bordwell, *Narration in the Fiction Film*.

28 Virginia Woolf, 'The Cinema'. *Collected Essays*, 4 Vols. (London: Hogarth Press, 1966), Vol. 2, 268–272 (269).

29 Woolf, 'The Cinema', 271, 272.

30 The American film critic Richard Brody describes Woolf's essay, more than eighty years after its first publication, as remaining 'one of the finest pieces of film criticism I have ever read'. Richard Brody, 'Virginia Woolf, Critic', *The New Yorker*, 24 February 2012.

31 See, for example, Steven Moore, *The Novel: An Alternative History* (London & New York: Continuum, 2010).

32 Roland Barthes, 'The Death of the Author' (1968). *Image-Music-Text* (London: Fontana, 1977), 142–148 (146).

33 Nöel Carroll, *Theorising the Moving Image* (Cambridge: Cambridge University Press, 1996), 26.

34 Bluestone, *Novels into Film*, viii; 21.

35 Thomas Leitch, 'Twelve Fallacies in Contemporary Adaptation Theory', *Criticism* 45: 2 (Spring 2003), 149–171 (156).

36 Leitch, 'Twelve Fallacies', 158.

37 See Marvin Carlson, 'Theatrical Performance: Illustration, Translation, Fulfillment, or Supplement?', *Theatre Journal* 37: 1 (1985), 5–11.

38 Charles Isherwood, 'Pages That Weren't Meant for Stages', *New York Times*, 21 November 2008.

39 Lyn Gardner, '*Waves* Sets a High Water-Mark for Multimedia Theatre', *Guardian*, 4 December 2006.

40 Ben Brantley, 'Six Lives Ebb and Flow, Interconnected and Alone', *New York Times*, 16 November 2008.

41 Gardner, '*Waves* Sets a High Water-Mark'.

42 Joanne Tompkins, *Theatre's Heterotopias: Performance and the Cultural Politics of Space* (Basingstoke & New York: Palgrave Macmillan, 2014), 143.

43 Isherwood, 'Pages That Weren't Meant for Stages'.

44 Michael Billington, Review of *Pride and Prejudice* at Regent's Park. *Guardian*, 26 June 2013; Review of *Jane Eyre* at Bristol Old Vic. *Guardian*, 18 September 2015.

45 Charles Spencer, Review of *The Portrait of a Lady* at the Theatre Royal, Bath. *Telegraph*, 25 July 2008.

46 Milan Kundera, *Jacques and His Master*, trans. Simon Callow (New York & London: Harper Perennial, 1986), 15–16. Kundera's remarks feature in the preface to his dramatic 'variation' on Diderot's *Jacques, the Fatalist*: he is at pains to stress the originality of his play, even while it remains a 'homage' to Diderot, and insist that *Jacques and His Master* is *not* an adaptation.

47 Vincent Murphy, *Page to Stage: The Craft of Adaptation* (Ann Arbor: University of Michigan Press, 2013), 77.

48 Neil Sinyard, 'Adaptation as Criticism: Four Films'. *Filming Literature: The Art of Screen Adaptation* (London & Sydney: Croom Helm, 1986), 117–142 (117).

49 Cox, *Reading Adaptations*, 55.

50 Cox, *Reading Adaptations*, 71.

51 Jonathan Miller, *Subsequent Performances* (London: Faber, 1986), 229.

52 Philip Hensher, 'You'll Never Catch Me Watching It', *Guardian*, 7 November 2005.

53 Hutcheon, *A Theory of Adaptation*, 58–60.

54 Robert Stam, 'Introduction: The Theory and Practice of Adaptation'. In Robert Stam and Alessandra Raengo, eds., *Literature and Film: A Guide to the Theory and Practice of Film Adaptation* (Oxford: Blackwell, 2004), 5.
55 Agota Kristof, *The Notebook*, trans. Alan Sheridan (New York: Grove Press, 1997), 29.
56 Leitch, 'Twelve Fallacies', 161.
57 Brian McFarlane, 'It Wasn't Like That in the Book', *Literature/Film Quarterly* 28: 3 (2000), 163–169 (165).
58 Wagner, *The Novel and the Cinema*, 223.
59 Dudley Andrew, 'The Well-Worn Muse: Adaptation in Film History and Theory'. In Syndy Conger and Janet Welsh, eds., *Narrative Strategies: Original Essays in Film and Prose Fiction* (Macomb: Western Illinois University Press, 1980), 9–17 (11–12).
60 Cardwell, *Adaptation Revisited*, 61–62.
61 Laera, ed., *Theatre and Adaptation*, 5.
62 J. D. Connor, 'The Persistence of Fidelity: Adaptation Theory Today', *M/C Journal (Journal of Media and Culture)* 10: 2 (2007), http://journal.media-culture.org.au/0705/15-connor.php. Accessed 10 March 2017.
63 Casie Hermansson, 'Flogging Fidelity: In Defense of the (Un)Dead Horse', *Adaptation* 8: 2 (2015), 149–160 (147, 157).
64 Christine Geraghty, *Now a Major Motion Picture: Film Adaptations of Literature and Drama* (New York and Plymouth: Rowan & Littlefield, 2008), 3.
65 Charles Spencer, Review of *The Curious Incident of the Dog in the Night-Time* at the Apollo Theatre, London. *Telegraph*, 8 June 2015.
66 Susannah Clapp, Review of *The Curious Incident of the Dog in the Night-Time* at the Apollo Theatre, London. *Guardian*, 17 March 2013.
67 Alexis Soloski, Review of *The Curious Incident of the Dog in the Night-Time* at the Ethel Barrymore Theatre, New York. *Guardian*, 6 October 2014.
68 Simon Stephens, interviewed by Duška Radosavljević. Laera, ed., *Theatre and Adaptation*, 255–268 (261).
69 Hutcheon, *A Theory of Adaptation*, 172.
70 Patrice Pavis, 'On Faithfulness: The Difficulties Experienced by the Text/Performance Couple', *Theatre Research International* 33: 2 (2008), 117–126 (120).
71 Kundera, *Jacques and His Master*, 16.

Chapter 2

1 Tim Etchells and Ant Hampton, *The Quiet Volume* (2010). Unpublished text of audio track and notebook. I am grateful to the artists for making this available to me.
2 Howard Hollands describes publishers' alerts that a 'page is intentionally blank' as 'a means of allaying the anxiety generated for and by the reader faced with what appears to be nothing on the page'. Hollands, 'Drawing a Blank: Picturing Nothing on the Page', *Performance Research* 9: 2 (2004), 24–33 (24).
3 Etchells and Hampton, *The Quiet Volume*.
4 Etchells and Hampton, *The Quiet Volume*.
5 Allsopp, 'Itinerant Pages: The Page as Performance Space', *Performance Research* 9: 2 (2004), 2–7 (5).
6 Etchells and Hampton, *The Quiet Volume*.
7 Ray Bradbury, *Fahrenheit 451* (London: Corgi, 1973), 147.
8 Amy Boyle Johnston, 'Ray Bradbury: *Fahrenheit 451* Misinterpreted', *LA Weekly*, 30 May 2007. http://www.laweekly.com/news/ray-bradbury-fahrenheit-451-misinterpreted-2149125. Accessed 10 March 2017.
9 Sam Weller, 'Ray Bradbury: The Art of Fiction, No. 203', *The Paris Review*, Spring 2010, No. 192. (The main body of this interview had originally been conducted in the late 1970s, but had remained unpublished.) http:/www.theparisreview.org/interviews/6012/the-art-of-fiction-no-203-ray-bradbury. Accessed 10 March 2017.
10 Weller, 'Ray Bradbury'.
11 Weller, 'Ray Bradbury'.
12 Alexander Smith, *Dreamthorp: A Book of Essays Written in the Country*. 1905. http://www.gutenberg.org/ebooks/18135. Accessed 10 March 2017.
13 Lyn Gardner, review of *Time Has Fallen Asleep in the Afternoon Sunshine* at Birmingham Central Library. *Guardian*, 3 April 2012. http://www.theguardian.com/stage/2012/apr/03/time-has-fallen-asleep-review. Accessed 10 March 2017.
14 Bradbury, *Fahrenheit 451*, 43.
15 Richard Hornby, 'Forgetting the Text: Derrida and the "Liberation" of the Actor', *New Theatre Quarterly* 18: 4 (2002), 355–358 (357–358).
16 Edgar Allan Poe, *The Fall of the House of Usher and Other Writings* (London & New York: Penguin, 1986), 451.

17 Lyn Gardner, 'The Face of the Future', *Guardian*, 19 November 1997.
18 Simon McBurney, *The Street of Crocodiles*. 1992. Programme note.
19 Sarah Cardwell, *Adaptation Revisited: Television and the Classic Novel* (Manchester & New York: Manchester University Press, 2002), 19. Hutcheon, *A Theory of Adaptation*, 6–9. McFarlane, *Novel to Film*, 194.
20 Francis Spufford, *The Child That Books Built* (London: Faber & Faber, 2002), 4.
21 Garrett Stewart, *The Look of Reading: Book, Painting, Text* (Chicago & London: University of Chicago Press, 2006), 2–3.
22 Bruno Schulz, *The Street of Crocodiles*. Trans. Celina Wieniewska (London & New York: Penguin, 2008), 31.
23 Schulz, *The Street of Crocodiles*, 21.
24 Schulz, *The Street of Crocodiles*, 65.
25 Georges Poulet, 'Criticism and the Experience of Interiority'. In Richard Macksey and Eugenio Donato, eds., *The Structuralist Controversy: The Languages of Criticism and the Sciences of Man* (Baltimore, MD: Johns Hopkins University Press, 1970), 56–72 (57).
26 Roland Barthes, *The Pleasure of the Text* (New York: Hill & Wang, 1990), 9–10.
27 F. Scott Fitzgerald, *The Great Gatsby* (London & New York: Penguin, 1990).
28 Oskar Eustis et al., 'An Evening of Gatsby with Elevator Repair Service at the 92nd Street Y'. 29 September 2010. http://www.youtube.com/watch?v=GzcvwyhtG3o. Accessed 10 March 2017.
29 Michael Feingold, '*Gatz* Tries a Novel Approach to Fitzgerald', *The Village Voice*, 10 October 2013. http://www.villagevoice.com/2010-10-13/theater/gatz-tries-a-novel-approach-to-fitzgerald/. Accessed 10 March 2017.
30 Catherine Love, 'By the Book: Adaptation, Work, and Elevator Repair Service's *Gatz*', *Contemporary Theatre Review* 26: 2 (2016), 183–195 (192).
31 Love, 'By the Book', 188.
32 Mikhail Bulgakov, *The Master and Margarita*. Trans. Michael Glenny (New England: Harvill Press, 1995).
33 Maria Kisel, 'Feuilletons Don't Burn: Bulgakov's "The Master and Margarita" and the Imagined "Soviet Reader"', *Slavic Review* 68: 3 (2009), 582–600 (582).

34 Roger Chartier and Peter Stallybrass, 'What Is a Book?' In Neil Fraistat and Julia Flanders, eds., *The Cambridge Companion to Textual Scholarship* (Cambridge & New York: Cambridge University Press, 2013), 188–204 (201).

35 Jorge Luis Borges with Norman Thomas de Giovanni, *Autobiographia 1899–1970* (Buenos Aires: El Ateneo, 1999), 26. Cited in Chartier and Stallybrass, 'What is a book?', 201.

36 George Bornstein and Ralph Williams, eds., *Palimpsest: Editorial Theory in the Humanities* (Ann Arbor: University of Michigan Press, 1993), 3.

37 Paul Eggert, 'Apparatus, Text, Interface: How to Read a Printed Critical Edition'. In Neil Fraistat and Julia Flanders, eds., *The Cambridge Companion to Textual Scholarship* (Cambridge & New York: Cambridge University Press, 2013), 97–118 (97).

38 Roland Barthes, 'From Work to Text' (1971). In Roland Barthes, ed., *Image-Music-Text*, trans. Stephen Heath (London: Fontana Books, 1977), 156–157.

39 Jerome McGann, *The Textual Condition* (Princeton, NJ: Princeton University Press, 1991), 4; 10.

40 McGann, *The Textual Condition*, 185.

41 McGann, *The Textual Condition*, 65–66.

42 For other articulations of this argument (after McGann) see Eggert, 'Apparatus, Text, Interface', 97–118; Peter Shillingsburg, 'Polymorphic, Polysemic, Protean, Reliable, Electronic Texts'. In George Bornstein and Ralph Williams, eds., *Palimpsest: Editorial Theory in the Humanities* (Ann Arbor: University of Michigan Press, 1993), 29–44.

43 Michael Alexander, *The Poetic Achievement of Ezra Pound* (Berkeley & Los Angeles: University of California Press, 1981), 144.

44 Hutcheon, *A Theory of Adaptation*, 21–22; Leitch, *Film Adaptation and Its Discontents*, 129; Milan Pribisic, 'The Pleasures of "Theater Film": Stage to Film Adaptation'. In Dennis Cutchins, Laurence Raw and James Welsh, eds., *Redefining Adaptation Studies* (Lanham, Toronto & Plymouth: Scarecrow Press, 2010), 147–159 (155–156).

45 While Sarah Cardwell does not use the metaphor of the palimpsest, she adopts a very similar model in her analysis of the limitations with the 'centre-based' model that has traditionally dominated adaptation criticism, in which 'each subsequent adaptation is understood to hold a

direct relationship with the culturally established original'. As Cardwell explains, this way of thinking about adaptation denies the relationship of individual adaptations to each other (which may be more significant than consideration of the 'original'), as well as closing down the possibility of examining adaptations in alternative ways (e.g. in their contribution to genre formation). Cardwell, *Adaptation Revisited*, 13–20.

46 Nicholas Lezard, 'The Book to End All Books', *Guardian*, 18 August 2001.

47 G. C. F. Mead and R. C. Clift, Introduction to Robert Burton, *The Essential Anatomy of Melancholy* (Mineola, New York: Dover, 2002), xxix.

48 Noga Arikha, 'As a Lute Out of Tune: Robert Burton's Melancholy', *The Public Domain Review*, 1 May 2013 (Open Knowledge Foundation). http://publicdomainreview.org/2013/05/01/as-a-lute-out-of-tune-robert-burtons-melancholy/. Accessed 10 March 2017.

49 Harold Fromm, 'Democritus Junior, and the Curse of Postmodernism', *The Hudson Review* 49: 2 (1996), 323–330 (323).

50 Burton, *The Essential Anatomy of Melancholy*, 3.

51 Arikha notes that by the time Burton was writing, humoural theory was already in dispute. The early seventeenth century produced revolutionary accounts of the circulation of blood in the body, in direct contradiction with the humoural system; this is unsurprising, since the concept of the humours was founded on the anatomical assumptions of Roman physicians who had never dissected a human body. Arikha, 'As a Lute out of Tune'.

52 Fromm, 'Democritus Junior, and the Curse of Postmodernism', 323.

53 Burton, *The Essential Anatomy of Melancholy*, 13.

54 Stan's Cafe, *The Anatomy of Melancholy*. Programme note, March 2013.

55 James Yarker, email correspondence with Frances Babbage, 15 February 2013.

56 Robert Burton, *The Anatomy of Melancholy*, adapted for the stage by Stan's Cafe (Birmingham: Stan's Cafe, 2013), 38; 39.

57 Yarker, email correspondence.

58 Stan's Cafe, *The Anatomy of Melancholy*, 18.

59 Eggert, 'Apparatus, Text, interface', 100.

60 Eggert, 'Apparatus, Text, interface', 100.

61 Eggert, 'Apparatus, Text, interface', 98.

62 Alexandra Coghlan, Review of *The Anatomy of Melancholy* at Oval House, 28 November 2013. http://www.theartsdesk.com/theatre/anatomy-melancholy-ovalhouse. Accessed 10 March 2017.

63 Lyn Gardner, Review of *The Anatomy of Melancholy* at Oval House. *Guardian*, 27 November 2013. http://www.theguardian.com/stage/2013/nov/27/anatomy-of-melancholy-review. Accessed 10 March 2017.

64 Hannah Tookey, Review of *The Anatomy of Melancholy* at Warwick Arts Centre. *A Younger Theatre*, 17 March 2013. http://www.ayoungertheatre.com/review-on-tour-the-anatomy-of-melancholy-warwick-arts-centre-stans-cafe/ Accessed 10 March 2017.

65 Nicola Fordham Hodges, Review of *The Anatomy of Melancholy* at Oval House in *Disability Arts Online*, 3 December 2013. http://www.disabilityartsonline.org.uk/the-anatomy-of-melancholy. Accessed 10 March 2017.

66 Jo Beggs, Review of *The Anatomy of Melancholy* at the Lowry, Salford, in *The Public Reviews* (North West), 25 April 2014. http://www.thereviewshub.com/the-anatomy-of-melancholy-the-lowry-salford/. Accessed 10 March 2017.

Chapter 3

1 Richard Kearney, *On Stories: Thinking in Action* (London & New York: Routledge, 2002), 3.

2 Mike Alfreds, *Then What Happens? Storytelling and Adapting for the Theatre* (London: Nick Hern Books, 2013), 138.

3 J. Hillis Miller, *Reading Narrative* (Norman, OK: University of Oklahoma Press, 1998), 47.

4 Cardwell, *Adaptation Revisited*, 98.

5 Richard Steadman-Jones, 'Odysseus and the Sirens: Archive, Exile, Voices', *Parallax* 19: 4 (2013), 20–35 (28).

6 Roland Barthes, *Image, Music, Text*, trans. Stephen Heath (London: Fontana, 1977), 146.

7 Jack Zipes, *Why Fairy Tales Stick: The Evolution and Relevance of a Genre* (New York & Abingdon: Routledge, 2006), 241.

8 For Zipes, the evolution of the Grimm brothers' 'Hansel and Gretel' reveals precisely such a betrayal of storytelling tradition. The tale reflects

the genuinely dark subjects of poverty, hunger and child abandonment; women are negatively depicted and punished, while the equally culpable male is not just forgiven but rewarded. While Zipes draws attention to selected retellings that do address the implications of such themes for changing contexts and eras, he argues that too often the tale has been reprinted and republished 'mindlessly' in a way that '[does] the brothers a disservice and ignore[s] deep social and political problems that threaten to shove our children into the witch's oven'. *Why Fairy Tales Stick*, 195–221 (221).

9 Wagner, *The Novel and the Cinema*, 222–231.

10 Zipes, *Breaking the Magic Spell: Radical Theories of Folk and Fairy Tales* (New York: Palgrave Macmillan, 2002 revised ed.), 210.

11 Bruno Bettelheim, *The Uses of Enchantment: The Meaning and Importance of Fairy Tales* (London & New York: Penguin, 1991), 5.

12 Marina Warner, *From the Beast to the Blonde: On Fairy Tales and Their Tellers* (London: Chatto & Windus, 1994), 212.

13 Bettelheim, *The Uses of Enchantment*, 69.

14 Warner, *From the Beast to the Blonde*, 212.

15 Spufford, *The Child That Books Built*, 56.

16 Warner, *From the Beast to the Blonde*, 213; Zipes, *Breaking the Magic Spell*, 22, 23.

17 Maria Tatar, *The Hard Facts of the Grimms' Fairy Tales* (Princeton, NJ: Princeton University Press, 1987), 161.

18 Tatar, *The Hard Facts*, 156–178. Tatar takes the example of the British folk tale 'Mr Fox', a version of the Bluebeard narrative in which the heroine, made curious by the advice above a doorway to 'be bold, be bold, but not too bold', discovers the murderous crimes of a potential suitor, who she then confronts before cutting him into a thousand pieces(170).

19 Tatar, *The Hard Facts*, 191.

20 Zipes identifies the utopian impulse in storytelling tradition most forcefully and frequently, but it is a perception shared by other commentators. Thus Tatar refers to the 'utopian moment' within the bleakest story that, for her, reflects not denial of darkness but the fact that 'as human beings we just need hope' and the belief 'that things can take a better turn'. Tatar in conversation with Krista Tippett, 'The Great Cauldron of Story: Why Fairy Tales Are for Adults Again', *On Being*, 14

March 2013. http://www.onbeing.org/?s=Maria+tatar&op=Search&form_build_id=&form_id=search_block_form. Accessed 10 March 2017.

21 Taffy Thomas in Michael Wilson, *Storytelling and Theatre* (New York & Basingstoke: Palgrave Macmillan, 2009), 192. I describe the mutual thievery between storytelling performance and theatre as only 'largely' benign, through an awareness that some professional storytellers *do* reject the idea of overlap, insisting instead on the specificity of a distinct and separate oral telling tradition (and perhaps also to protect the funding that supports this).

22 Emma Rice, *The Essay*: 'On Directing'. Broadcast on BBC Radio 3, 14 February 2012.

23 Educational pack for *The Red Shoes* (Kneehigh, 2010), 4.

24 Emma Rice, 'Foreword'. In Kneehigh Theatre, ed., *Tristan & Yseult, The Bacchae, The Wooden Frock, The Red Shoes* (London: Oberon Books, 2005), 11. Theatre-makers such as Rice and Teresa Ludovico are frequently able to draw on Bettelheim's thinking with none – or very few – of the qualms about rigidity of analysis that Zipes and other critics have expressed; to some degree, it would seem that the live, collaborative and already intertextual context of performance automatically contests or offsets that problematic 'fixity' of interpretation.

25 Rice, 'On Directing'.

26 Elias Bredsdorff, *Hans Christian Andersen: The Story of His Life and Work, 1805–1875* (London: Phaidon, 1979), 152.

27 Bredsdorff, *Hans Christian Andersen*, 152, 153.

28 Elisabeth Mahoney, Review of *The Red Shoes* at the Asylum, Blackwater (Cornwall). *Guardian*, 3 August 2010. https://www.theguardian.com/stage/2010/aug/03/red-shoes-review. Accessed 10 March 2017.

29 Kneehigh Theatre, *The Red Shoes*, 183.

30 Interview with Emma Rice, 'From the Community to the West End'. In Duška Radosavljević, ed., *The Contemporary Ensemble: Interviews with theatre-makers* (Abingdon & New York: Routledge, 2013), 98–108 (104).

31 Educational pack, *The Red Shoes*.

32 Kneehigh Theatre, *The Red Shoes*, 203.

33 Hans Christian Andersen, 'The Red Shoes' (1845). http://hca.gilead.org.il/red_shoe.html. Accessed 10 March 2017.

34 Kneehigh Theatre, *The Red Shoes*, 203.

35 Miriam Gillinson, 'A Recreation, a Reinterpretation – and Certainly Not Magic'. Review of *The Red Shoes* at Battersea Arts Centre. *Culture Wars*, 5 March 2011. http://www.culturewars.org.uk/index.php/site/article/a_recreation_a_reinterpretation_and_certainly_not_magic/. Accessed 10 March 2017.

36 Gillinson, Review of *The Red Shoes*.

37 Pullman, commenting on his own retelling of *Puss in Boots* (London: Corgi Childrens, 2001). http://www.philip-pullman.com/. Accessed 10 March 2017.

38 It has been popularly believed that the Grimms gathered this material by wandering the German countryside and urging peasants to share their tales, but according to Zipes this is a myth; in fact, the majority of storytellers invited to the brothers' home in the town of Kassel were mainly educated young women from the middle class or aristocracy. Jack Zipes, *When Dreams Came True: Classical Fairy Tales and Their Tradition* (London & New York: Routledge, 1999), 69, 70.

39 The fairy tales of the seventeenth-century French author Charles Perrault rival those of the Grimms in their 'authoritative' status. While it is admittedly partisan to specify a single individual or work from the contemporary period, Angela Carter's subversive reinvention of classic fairy tales in *The Bloody Chamber* (London: Gollancz, 1979) was a landmark publication in the context of the feminist movement and has proved highly inspirational since, for literature, feminist theory and in the arts. Maria Tatar's edition *The Classic Fairy Tales* collects and compares multiple versions of six popular narratives – 'Little Red Riding Hood', 'Beauty and the Beast', 'Cinderella', 'Snow White', 'Bluebeard', and 'Hansel and Gretel' – and carefully traces the journeys of each from very early manifestations through to late twentieth-century retellings (New York & London: Norton, 1999). Other publications pursue the same project in more exhaustive detail by concentrating on a single tale. See, for example, Neil Philip, *The Cinderella Story* (London & New York: Penguin, 1989); Jack Zipes, *The Trials and Tribulations of Little Red Riding Hood* (London & New York: Routledge, 1993).

40 Pullman, *Grimm Tales for Young and Old* (London & New York: Penguin, 2012), xviii–xix; xiii.

41 Pullman, *I Was a Rat! or The Scarlet Slippers* (London: Random House, 2000), 8.

42 'Rapunzel', 'Snow White', 'Thumbelina' (and the male story equivalent, 'Tom Thumb') and 'Hans-my-Hedgehog' exemplify the childless couple motif. The same theme is worked through in a different way with a story like 'The Gingerbread Man', or with 'Pinocchio' (in which there is a single 'parent'). With many such stories, there is an underlying moral that you should be careful what you wish for: very frequently, the unusual nature of the child or rashness of the original wish formulation results in complications, whether dark or comic, that constitute the narrative itself. By contrast, Bob and Joan express no longing for a child; it is rather in gradually building an adoptive relationship with the rat boy that they come to feel, retrospectively, that their life before his arrival had begun to lose 'purpose'. Pullman, *I Was a Rat!*, 113.

43 Pullman, *I Was a Rat!*, 12.

44 Pullman, *I Was a Rat!*, 109.

45 Pullman, *I Was a Rat!*, 158.

46 Pullman, *I Was a Rat!*, 169.

47 Pullman, *I Was a Rat!*, 5.

48 Pullman, *I Was a Rat!*, 45; 110, 111; 121.

49 If Pullman's book was topical at the time of writing, it became so again in the period of Ludovico's adaptation with Kate Middleton's marriage into the British royal family in 2011. In an interview, Pullman remarked that for him *I Was a Rat!* 'says something, again in a political way, about us and about how we regard our monarchy, and the magic we believe clings to it'. Pullman interviewed in the *Liverpool Echo*, 8 May 2013.

50 Pullman, Review of Blake Morrison, *As If* (London: Granta, 1997). *The Independent*, 1 February 1997.

51 Pullman, *I Was a Rat!*, 29; 55.

52 Pullman, *I Was a Rat!*, 69 (illustration); 76 (billboard).

53 Pullman, 'The Art of Reading in Colour', *Index on Censorship* 33: 4 (2004), 156–163 (161). http://ioc.sagepub.com/content/33/4/156. Accessed 10 March 2017.

54 Pullman, 'The Art of Reading in Colour', 162–163.

55 Pullman, 'All Around You Is Silence', *Guardian*, 5 June 2003.

56 Peter Bailey, email correspondence with Frances Babbage, 16 May 2013.

57 *The Snow Queen* and *The Mermaid Princess* were the result of commissions by Tokyo's Setagaya Public Theatre, following the popular success in Japan of Ludovico's *Beauty and the Beast*, and were first

performed by a Japanese cast; the dates given here refer to European versions of the productions, staged subsequently.

58 The generally excellent reviews of *I Was a Rat!* typically emphasize the show's cross-generational appeal. See, for example, Laura Thompson in the *Telegraph*, 17 February 2013; Pat Ashworth in *The Stage*, 20 February 2013; Maxie Szalwinska in *The Sunday Times*, 24 February 2013.

59 Teresa Ludovico interviewed by Frances Babbage, 20 May 2013. Simultaneous translation by Alberto Prandini.

60 Wendy Parsons and Catriona Nicholson, 'Talking to Philip Pullman: An Interview', *The Lion and the Unicorn* 23: 1 (1999), 116–134 (122).

61 Ludovico, interview with Babbage.

62 Wright's adaptation of *His Dark Materials* was significantly reinterpreted by the Warwick youth theatre company Playbox in a critically well-received 2006 production. *The Firework Maker's Daughter* has been adapted by the British physical theatre company Told By an Idiot (2005), as well as by playwright Stephen Russell for Birmingham Stage (2010). An opera based on the book, co-authored by Glyn Maxwell (librettist) and David Bruce (composer), opened at Hull Truck Theatre in 2013.

63 Interview with Nicholas Hytner by Robert Butler at the National Theatre, 6 January 2004.

64 'A Wizard with Worlds'. Kate Kellaway in conversation with Philip Pullman, *The Observer*, 22 October 2000.

65 Pullman, 'Reading in the Borderland: The Space Between the Words, the Reader and the Pictures'. Open University 40th Anniversary Lecture, 21 October 2011. https://www.youtube.com/watch?v=xKYDp3mjThU. Accessed 10 March 2017.

66 Ludovico, interview with Babbage.

67 Interview with Frank Moon. *I Was a Rat!* publicity material. http://www.iwasarat.co.uk/. Accessed 16 April 2014.

68 Ross Chambers, *Loiterature* (Lincoln: University of Nebraska Press, 1999), 19.

69 Pullman, 'Imaginary Friends: Philip Pullman on Fairy Tales', *New Statesman*, 13 December 2011. http://www.newstatesman.com/culture/2014/06/imaginary-friends-philip-pullman-fairy-tales. Accessed 5 May 2017.

70 Pullman, *I Was a Rat!*, 158.

71 Kenneth Gross, *Puppet: An Essay on Uncanny Life* (Chicago & London: University of Chicago Press, 2011), 33.

72 Ludovico works regularly in Japan and explained to me that her use of cherry blossom, specifically, reflected the meaning of the flower in Japanese culture. Cherry blossom features strongly in the Hanami festivals in March and April, and adorns shrines. The cherry blossom suggests beauty and fragility, blooming in great force but always fleetingly; metaphorically, it signals both the joy and ephemerality of life. Ludovico, interview with Babbage.

73 Pullman, *I Was a Rat!*, 175.

74 Spufford, *The Child That Books Built*, 9.

75 Bettelheim, *The Uses of Enchantment*, 93.

76 Pullman, *I Was a Rat!*, 173.

77 Pullman, 'Reading in the Borderland'. In this lecture Pullman makes the connection to Keats; the poet famously uses the term 'Negative Capability' in a letter to his brothers (1817) to describe a desirable state where one is 'capable of being in uncertainties, Mysteries, doubts, without any irritable reaching after fact and reason'. Robert Gittings, ed., *Selected Poems and Letters of Keats* (London: Heinemann, 1966), 40, 41.

78 Philip Pullman, 'Theatre – The True Key Stage', *Guardian*, 30 March 2004.

Chapter 4

1 Josephine Machon, *Immersive Theatres* (Basingstoke & New York: Palgrave Macmillan, 2013), 36–37.

2 Norman Holland, *The Dynamics of Literary Response* (New York: Norton, 1973), 66.

3 Mary Jacobsen, 'Looking for Literary Space: The Willing Suspension of Disbelief Re-Visited', *Research in the Teaching of English* 16: 1 (February 1982), 21–38.

4 Mikhail Bulgakov, *The Master and Margarita*, trans. Michael Glenny (London: Harvill Press, 1967), 270.

5 Martin Heidegger, 'Building, Dwelling, Thinking'. In Heidegger, ed., *Poetry, Language, Thought*, trans. Albert Hofstadter (New York: Harper & Row, 1971), 145–161 (156).

6 For example, the first licensed stage version of *Dracula*, mounted by actor-manager Hamilton Deane in 1924, set the first two acts in Jonathan Harker's Hampstead study and the third in Mina Harker's bedroom. Many of the most memorable landscapes of Stoker's novel – Dracula's castle, the voyage to England, a Whitby graveyard – were cut altogether to render the adaptation manageable and affordable. Harry Ludlam, *A Biography of Bram Stoker* (London: Nel Books, 1977), 171–173.

7 Elaine Scarry, *Dreaming by the Book* (New York: Farrar, Straus & Giroux, 1999).

8 Bulgakov, *The Master and Margarita*, 280.

9 Holland, *The Dynamics of Literary Response*.

10 Heidegger, 'Building, Dwelling, Thinking', 154.

11 Parsons and Nicholson, 'Talking to Philip Pullman', 116–134 (122).

12 Spufford, *The Child That Books Built*, 21–22.

13 Jacobsen, 'Looking for Literary Space', 25.

14 Jacobsen, 'Looking for Literary Space', 27.

15 Jacobsen, 'Looking for Literary Space', 28–30.

16 Students had not been told the authors of the texts, but might have grasped the qualities of each style instinctively (it was a Composition course).

17 Jacobsen, 'Looking for Literary Space', 37.

18 Dan Rebellato, 'When We Talk of Horses: Or, What Do We See When We See a Play?' *Performance Research* 14: 1 (2009), 17–28 (25).

19 Rebellato, 'When We Talk of Horses', 23.

20 It is impossible, of course, to acknowledge the experiences of every spectator at any production, and especially in a show constructed in this fashion. However, the online forums that made it possible to share spectator experiences of *The Masque of the Red Death* do collectively convey giddiness, delight, feeling overwhelmed, a sense of abandon and something very like fear. See, for instance, https://westendwhingers.wordpress.com/2007/09/19/review-masque-of-the-red-death-punchdrunk-national-theatre-at-battersea-arts-centre/. Accessed 10 March 2017.

21 David Jubb, 'Co-producing the Future of Theatre', *The Masque of the Red Death*, programme. BAC 2008.

22 Jubb, 'Co-producing the Future of Theatre'.

23 Jubb, 'Co-producing the Future of Theatre'; Steve Tompkins, 'Architectural Improvisation', *Masque* programme, 2008.

24 On 13 March 2015 the Battersea Arts Centre suffered a major fire, the cause of which is still uncertain; a large part of the roof was destroyed in the blaze, and both the Grand Hall and Lower Hall were seriously damaged. Despite this, the venue determinedly went ahead with two planned performances the day after the disaster. Perhaps a legacy of the Playground Projects initiative is that this revealed the *whole* site as, potentially, a performance site; up to and following the fire, the BAC was still enabling artists to make theatre in 80-odd rooms. 'Interview with David Jubb', *London Calling*, 30 June 2015. http://londoncalling.com/features/interview-with-david-jubb-artistic-director-of-battersea-arts-centre. Accessed 10 March 2017.

25 Felix Barrett in interview with Josephine Machon. Machon, *Immersive Theatres*, 159.

26 'Immy', comment posted 11.24pm 28 September 2007. https://westendwhingers.wordpress.com/2007/09/19/review-masque-of-the-red-death-punchdrunk-national-theatre-at-battersea-arts-centre/. Accessed 10 March 2017.

27 Edgar Allan Poe, 'The Masque of the Red Death'. In David Galloway, ed., *The Fall of the House of Usher and Other Writings* (London & New York: Penguin, 1986), 254–260 (256).

28 Poe, 'The Philosophy of Composition'. In Galloway, ed., *The Fall of the House of Usher and other Writings*, 480–492 (480).

29 Poe, 'The Philosophy of Composition', 482.

30 Poe, 'The Philosophy of Composition', 488.

31 Poe, 'The American Drama'. In Galloway, ed., *The Fall of the House of Usher and Other Writings*, 449.

32 Poe, 'The Philosophy of Composition', 481.

33 Poe, 'The Philosophy of Composition', 482.

34 Spectators can buy a programme which contains brief summaries of the highlighted stories. However, this is more of a souvenir than a guide: once inside the building, there is no opportunity to study it and no information included about how to negotiate the site.

35 Poe, 'The American Drama', 448–477 (456–457). It should be acknowledged that Poe's various tales 'of the grotesque and arabesque'

do overlap significantly, employing certain motifs regularly enough that a non-specialist reader may struggle to keep the narratives distinct (premature burial, for example, recurs in at least five of Poe's stories).

36 Poe, 'The Philosophy of Composition', 482.

37 Lyn Gardner, 'We Make Our Own Ghosts Here'. *Guardian*, 12 September 2007. http://www.theguardian.com/stage/2007/sep/12/theatre.edgarallanpoe. Accessed 10 March 2017.

38 The reviews of critics such as Michael Billington and Charles Spencer comment on the production's appropriation of the building, noting appreciatively the way Punchdrunk extended and radically transformed its internal spaces. See http://www.theguardian.com/stage/2007/oct/04/theatre and http://www.telegraph.co.uk/culture/theatre/drama/3668321/The-Masque-of-the-Red-Death-A-night-of-delicious-terror.html. Accessed 10 March 2017.

39 Shoshana Felman, 'On Reading Poetry: Reflections on the Limits and Possibilities of Psychoanalytical Approaches'. In John Muller and William Richardson, eds., *The Purloined Poe: Lacan, Derrida and Psychoanalytical Reading* (Baltimore & London: Johns Hopkins University Press, 1988), 133–156 (135).

40 Poe, 'The Philosophy of Composition', 490.

41 See for example Rose Biggin, 'Reading Fan Mail: Communicating Immersive Experience in Punchdrunk's *Faust* and *The Masque of the Red Death*', *Participations (Journal of Audience & Reception Studies)* 12: 1 (2015), 301–317 (308); Jan Wozniak, 'The Value of Being Together? Audiences in Punchdrunk's *The Drowned Man*', *Participations* 12: 1 (2015), 318–332.

42 Barrett in Machon, *Immersive Theatres*, 162.

43 'Webcowgirl's review of *The Masque of the Red Death* at Battersea Arts Centre, 20 December 2007. https://webcowgirl.wordpress.com/2008/01/06/punchdrunk-productions-masque-of-the-red-death-battersea-arts-centre/. Accessed 10 March 2017.

44 Kelly Nestruck, 'For Your Eyes Only: Theatre Just for You', *Guardian* theatre blog, 11 May 2009. http://www.theguardian.com/stage/theatreblog/2009/may/08/one-on-one-theatre. Accessed 10 March 2017.

45 Anonymous review of *The Masque of the Red Death*, *Evening Standard*, 3 October 2007. http://www.standard.co.uk/goingout/theatre/interactive-black-tie-and-tales-7399759.html. Accessed 10 March 2017.

46 Biggin, 'Reading Fan Mail', 308.
47 Wozniak, 'The Value of Being Together?', 329.
48 Biggin, 'Reading Fan Mail'; Wozniak, 'The Value of Being Together?' Adam Alston, 'Audience Participation and Neoliberal Value: Risk, Agency and Responsibility in Immersive Theatre', *Performance Research* 18: 2 (2013), 128–138.
49 Christopher Semtner, *Edgar Allan Poe's Richmond: The Raven in the Silver City* (Charleston, SC: The History Press, 2012), 21–22.
50 In a later iteration in 2013, Retz reworked *The Trial* as an event running across a single evening. This truncation increased the sense of unstoppable momentum, but somewhat diminished opportunities for participant reflection, as well as reducing periods of waiting around which, in the two-part version, arguably reinforced the theme of helplessness in the face of bureaucracy.
51 Felix Mortimer, email correspondence with Frances Babbage, 23 July 2013.
52 Sky Arts documentary on the making of *The Trial*, May 2013. https://www.youtube.com/watch?v=klTQg88CdIw. Accessed 10 March 2017.
53 Allen Thiher, 'Kafka's legacy', *Modern Fiction Studies* 26: 4 (1980), 543–561 (561).
54 Ruth Gross, 'Kafka's Short Fiction'. In Julian Preece, ed., *The Cambridge Companion to Kafka* (Cambridge & New York: Cambridge University Press, 2002), 80–94 (91).
55 Franz Kafka, *The Trial*, trans. Idris Parry (London & New York: Penguin, 1994), 174.
56 Kafka, *The Trial*, 178.
57 Hannah Arendt, 'Franz Kafka, Appreciated Anew'. In Susannah Young-Ah Gottlieb, ed., *Reflections on Literature and Culture* (Stanford, CA: Stanford University Press, 2007), 94–109 (98).
58 Arendt, 'Franz Kafka, Appreciated Anew', 98.
59 See Gregor Kalinowski, '"Fräulein Bürstners weißte Bluse": Making Sense Stick in Kafka's *The Trial*', *German Quarterly* 83: 4 (2010), 449–464 (449–450).
60 Simon O. Lesser, 'The Source of Guilt and the Sense of Guilt: Kafka's *The Trial*', *Modern Fiction Studies* 8: 1 (1962), 44–60 (45–47).
61 Erich Heller, *Kafka* (London: Fontana, 1974), 9.

62 Kafka, *The Trial*, 1.
63 Kafka, *The Trial*, 12.
64 Kafka, *The Trial*, 22.
65 Kafka, *The Trial*, 64.
66 Kafka, *The Trial*, 70–71.
67 Philip Weinstein, *Unknowing: The Work of Modernist Fiction* (Ithaca & London: Cornell University Press, 2005), 2.
68 Weinstein, *Unknowing*, 2.
69 Osman Durrani, 'Editions, Translations, Adaptations'. In Preece, ed., *The Cambridge Companion to Kafka*, 206–225 (217).
70 Michelle Woods, *Kafka Translated: How Translators have Shaped our Reading of Kafka* (New York & London: Bloomsbury, 2014), 193.
71 Steven Berkoff, *The Trial* (Oxford: Amber Lane Press, 1981), page unnumbered.
72 Berkoff, *The Trial*, page unnumbered.
73 For accounts of the Young Vic production and its impression on audiences, see for example Dominic Cavendish, Review of *The Trial* for the *Telegraph*, 27 June 2015; Sarah Hemming, Review of *The Trial* for the *Financial Times*, 29 June 2015.
74 Stevie Chick, '50 Years On: *The Trial* Revisited', *The Quietus*, 24 September 2012. http://thequietus.com/articles/10132-the-trial-orson-welles-50-years-on. Accessed 10 March 2017.
75 Miriam Gillinson, 'Retz's *The Trial* Review, or Death as a Get-out Clause', *Sketches on Theatre*, 5 April 2013. http://sketchesontheatre.blogspot.co.uk/2013/04/retz-trial-review-or-death-as-get-out.html. Accessed 10 March 2017.
76 Retz, *The Trial*: April–May 2013.
77 In my own case, a hastily improvised excuse rang hollow as soon as it was uttered. The guard said simply: 'That's not true, is it?', and I admitted it.
78 Mélanie Binette, 'Spatial Encounters: Spectatorship in Immersive Performances'. MA dissertation (Montréal, Québec: Concordia University, 2014).
79 Susan Sontag, 'The Unseen Alphabet: Kafka's Inner World.' *Vogue*, 1 July 1983. 202–203, 253 (203).
80 Sontag, 'The Unseen Alphabet', 203.

Chapter 5

1 '"Staging the Unstageable": The Story Behind *Curious Incident*.' Mark Haddon in conversation. http://www.curiousonstage.com/staging-unstageable-story-behind-curious-incident/. Accessed 10 March 2017.

2 Hans-Thies Lehmann, *Postdramatic Theatre*, trans. Karen Jürs-Munby (London & New York: Routledge, 2006). For Lehmann's far wider (yet inevitably still only representative) 'panorama' of postdramatic artists and influential predecessors, see Lehmann, *Postdramatic Theatre*, 23–24.

3 Lehmann, *Postdramatic Theatre*, 23.

4 Denis Diderot, *Jacques the Fatalist*, trans. David Coward (Oxford & New York: Penguin, 1999), 12.

5 J. Robert Loy, *Diderot's Determined Fatalist* (New York: King's Crown Press, 1950), 1–5; 184–185.

6 Introduction to Marcel Proust, *In Search of Lost Time, Vol. 1: Swann's Way*, trans. C. K. Scott Moncrieff and ed. William Carter (New Haven & London: Yale University Press, 2013), ix.

7 Cartoon by David Sipress, *The New Yorker*, 24 December 2007.

8 Roger Shattuck, *Proust's Way: A Field Guide to* In Search of Lost Time (London & New York: Penguin, 2000), 2.

9 David Letzler, 'Encyclopedic Novels and the Cruft of Fiction: *Infinite Jest*'s Endnotes', *Studies in the Novel* 44: 3 (2012), 304–324.

10 Lisa Schwartzbaum, '*Infinite Jest*: Too Much of a Good Thing?', *Entertainment Weekly*, 14 March 2008.

11 David Foster Wallace interviewed by Michael Silverblatt, *Bookworm*, 11 April 1996. https://www.youtube.com/watch?v=ZKCMTHX5WHk. Accessed 10 March 2017.

12 Marcel Proust, *The Way by Swann's*, trans. Lydia Davis (London & New York: Penguin, 2002), 184–186.

13 Diderot, *Jacques the Fatalist*, 3.

14 David Foster Wallace, *Infinite Jest* (London: Abacus, 1996), 233–234.

15 Mikhail Bakhtin, 'Forms of Time and of the Chronotope in the Novel'. *The Dialogical Imagination*, trans. Caryl Emerson and Michael Holquist (Austin: University of Texas Press, 1981), 84–258 (84).

16 Bakhtin, 'Forms of Time and of the Chronotope in the Novel', 135; 246.

17 Bakhtin, 'Forms of Time and of the Chronotope in the Novel', 248.
18 Bakhtin, 'Forms of Time and of the Chronotope in the Novel', 157.
19 Sue Vice, *Introducing Bakhtin* (Manchester & New York: Manchester University Press, 1997), 205.
20 SheShePop, *Infinite Jest – Footnote 24*. http://www.sheshepop.de/en/productions/archive/infinite-jest-footnote-24.html. Accessed 10 March 2017.
21 Emma Lee-Moss, '*Infinite Jest* at 20: Still a Challenge, Still Brilliant', *Guardian*, 15 February 2016.
22 Dave Eggers, Foreword to Wallace, *Infinite Jest*, viii–ix.
23 Wallace interviewed by Michael Silverblatt, *Bookworm*, 15 May 1997. http://www.smallbytes.net/~bobkat/bookworm.html. Accessed 10 March 2017.
24 Wallace, *Infinite Jest*, 1012.
25 Letzler, 'Encyclopedic Novels and the Cruft of Fiction', 305.
26 Larry McCaffery, 'An Expanded Interview with David Foster Wallace' (1993). In Stephen Burn, ed., *Conversations with David Foster Wallace* (Jackson, MS: University Press of Mississippi, 2012), 21–52 (26).
27 Wallace, *Infinite Jest*, 12.
28 Wallace, *Infinite Jest*, 785.
29 Laura Miller, 'The Salon Interview: David Foster Wallace' (1996). In Burn, ed., *Conversations with David Foster Wallace*, 58–65 (59).
30 Bakhtin, 'Forms of Time and of the Chronotope in the Novel', 157.
31 Bakhtin, 'Forms of Time and of the Chronotope in the Novel', 157.
32 Nicola Johnson and Helen Keane, 'Internet Addiction? Temporality and Life Online in the Networked Society', *Time & Society* (2015), 1–19 (7–8).
33 Wallace, *Infinite Jest*, 859–860.
34 Michael Earley, 'A Day in Dystopia', *Financial Times*, 22 June 2012. https://www.ft.com/content/3e80b10a-b95c-11e1-b4d6-00144feabdc0. Accessed 10 March 2017.
35 Matthias Lilienthal in conversation with Göksu Kunak, in connection with the Beirut mounting of Lilienthal's *X-Apartments*. *IBRAAZ* 29 July 2013. http://www.ibraaz.org/interviews/90. Accessed 10 March 2017.
36 Lilienthal in conversation with Kunak.
37 Abigail Wick, 'An Old-Fashioned *Infinite Jest* Invades Berlin', *NPR Now* (US National Public Radio), 16 July 2012. http://www.npr.org/

sections/nprberlinblog/2012/07/16/156853184/an-old-fashioned-infinite-jest-invades-berlin. Accessed 10 March 2017.

38 William Skidelsky, 'Tennis Review – the Best Writer on the Game Ever', *Guardian*, 24 June 2016.

39 Gob Squad, *The Conversationalist*, 2012 (DVD).

40 Gob Squad, 'Remote Acting through Headphones'. *Gob Squad and the Impossible Attempt to Make Sense of It All* (Gob Squad, 2010), 71–74 (72).

41 Wallace, *Infinite Jest*, 27–28.

42 Gob Squad, *Gob Squad and the Impossible Attempt to Make Sense of It All*, 58.

43 Lehmann, *Postdramatic Theatre*, 151–152.

44 Urška Brodar, 'Endless Party', trans. Sunčan Stone, *Maska* 155–156 (Summer 2013), 78–84 (84).

45 Aaron Wiener, '*Infinite Jest*! Live! On Stage! One Entire Day Only!' *Culturebox*, 18 June 2012. http://www.slate.com/articles/arts/culturebox/2012/06/infinite_jest_on_stage_berlin_theater_adaptation_of_david_foster_wallace_s_novel_.html. Accessed 10 March 2017. Giovanni Marchini Camia, 'A Performance of Staggering Proportions', *ExBerliner*, 18 June 2012. http://www.exberliner.com/culture/stage/a-performance-of-staggering-proportions/. Accessed 10 March 2017. Earley, 'A Day in Dystopia'.

46 Camia, 'A Performance of Staggering Proportions'.

47 Anne Marie Donahue, 'David Foster Wallace Winces at the Suggestion That His Book Is Sloppy in Any Sense'. In Burn, ed., *Conversations with David Foster Wallace*, 70–72 (71–72).

48 Daniel Brunet, 'The Essentiality of Innovation', TCG Circle, 2013. http://www.tcgcircle.org/2013/05/the-essentiality-of-innovation/. Accessed 10 March 2017.

49 Earley, 'A Day in Dystopia'; Brodar, 'Endless Party'.

50 Donahue, 'David Foster Wallace Winces at the Suggestion That His Book Is Sloppy in Any Sense', 71.

51 Marcus Canning, 'Berlin Performs David Foster Wallace', *Real Time* 112 (December–January 2012). http://www.realtimearts.net/article/112/10915. Accessed 10 March 2017.

52 Lehmann, *Postdramatic Theatre*, 152.

53 Kundera, *Jacques and His Master*, 17.

54 Kundera, *Jacques and His Master*, 25.
55 Kundera, *Jacques and His Master*, 41.
56 Diderot, *Jacques the Fatalist*, 21.
57 Tim Jones, 'Milan Kundera's *Slowness* – Making It Slow', *Review of European Studies* 1: 2 (2009), 64–75.
58 Kundera, *Jacques and His Master*, 10.
59 Kundera, *Jacques and His Master*, 16–17.
60 Kundera, *Jacques and His Master*, 15–17; Diderot, *Jacques the Fatalist*, 237.
61 Dawn Sova, *Banned Books: Literature Suppressed on Sexual Grounds* (New York: Facts on File, 2006), 157–159.
62 Diderot, *Jacques the Fatalist*, 185.
63 Diderot, *Jacques the Fatalist*, 199.
64 Whitney Mannies argues that the structure and style of *Jacques the Fatalist* is informed by and actively promotes its author's philosophical perspective. Mannies, 'The Style of Materialist Skepticism: Diderot's *Jacques le Fataliste*', *Philosophy and Literature* 39: 1A (2015), A32–A48.
65 See Peter France, 'Public Theatre and Private Theatre in the Writings of Diderot', *The Modern Language Review* 64: 3 (1969), 522–528; Graham Ley, 'The Significance of Diderot', *New Theatre Quarterly* 11: 44 (1995), 342–354.
66 See France, 'Public Theatre and Private Theatre in the Writings of Diderot', 522–528; Ley, 'The Significance of Diderot', 342–354; Peter Brooks, *The Melodramatic Imagination* (New Haven & London: Yale University Press, 1995), 82–85 (84).
67 Diderot, *The Paradox of Acting – Primary Source Edition* (London: Chatto & Windus, 1883), 7. See also Joseph Roach Jr., 'Diderot and the Actor's Machine', *Theatre Survey* 22: 1 (1981), 51–68 (66).
68 Philipp Blom, *A Wicked Company: The Forgotten Radicalism of the European Enlightenment* (New York: Basic Books, 2010), 47–52.
69 David Coward, Introduction to *Jacques the Fatalist*, xii–xiii.
70 John Lough, *The* Encyclopédie *in Eighteenth-Century England* (Newcastle: Oriel Press, 1970), 2.
71 Lough, *The* Encyclopédie *in Eighteenth-Century England*, 19.
72 Diderot, *Jacques the Fatalist*, 77.
73 Loy, *Diderot's Determined Fatalist*, 52.

74 Loy, *Diderot's Determined Fatalist*, 52.

75 Milan Kundera and Arthur Holmberg, 'Interview: Milan Kundera', *Performing Arts Journal* 9: 1 (1985), 25–27 (26).

76 Mannies, 'The Style of Materialist Skepticism: Diderot's *Jacques le Fataliste*', A34.

77 Bakhtin, 'Forms of Time and of the Chronotope in the Novel', 244.

78 Bakhtin, 'Forms of Time and of the Chronotope in the Novel', 160–163.

79 Blake Stevens, 'Transposition of Spectacle and Time: The Entr'Acte in the *Tragédie en Musique*', *Eighteenth-Century Music* 11: 1 (2014), 11–29 (16).

80 Some artists and indeed some audiences were unhappy with the disruptive effect of the entr'acte. Rousseau insisted that whatever entertainment was presented should sustain whatever affective state the prior action had established (Stevens, 'Transposition of Spectacle and Time', 17–18). In the early twentieth century, literary magazines including *The Musical World* and *The Athenaeum* featured letters criticizing the lack of care often evident in the entr'acte, one correspondent declaring it 'a very real blot on our methods of theatrical production'. Doris Odlum, 'Entr'Acte Music in the Theatre'. Letter to the Editor, *The Athenaeum*, 12 September 1919.

81 Diderot, *Jacques the Fatalist*, 41.

82 Publicity material for *The Weiss Effect*, Bozar Studio Theatre, Brussels, March 2016. http://www.bozar.be/en/activities/99530-het-weiss-effect. Accessed March 10 2017.

83 Ans Van den Eede in correspondence with Frances Babbage, October 2016.

84 Louise Van den Eede and Ans Van den Eede, *Where the World is Going, That's Where We are Going*, trans. Wannes Gyselinck (2012). Unpublished performance text.

85 The use of He and She echoes Diderot's employment of similar identifications in his novels, most noticeably the conversation between 'Me' and 'Him' that structures *Rameau's Nephew* (1805).

86 Van den Eede and Van den Eede, *Where the World is Going.*

87 Diderot, *Jacques the Fatalist*, 48.

88 Diderot, *Jacques the Fatalist*, 41.

89 Van den Eede and Van den Eede, *Where the World is Going.*

90 Stewart Pringle, Review of *Where the World is Going, That's Where We are Going* (Edinburgh Festival), *Fest*, 13 August 2014. https://www.festmag.co.uk/theatre/102419-where-world-going-thats-where-were-going. Accessed 10 March 2017.
91 Van den Eede and Van den Eede, *Where the World is Going.*
92 Van den Eede and Van den Eede, *Where the World is Going.*
93 Van den Eede and Van den Eede, *Where the World is Going.*
94 Van den Eede and Van den Eede, *Where the World is Going.*
95 Herbert Josephs and Jack Undank, eds., *Diderot: Digression and Dispersion* (Lexington, KY: French Forum Publishers, 1984), 14.
96 Diderot, *Jacques the Fatalist*, 21.
97 George Steiner, *Lessons of the Masters* (Cambridge, MA & London: Harvard University Press, 2003), 60–61.
98 Proust, *The Way by Swann's*, trans. Davis, 85.
99 Shattuck, *Proust's Way*, 33.
100 Adam Watt, *The Cambridge Introduction to Marcel Proust* (Cambridge & New York: Cambridge University Press, 2011), 6.
101 Barthes, Deleuze, Genette et al., 'Proust Round Table'. Gilles Deleuze, *Two Regimes of Madness: Texts and Interviews 1975–1995* (New York: Columbia University, 2007), 29–60 (29).
102 *In Our Time: Proust*, BBC Radio 4. Broadcast 17 April 2003. Accessed on BBC iplayer, 10 March 2017.
103 Shattuck, *Proust's Way*, 38.
104 Bakhtin, 'Forms of Time and of the Chronotope in the Novel', 247–248.
105 Bakhtin, 'Forms of Time and of the Chronotope in the Novel', 140.
106 Proust, *The Way by Swann's*, 184–185.
107 Proust, *In Search of Lost Time, Vol. 6: Time Regained*, trans. Andreas Mayor and Terence Kilmartin, revised by DJ Enright (London: Vintage, 2000), 223.
108 Geraghty, *Now A Major Motion Picture*, 51–57.
109 Van den Eede and Van den Eede, *Where the World is Going.*
110 Proust, *The Way by Swann's*, 430.
111 Proust, *The Way by Swann's*, 429.
112 Shattuck, *Proust's Way*, 191.
113 Peter Jaeger, 'Poetics with Examples', *Evening Will Come* 53 (May 2015). http://www.thevolta.org/ewc53-pjaeger-p1.html. Accessed 10 March 2017. See also Jaeger, '*Martyrologies*', *Performance Research* 20: 1 (2015), 13–17.

114 Walter Benjamin, *Arcades Project*, trans. Howard Eiland and Kevin McLaughlin (Cambridge, MA & London: Harvard University Press, 2002).

115 J. M. Coetzee, 'The Marvels of Walter Benjamin', *New York Review of Books*, 11 January 2001. http://www.nybooks.com/articles/2001/01/11/the-marvels-of-walter-benjamin/. Accessed 10 March 2017.

116 Benjamin cited in Jaeger, *A Field Guide to Lost Things* (Manchester, MA: if p then q, 2015), 7.

117 Shattuck, *Proust's Way*, xv; Patrick Alexander, *Marcel Proust's Search for Lost Time: A Reader's Guide* (New York: Vintage, 2007), page unnumbered; P. A. Spalding, *A Reader's Handbook to Proust: An Index Guide to Remembrance of Things Past* (London: Chatto & Windus, 1952), 135.

118 Spalding, *A Reader's Handbook to Proust*, vii.

119 Thomas Baldwin, *The Material Object in the Work of Marcel Proust* (Oxford & Bern: Peter Lang, 2005), 103.

120 Jaeger, *A Field Guide to Lost Things*, 9.

121 Jaeger, *A Field Guide to Lost Things*, 36.

122 Jaeger, *A Field Guide to Lost Things*, 31.

123 Mrs William Starr Dana, *How to Know the Wild Flowers* (New York: Charles Scribner's Sons, 1895).

124 Jaeger, in conversation with Frances Babbage. 14 November 2016.

125 Kenneth Goldsmith, 'Uncreative Writing', *The Chronicle of Higher Education*, 11 September 2011.

126 Benjamin, *Arcades Project*, x.

127 Jaeger, in conversation with Babbage.

128 Adrian Heathfield and Tehching Hsieh, *Out of Now: The Lifeworks of Tehching Hsieh* (London, LADA & Cambridge, MA: MIT Press, 2009), 22.

129 Barthes, Deleuze, Genette et al., 'Proust Round Table', 29–30.

130 Lehmann, *Postdramatic Theatre*, 157.

131 Eggers, Foreword to Wallace, *Infinite Jest*, vii.

Conclusion

1 Thomas Leitch, 'Twelve Fallacies in Contemporary Adaptation Theory', *Criticism* 45: 2 (2003): 149–171 (166).

2 Kenneth Goldsmith, 'Uncreative Writing', *The Chronicle of Higher Education*, 11 September 2011.

3 See https://www.artangel.org.uk/project/a-room-for-london/. Accessed 10 March 2017.

Bibliography

Ackerman, Alan. *The Portable Theater: American Literature and the Nineteenth-Century Stage*. Baltimore, MD: Johns Hopkins University Press, 1999.

Alexander, Michael. *The Poetic Achievement of Ezra Pound*. Berkeley & Los Angeles: University of California Press, 1981.

Alexander, Patrick. *Marcel Proust's Search for Lost Time: A Reader's Guide*. New York: Vintage, 2007.

Alfreds, Mike. *Then What Happens? Storytelling and Adapting for the Theatre*. London: Nick Hern Books, 2013.

Allsopp, Ric. 'Itinerant Pages: The Page as Performance Space'. *Performance Research* 9:2. 2004. 2–7.

Alston, Adam. 'Audience Participation and Neoliberal Value: Risk, Agency and Responsibility in Immersive Theatre'. *Performance Research* 18:2. 2013. 128–138.

Andersen, Hans Christian. 'The Red Shoes'. 1845. http://hca.gilead.org.il/red_shoe.html.

Andrew, Dudley. 'The Well-Worn Muse: Adaptation in Film History and Theory'. In Syndy Conger and Janet Welsh, eds., *Narrative Strategies: Original Essays in Film and Prose Fiction*. Macomb: Western Illinois University Press, 1980. 9–17.

Andrew, Dudley. *Concepts in Film Theory*. Oxford: Oxford University Press, 1984.

Arendt, Hannah. 'Franz Kafka, Appreciated Anew'. In Susannah Young-Ah Gottlieb, ed.,. *Reflections on Literature and Culture*. Stanford, CA: Stanford University Press, 2007. 94–109.

Arikha, Noga. 'As a Lute out of Tune: Robert Burton's Melancholy'. *The Public Domain Review*, 1 May 2013. Open Knowledge Foundation. http://publicdomainreview.org/2013/05/01/as-a-lute-out-of-tune-robert-burtons-melancholy/

Babbage, Frances. 'Staging Angela Carter'. In Kelly Jones, Benjamin Poore and Robert Dean, eds., *Contemporary Gothic Drama*. Basingstoke: Palgrave Macmillan, forthcoming (2018).

Bakhtin, Mikhail. 'Forms of Time and of the Chronotope in the Novel'. *The Dialogical Imagination*, trans. Caryl Emerson and Michael Holquist. Austin: University of Texas Press, 1981. 84–258.

Baldwin, Thomas. *The Material Object in the Work of Marcel Proust*. Oxford & Bern: Peter Lang, 2005.

Barthes, Roland. *Image-Music-Text*. London: Fontana, 1977.

Barthes, Roland. *The Pleasure of the Text*. New York: Hill & Wang, 1990.

Barthes, Roland, Gilles Deleuze, Gérard Genette et al. 'Proust Round Table'. Gilles Deleuze, *Two Regimes of Madness: Texts and Interviews 1975–1995*. New York: Columbia University, 2007. 29–60.

Bazin, Andre. *What Is Cinema?* Vol.1, trans. Hugh Gray. Berkeley: University of California Press, 1967.

Beggs, Jo. Review of *The Anatomy of Melancholy*. *The Public Reviews*, North West. 25 April 2014.

Beja, Morris. *Film and Literature*. New York: Longman, 1979.

Benjamin, Walter. *Arcades Project*, trans. Howard Eiland and Kevin McLaughlin. Cambridge, MA & London: Harvard University Press, 2002.

Berkoff, Steven. *The Trial*. Oxford: Amber Lane Press, 1981.

Bettelheim, Bruno. *The Uses of Enchantment: The Meaning and Importance of Fairy Tales*. London & New York: Penguin, 1991.

Biggin, Rose. 'Reading Fan Mail: Communicating Immersive Experience in Punchdrunk's *Faust* and *The Masque of the Red Death*'. *Participations* 12:1. 2015. 301–317.

Billington, Michael. Review of *The Masque of the Red Death*. *Guardian*, 4 October 2007.

Billington, Michael. Review of *Pride and Prejudice*. *Guardian*, 26 June 2013.

Billington, Michael. Review of *Jane Eyre*. *Guardian*, 18 September 2015.

Binette, Mélanie. 'Spatial Encounters: Spectatorship in Immersive Performances'. MA dissertation. Montréal, Québec: Concordia University, 2014.

Blom, Philipp. *A Wicked Company: The Forgotten Radicalism of the European Enlightenment*. New York: Basic Books, 2010.

Bluestone, George. *Novels into Film*. Berkeley: University of California Press, 1957.

Bolton, Philip, ed. *Dickens Dramatised*. Boston, MA: G.K Hall, 1987.

Bolton, Philip, ed. *Scott Dramatised*. London & New York: Mansell, 1992.

Bolton, Philip, ed. *Women Writers Dramatised*. London & New York: Mansell, 1999.

Bordwell, David. *Narration in the Fiction Film*. London: Methuen, 1985.

Bordwell, David and Kristin Thompson. *Film Art: An Introduction*. New York: McGraw-Hill, 2001.

Bornstein, George and Ralph Williams, eds. *Palimpsest: Editorial Theory in the Humanities*. Ann Arbor: University of Michigan Press, 1993.

Bradbury, Ray. *Fahrenheit 451*. London: Corgi, 1973.

Bradley, John, ed. *Henry James on Stage and Screen*. Basingstoke: Palgrave Macmillan, 2000.

Bragg, Melvyn and guests. 'In Our Time: Proust', BBC Radio 4. Broadcast 17 April 2003. BBC iplayer.

Brantley, Ben. 'Six Lives Ebb and Flow, Interconnected and Alone', *New York Times*, 16 November 2008.

Bredsdorff, Elias. *Hans Christian Andersen: The Story of his Life and Work, 1805–75*. London: Phaidon, 1979.

Brodar, Urška. 'Endless Party'. Trans. Sunčan Stone. *Maska* 155/156. 2013. 78–84.

Brody, Richard. 'Virginia Woolf, Critic'. *The New Yorker*, 24 February 2012.

Brooks, Peter. *The Melodramatic Imagination*. New Haven & London: Yale University Press, 1995.

Brunet, Daniel. 'The Essentiality of Innovation'. TCG Circle, 2013. http://www.tcgcircle.org/2013/05/the-essentiality-of-innovation/

Bulgakov, Mikhail. *The Master and Margarita*, trans. Michael Glenny. New England: Harvill Press, 1995.

Burton, Robert. *The Essential Anatomy of Melancholy*, eds. G. C. F. Mead and R. C. Clift. Mineola, New York: Dover, 2002.

Burton, Robert. *The Anatomy of Melancholy*, adapted for the stage by Stan's Cafe. Birmingham: Stan's Cafe, 2013.

Camia, Giovanni Marchini. 'A Performance of Staggering Proportions'. *ExBerliner*, 18 June 2012. http://www.exberliner.com/culture/stage/a-performance-of-staggering-proportions/

Canning, Marcus. 'Berlin Performs David Foster Wallace'. *Real Time* 112. December–January 2012. http://www.realtimearts.net/article/112/10915

Cardwell, Sarah. *Adaptation Revisited: Television and the Classic Novel*. Manchester & New York: Manchester University Press, 2002.

Carlson, Marvin. 'Theatrical Performance: Illustration, Translation, Fulfillment, or Supplement?' *Theatre Journal* 37:1. 1985. 5–11.

Carlson, Marvin. Review of Lyubimov's *Three Sisters*. *Journal of Dramatic Theory and Criticism*. Fall 1989. 177–181.

Carlson, Marvin. *The Haunted Stage: The Theatre as Memory Machine*. Ann Arbor: University of Michigan Press, 2003.

Carroll, Nöel. *Theorising the Moving Image*. Cambridge: Cambridge University Press, 1996.

Cartmell, Deborah and Imelda Whelehan, eds. *Adaptations: From Text to Screen, Screen to Text*. London: Routledge, 1999.

Carter, Angela. *The Bloody Chamber*. London: Gollancz, 1979.

Cavendish, Dominic. Review of *The Trial*. *Telegraph*, 27 June 2015.

Chambers, Ross. *Loiterature*. Lincoln, NE: University of Nebraska Press, 1999.

Chartier, Roger and Peter Stallybrass. 'What Is a Book?' In Neil Fraistat and Julia Flanders, eds., *The Cambridge Companion to Textual Scholarship*. Cambridge & New York: Cambridge University Press, 2013. 188–204.

Chick, Stevie. '50 Years On: *The Trial* Revisited'. *The Quietus*, 24 September 2012. http://thequietus.com/articles/10132-the-trial-orson-welles-50-years-on

Clapp, Susannah. Review of *The Curious Incident of the Dog in the Night-Time*. *Guardian*, 17 March 2013.

Clery, E. J. and Robert Miles, eds. *Gothic Documents: A Sourcebook, 1700–1820*. Manchester & New York: Manchester University Press, 2000.

Coetzee, J. M. 'The Marvels of Walter Benjamin'. *New York Review of Books*, 11 January 2001. http://www.nybooks.com/articles/2001/01/11/the-marvels-of-walter-benjamin/

Coghlan, Alexandra. Review of *The Anatomy of Melancholy*, 28 November 2013. http://www.theartsdesk.com/theatre/anatomy-melancholy-ovalhouse.

Conger, Syndy and Janet Welsh, eds. *Narrative Strategies: Original Essays in Film and Prose Fiction*. Macomb: Western Illinois University Press, 1980. 9–17.

Connor, J. D. 'The Persistence of Fidelity: Adaptation Theory Today'. *M/C Journal* 10:2. 2007. http://journal.media-culture.org.au/0705/15-connor.php.

Cox, Philip. *Reading Adaptations: Novels and Verse Narratives on the Stage, 1790–1840*. Manchester & New York: Manchester University Press, 2000.

Dana, Mrs William Starr. *How to Know the Wild Flowers*. New York: Charles Scribner's Sons, 1895.

Dickens, Charles. *Nicholas Nickleby*. 1839. Ed. Michael Slater. Harmondsworth: Penguin, 1978.

Diderot, Denis. *The Paradox of Acting – Primary Source Edition*. London: Chatto & Windus, 1883.

Diderot, Denis. *Jacques the Fatalist*, trans. David Coward. Oxford & New York: Penguin, 1999.

Donahue, Anne Marie. 'David Foster Wallace Winces at the Suggestion That His Book Is Sloppy in Any Sense'. In Stephen Burn, ed., *Conversations with David Foster Wallace*. Jackson, MS: University Press of Mississippi, 2012. 70–72.

Durrani, Osman. 'Editions, Translations, Adaptations'. In Julian Preece, ed., *The Cambridge Companion to Kafka*. Cambridge & New York: Cambridge University Press, 2002. 206–225.

Earley, Michael. 'A Day in Dystopia'. *Financial Times*, 22 June 2012. https://www.ft.com/content/3e80b10a-b95c-11e1-b4d6-00144feabdc0

Eggert, Paul. 'Apparatus, Text, Interface: How to Read a Printed Critical Edition'. In Neil Fraistat and Julia Flanders, eds., *The Cambridge Companion to Textual Scholarship*. Cambridge & New York: Cambridge University Press, 2013. 97–118.

Eisenstein, Sergei. 'Dickens, Griffith and the Film Today'. In Jay Leyda, ed. and trans., *Film Form: Essays in Film Theory* and Orlando, FL: Harcourt Brace, 1969. 195–255.

Elder, Bruce. '"Doing the Inexpressible Uncommonly Well": The Theatre of Steven Berkoff'. *Theatre Quarterly* 31. Autumn 1978. 37–43.

Elliott, Kamilla. *Rethinking the Novel/Film Debate*. Cambridge: Cambridge University Press, 2003.

Etchells, Tim and Ant Hampton. *The Quiet Volume*. 2010. Unpublished text of audio track and notebook.

Eustis, Oskar et al. 'An Evening of Gatsby with Elevator Repair Service at the 92nd Street Y'. 29 September 2010. http://www.youtube.com/watch?v=GzcvwyhtG3o.

Feingold, Michael. '*Gatz* Tries a Novel Approach to Fitzgerald'. *The Village Voice*, 10 October 2013. http://www.villagevoice.com/2010-10-13/theater/gatz-tries-a-novel-approach-to-fitzgerald/

Felman, Shoshana. 'On Reading Poetry: Reflections on the Limits and Possibilities of Psychoanalytical Approaches'. In John Muller and William Richardson, eds., *The Purloined Poe: Lacan, Derrida and Psychoanalytical Reading*. Baltimore & London: Johns Hopkins University Press, 1988. 133–156.

Fitzgerald, F. Scott. *The Great Gatsby*. London & New York: Penguin, 1990.

France, Peter. 'Public Theatre and Private Theatre in the Writings of Diderot'. *The Modern Language Review* 64:3. 1969. 522–528.

Fromm, Harold. 'Democritus Junior, and the Curse of Postmodernism'. *The Hudson Review* 49:2. 1996. 323–330.

Gardner, Lyn. 'The Face of the Future'. *Guardian*, 19 November 1997.

Gardner, Lyn. '*Waves* Sets a High Water-Mark for Multimedia Theatre'. *Guardian*, 4 December 2006.

Gardner, Lyn. 'We Make Our Own Ghosts Here'. *Guardian*, 12 September 2007. http://www.theguardian.com/stage/2007/sep/12/theatre.edgarallanpoe.

Gardner, Lyn. Review of *Time Has Fallen Asleep in the Afternoon Sunshine*. 3 April 2012. http://www.theguardian.com/stage/2012/apr/03/time-has-fallen-asleep-review.

Gardner, Lyn. Review of *The Anatomy of Melancholy*. *Guardian*, 27 November 2013. http://www.theguardian.com/stage/2013/nov/27/anatomy-of-melancholy-review.

Geraghty, Christine. *Now a Major Motion Picture: Film Adaptations of Literature and Drama*. Lanham, MD: Rowman & Littlefield, 2008.

Gillinson, Miriam. 'A recreation, A Reinterpretation – and Certainly Not Magic'. *Culture Wars*, 5 March 2011. http://www.culturewars.org.uk/index.php/site/article/a_recreation_a_reinterpretation_and_certainly_not_magic/

Gillinson, Miriam. 'Retz's *The Trial*, or Death as a Get-Out Clause'. *Sketches on Theatre*, 5 April 2013. http://sketchesontheatre.blogspot.co.uk/2013/04/retz-trial-review-or-death-as-get-out.html.

Glavin, John. *After Dickens: Reading, Adaptation and Performance*. Cambridge: Cambridge University Press, 1999.

Gob Squad. *Gob Squad and the Impossible Attempt to Make Sense of It All*. Gob Squad, 2010.

Gob Squad. *The Conversationalist*. 2012 [DVD].

Goldsmith, Kenneth. 'Uncreative Writing'. *The Chronicle of Higher Education*, 11 September 2011.

Gross, Kenneth. *Puppet: An Essay on Uncanny Life*. Chicago & London: University of Chicago Press, 2011.

Gross, Ruth. 'Kafka's Short Fiction'. In Julian Preece, ed., *The Cambridge Companion to Kafka*. Cambridge & New York: Cambridge University Press, 2002. 80–94.

Haddon, Mark. '"Staging the Unstageable": The Story Behind *Curious Incident*'. No date. http://www.curiousonstage.com/staging-unstageable-story-behind-curious-incident/

Heathfield, Adrian and Tehching Hsieh. *Out of Now: The Lifeworks of Tehching Hsieh*. London, LADA & Cambridge, MA: MIT Press, 2009.

Heidegger, Martin. 'Building, Dwelling, Thinking'. *Poetry, Language, Thought*, trans. Albert Hofstadter. New York: Harper & Row, 1971, 145–161.

Heller, Erich. *Kafka*. London: Fontana, 1974.

Hemming, Sarah. Review of *The Trial*. *Financial Times*, 29 June 2015.

Hensher, Philip. 'You'll Never Catch Me Watching It'. *Guardian*, 7 November 2005.

Hermansson, Casie. 'Flogging Fidelity: In Defense of the (Un)Dead Horse'. *Adaptation* 8:2. 2015. 149–160.

Hodges, Nicola Fordham. Review of *The Anatomy of Melancholy*. *Disability Arts Online*, 3 December 2013. http://www.disabilityartsonline.org.uk/the-anatomy-of-melancholy.

Hof van Eede. Publicity Material for *The Weiss Effect*, Bozar Studio Theatre, Brussels, March 2016. http://www.bozar.be/en/activities/99530-het-weiss-effect.

Holland, Norman. *The Dynamics of Literary Response*. New York: Norton, 1973.

Hollands, Howard. 'Drawing a Blank: Picturing Nothing on the Page'. *Performance Research* 9:2. 2004. 24–33.

Hornby, Richard. 'Forgetting the Text: Derrida and the "Liberation" of the Actor'. *New Theatre Quarterly* 18:4. 2002. 355–358.

Hutcheon, Linda. *A Theory of Adaptation*. London & New York: Routledge, 2006.

Hytner, Nicholas. Interviewed by Robert Butler at the National Theatre, 6 January 2004. http://www.stagework.org.uk/webdav/harmonise@Page%252F@id=6026&Section%252F@id=406.html.

Innes, Christopher. 'Adapting Dickens to the Modern Eye: *Nicholas Nickleby* and *Little Dorrit*'. In Peter Reynolds, ed., *Novel Images: Literature in Performance*. London & New York: Routledge, 1993. 64–79.

Isherwood, Charles. 'Pages That Weren't Meant for Stages'. *New York Times*, 21 November 2008.

Jacobsen, Mary. 'Looking for Literary Space: The Willing Suspension of Disbelief Re-Visited'. *Research in the Teaching of English* 16.1. 1982. 21–38.

Jaeger, Peter. *A Field Guide to Lost Things*. Manchester: if p then q, 2015.

Jaeger, Peter. 'Poetics with Examples'. *Evening Will Come* 53. May 2015. http://www.thevolta.org/ewc53-pjaeger-p1.html.

Jaeger, Peter. '*Martyrologies*'. *Performance Research* 20:1. 2015. 13–17.

Johnson, Nicola and Helen Keane. 'Internet Addiction? Temporality and Life Online in the Networked Society'. *Time & Society* 2015. 1–19.

Johnston, Amy Boyle. 'Ray Bradbury: *Fahrenheit 451* Misinterpreted'. *LA Weekly*, 30 May 2007. http://www.laweekly.com/news/ray-bradbury-fahrenheit-451-misinterpreted-2149125.

Jones, Tim. 'Milan Kundera's *Slowness* – Making It Slow'. *Review of European Studies* 1:2. 2009. 64–75.

Josephs, Herbert and Jack Undank, eds. *Diderot: Digression and Dispersion*. Lexington, KY: French Forum Publishers, 1984.

Jubb, David. 'Co-producing the Future of Theatre'. *The Masque of the Red Death*, programme. BAC, 2008.

Jubb, David. Interviewed in *London Calling*, 30 June 2015. http://londoncalling.com/features/interview-with-david-jubb-artistic-director-of-battersea-arts-centre.

Kafka, Franz. *The Trial*, trans. Idris Parry. London & New York: Penguin, 1994.

Kalinowski, Gregor. '"Fräulein Bürstners weißte Bluse": Making Sense Stick in Kafka's *The Trial*'. *German Quarterly* 83:4. 2010. 449–464.

Kearney, Richard. *On Stories: Thinking in Action*. London & New York: Routledge, 2002.

Keats, John. *Selected Poems and Letters of Keats*. Ed. Robert Gittings. London: Heinemann, 1966.

Kellaway, Kate. 'A Wizard with Worlds'. Kellaway in conversation with Philip Pullman. *The Observer*, 22 October 2000.

Kisel, Maria. 'Feuilletons Don't Burn: Bulgakov's "The Master and Margarita" and the Imagined "Soviet Reader"'. *Slavic Review* 68:3. 2009. 582–600.

Kneehigh. *Tristan & Yseult, The Bacchae, The Wooden Frock, The Red Shoes*. London: Oberon Books, 2005.

Kneehigh. Educational pack for *The Red Shoes*. Kneehigh, 2010. http://www.kneehigh.co.uk/page/educational_packs.php.

Kristof, Agota. *The Notebook*, trans. Alan Sheridan. New York: Grove Press, 1997.

Kundera, Milan. *Jacques and His Master*, trans. Simon Callow. New York & London: Harper Perennial, 1986.

Kundera, Milan and Arthur Holmberg. 'Interview: Milan Kundera'. *Performing Arts Journal* 9:1. 1985. 25–27.

Lacey, Stephen. 'British Theatre and Commerce, 1979–2000'. In Baz Kershaw, ed., *The Cambridge History of British Theatre*, Vol. 3. Cambridge: Cambridge University Press, 2004. 426–447.

Laera, Margherita, ed. *Theatre and Adaptation: Return, Rewrite, Repeat.* London & New York: Bloomsbury, 2014.

Ledger, Sally and Holly Furneaux. *Charles Dickens in Context.* Cambridge & New York: Cambridge University Press, 2011.

Lee-Moss, Emma. '*Infinite Jest* at 20: Still a Challenge, Still Brilliant'. *Guardian*, 15 February 2016.

Lehmann, Hans-Thies. *Postdramatic Theatre*, trans. Karen Jürs-Munby. London & New York: Routledge, 2006.

Leitch, Thomas. 'Twelve Fallacies in Contemporary Adaptation Theory'. *Criticism* 45:2. 2003. 149–171.

Leitch, Thomas. *Film Adaptation and Its Discontents.* Baltimore, MD: Johns Hopkins University Press, 2007.

Lesser, Simon O. 'The Source of Guilt and the Sense of Guilt: Kafka's *The Trial*'. *Modern Fiction Studies* 8:1. 1962. 44–60.

Letzler, David. 'Encyclopedic Novels and the Cruft of Fiction: *Infinite Jest*'s Endnotes'. *Studies in the Novel* 44:3. 2012. 304–324.

Lewis, C. S. *The Magician's Nephew.* Harmondsworth: Penguin, 1963.

Ley, Graham. 'The Significance of Diderot'. *New Theatre Quarterly* 11:44. 1995. 342–354.

Lezard, Nicholas. 'The Book to End All Books'. *Guardian*, 18 August 2001.

Lilienthal, Matthias. In Conversation with Göksu Kunak. *IBRAAZ* 29 July 2013. http://www.ibraaz.org/interviews/90

Lough, John. *The* Encyclopédie *in Eighteenth-Century England.* Newcastle: Oriel Press, 1970.

Love, Catherine. 'By the Book: Adaptation, Work, and Elevator Repair Service's *Gatz*'. *Contemporary Theatre Review* 26:2. 2016. 183–195.

Loy, J. Robert. *Diderot's Determined Fatalist.* New York: King's Crown Press, 1950.

Ludlam, Harry. *A Biography of Bram Stoker, Creator of Dracula.* London: New English Library, 1977.

MacCabe, Colin, Kathleen Murray and Rick Warner, eds. *True to the Spirit: Film Adaptation and the Question of Fidelity.* Oxford & New York: Oxford University Press, 2011.

MacDonald, Gina and Andrew MacDonald, eds. *Jane Austen on Screen.* Cambridge & New York: Cambridge University Press, 2003.

Machon, Josephine. *Immersive Theatres.* Basingstoke & New York: Palgrave Macmillan, 2013.

Mannies, Whitney. 'The Style of Materialist Skepticism: Diderot's *Jacques le Fataliste*'. *Philosophy and Literature* 39:1A. 2015. A32–A48.

McCaffery, Larry. 'An Expanded Interview with David Foster Wallace'. 1993. In Stephen Burn, ed., *Conversations with David Foster Wallace*. Jackson: University Press of Mississippi, 2012. 21–52.

McFarlane, Brian. *Novel to Film*. Oxford: Clarendon Press, 1996.

McFarlane, Brian. 'It Wasn't Like That in the Book'. *Literature/Film Quarterly* 28:3. 2000. 163–169.

McGann, Jerome. *The Textual Condition*. Princeton, NJ: Princeton University Press, 1991.

Mee, Susie. 'Chekhov's *Three Sisters* and the Wooster Group's *Brace Up!*' *TDR* 36:4. 1992. 143–153.

Miller, J. Hillis. *Reading Narrative*. Norman: University of Oklahoma Press, 1998.

Miller, Jonathan. *Subsequent Performances*. London: Faber, 1986.

Miller, Laura. 'The Salon Interview: David Foster Wallace'. 1996. In S. Burn, ed., *Conversations with David Foster Wallace*. Jackson, MS: University Press of Mississippi, 2012. 58–65.

Moore, Steven. *The Novel: An Alternative History*. London & New York: Continuum, 2010.

Murphy, Vincent. *Page to Stage: the Craft of Adaptation*. Ann Arbor: University of Michigan Press, 2013.

Naremore, James, ed. *Film Adaptation*. New Brunswick, NJ: Rutgers University Press, 2000.

Nestruck, Kelly. 'For Your Eyes Only: Theatre Just for You'. *Guardian*, 11 May 2009. http://www.theguardian.com/stage/theatreblog/2009/may/08/one-on-one-theatre

Nicoll, Allardyce. *A History of English Drama 1660–1900*, Vol. 4. Cambridge: Cambridge University Press, 2009.

Odlum, Doris. 'Entr'Acte Music in the Theatre'. Letter to the Editor, *The Athenaeum*, 12 September 1919.

Parsons, Wendy and Catriona Nicholson. 'Talking to Philip Pullman: An Interview'. *The Lion and the Unicorn* 23:1. 1999. 116–134.

Pavis, Patrice. 'On Faithfulness: The Difficulties Experienced by the Text/Performance Couple'. *Theatre Research International* 33:2. 2008. 117–126.

Philip, Neil. *The Cinderella Story*. London & New York: Penguin, 1989.

Poe, Edgar Allan. *The Fall of the House of Usher and Other Writings*. London & New York: Penguin, 1986.

Poore, Benjamin. *Heritage, Nostalgia and Modern British Theatre: Staging the Victorians*. Basingstoke: Palgrave Macmillan, 2011.

Poulet, Georges. 'Criticism and the Experience of Interiority'. In Richard Macksey and Eugenio Donato, eds., *The Structuralist Controversy: The Languages of Criticism and the Sciences of Man*. Baltimore, MD: Johns Hopkins University Press, 1970. 56–72.

Pribisic, Milan. 'The Pleasures of "Theater Film": Stage to Film Adaptation'. In Dennis Cutchins, Laurence Raw and James Welsh, eds., *Redefining Adaptation Studies*. Lanham, Toronto & Plymouth: Scarecrow Press, 2010. 147–159.

Pringle, Stewart. Review of *Where the World is Going, That's Where We are Going*. *Fest*, 13 August 2014. https://www.festmag.co.uk/theatre/102419-where-world-going-thats-where-were-going

Proust, Marcel. *In Search of Lost Time, Vol. 6: Time Regained*, trans. Andreas Mayor and Terence Kilmartin, revised by D. J. Enright. London: Vintage, 2000.

Proust, Marcel. *The Way by Swann's*, trans. Lydia Davis. London & New York: Penguin, 2002.

Proust, Marcel. *In Search of Lost Time, Vol. 1: Swann's Way*, trans. C. K. Scott Moncrieff and ed. William Carter. New Haven & London: Yale University Press, 2013.

Pullman, Philip. Review of Blake Morrison, *As If*. London: Granta, 1997. *The Independent*, 1 February 1997.

Pullman, Philip. *I Was a Rat! or The Scarlet Slippers*. London: Random House, 2000.

Pullman, Philip. 'All Around You Is Silence'. *Guardian*, 5 June 2003.

Pullman, Philip. 'Theatre – the True Key Stage'. *Guardian*, 30 March 2004.

Pullman, Philip. 'The Art of Reading in Colour'. *Index on Censorship* 33: 4, 2004. 156–163. http://ioc.sagepub.com/content/33/4/156.

Pullman, Philip. 'Imaginary Friends: Philip Pullman on Fairy Tales'. *New Statesman*, 13 December 2011. http://www.newstatesman.com/culture/2014/06/imaginary-friends-philip-pullman-fairy-tales (Accessed 5 May 2017).

Pullman, Philip. 'Reading in the Borderland: The Space Between the Words, the Reader and the Pictures'. Open University 40th Anniversary Lecture, 21 October 2011. http://data.open.ac.uk/page/youtube/PLD01AF70D1BD703C8/PLTSTpNxgs88xyzo0jVg-Lo2AamJ_OL8DH

Pullman, Philip. *Grimm Tales for Young and Old*. London & New York: Penguin, 2012.

Radosavljević, Duška, ed. *The Contemporary Ensemble: Interviews with Theatre-Makers*. Abingdon & New York: Routledge, 2013.

Rebellato, Dan. 'When We Talk of Horses: Or, What Do We See When We See a Play?' *Performance Research* 14:1. 2009. 17–28.

Retz. *The Trial:* Sky Arts Documentary on the Making of *The Trial*, May 2013. https://www.youtube.com/watch?v=klTQg88CdIw

Rice, Emma. *The Essay*: 'On Directing'. Broadcast on BBC Radio 3, 14 February 2012.

Roach Jr., Joseph. 'Diderot and the Actor's Machine'. *Theatre Survey* 22:1. 1981. 51–68.

Saggini, Francesca. *The Gothic Novel and the Stage*. London & New York: Routledge, 2015.

Sanders, Julie. *Adaptation and Appropriation*. Abingdon & New York: Routledge, 2006.

Scarry, Elaine. *Dreaming by the Book*. New York: Farrar, Straus & Giroux, 1999.

Schulz, Bruno. *The Street of Crocodiles*, trans. Celina Wieniewska. London & New York: Penguin, 2008.

Schwartzbaum, Lisa. '*Infinite Jest*: Too Much of a Good Thing?' *Entertainment Weekly*, 14 March 2008.

Semtner, Christopher. *Edgar Allan Poe's Richmond: The Raven in the Silver City*. Charleston, SC: The History Press, 2012.

Shattuck, Roger. *Proust's Way: A Field Guide to* In Search of Lost Time. London: Penguin, 2000.

Shelley, Mary. Letter to Leigh Hunt. 9 September 1823. In Florence Marshall, ed., *The Life and Letters of Mary Wollstonecraft Shelley*, Vol. 2. Project Gutenberg, E Book, 2011. http://www.gutenberg.org/files/37956/37956-h/37956-h.htm#CHAPTER_XIX

SheShePop. *Infinite Jest – Footnote 24*. http://www.sheshepop.de/en/productions/archive/infinite-jest-footnote-24.html.

Shillingsburg, Peter. 'Polymorphic, Polysemic, Protean, Reliable, Electronic Texts'. In George Bornstein and Ralph Williams, eds., *Palimpsest: Editorial Theory in the Humanities*. Ann Arbor: University of Michigan Press, 1993. 29–44.

Silverblatt, Michael. Interview with David Foster Wallace. *Bookworm*, 11 April 1996. https://www.youtube.com/watch?v=ZKCMTHX5WHk.

Silverblatt, Michael. Interview with David Foster Wallace. *Bookworm*, 15 May 1997. http://www.smallbytes.net/~bobkat/bookworm.html.

Sinyard, Neil. 'Adaptation as Criticism: Four Films'. *Filming Literature: the Art of Screen Adaptation*. London & Sydney: Croom Helm, 1986. 117–142.
Sipress, David. 'That's the Guy I Hired to Read Proust for Me'. Cartoon. *The New Yorker*, 24 December 2007.
Skidelsky, William. 'Tennis Review – The Best Writer on the Game Ever'. *Guardian*, 24 June 2016.
Smith, Alexander. *Dreamthorp: A Book of Essays Written in the Country*. 1905. http://www.gutenberg.org/ebooks/18135.
Soloski, Alexis. Review of *The Curious Incident of the Dog in the Night-Time*. *Guardian*, 6 October 2014.
Sontag, Susan. 'The Unseen Alphabet: Kafka's Inner World'. *Vogue*, 1 July 1983. 202–203.
Sova, Dawn, *Banned Books: Literature Suppressed on Sexual Grounds*. New York: Facts on File, 2006.
Spalding, Philip. *A Reader's Handbook to Proust: An Index Guide to Remembrance of Things Past*. London: Chatto & Windus, 1952.
Spencer, Charles. '*The Masque of the Red Death*: A Night of Delicious Terror'. *Telegraph*, 4 October 2007. http://www.telegraph.co.uk/culture/theatre/drama/3668321/The-Masque-of-the-Red-Death-A-night-of-delicious-terror.html
Spencer, Charles. Review of *The Portrait of a Lady*. *Telegraph*, 25 July 2008.
Spencer, Charles. Review of *The Curious Incident of the Dog in the Night-Time*. *Telegraph*, 8 June 2015.
Spufford, Francis. *The Child That Books Built*. London: Faber & Faber, 2002.
Stam, Robert and Alessandra Raego, eds. *Literature and Film: A Guide to the Theory and Practice of Film Adaptation*. Oxford: Blackwell, 2004.
Steadman-Jones, Richard. 'Odysseus and the Sirens: Archive, Exile, Voices'. *Parallax* 19:4. 2013. 20–35.
Steiner, George. *Lessons of the Masters*. Cambridge, MA & London: Harvard University Press, 2003.
Stephens, Simon. Interviewed by Duška Radosavljević. In Margherita Laera, ed., *Theatre and Adaptation: Return, Rewrite, Repeat*. London & New York: Bloomsbury, 2014. 255–268.
Stevens, Blake. 'Transposition of Spectacle and Time: the Entr'Acte in the *Tragédie en Musique*'. *Eighteenth-Century Music* 11:1. 2014. 11–29.
Stewart, Garrett. *The Look of Reading: Book, Painting, Text*. Chicago & London: University of Chicago Press, 2006.

Stoneman, Patsy. *Brontë Transformations: Cultural Dissemination of 'Jane Eyre' and 'Wuthering Heights'.* London & New York: Prentice Hall & Harvester Wheatsheaf, 1995.

Stoneman, Patsy, ed. *Jane Eyre on Stage, 1848–1898.* London & New York: Routledge, 2007.

Tatar, Maria. *The Hard Facts of the Grimms' Fairy Tales.* Princeton, NJ: Princeton University Press, 1987.

Tatar, Maria, ed. *The Classic Fairy Tales.* New York & London: Norton, 1999.

Tatar, Maria. In conversation with Krista Tippett. 'The Great Cauldron of Story: Why Fairy Tales Are for Adults Again'. *On Being*, 14 March 2013. http://www.onbeing.org/program/the-great-cauldron-of-story-maria-tatar-on-why-fairy-tales-are-for-adults-again/transcript/5076.

Thiher, Allen. 'Kafka's Legacy'. *Modern Fiction Studies* 26:4. 1980. 543–561.

Thorp, Willard. 'The Stage Adventures of Some Gothic Novels'. *PMLA* 43:2. 1928. 476–486.

Tompkins, Joanne. *Theatre's Heterotopias: Performance and the Cultural Politics of Space.* Basingstoke & New York: Palgrave Macmillan, 2014.

Tompkins, Steve. 'Architectural Improvisation'. *Masque of the Red Death*, Punchdrunk programme. 2008.

Tookey, Hannah. Review of *The Anatomy of Melancholy. A Younger Theatre*, 17 March 2013. http://www.ayoungertheatre.com/review-on-tour-the-anatomy-of-melancholy-warwick-arts-centre-stans-cafe/

Van den Eede, Louise and Ans Van den Eede. *Where the World is Going, That's Where We are Going.* Trans. Wannes Gyselinck. 2012. Unpublished performance text.

Vice, Sue. *Introducing Bakhtin.* Manchester & New York: Manchester University Press, 1997.

Wagner, Geoffrey. *The Novel and the Cinema.* Rutherford, NJ: Fairleigh Dickinson University Press, 1975.

Wallace, David Foster. *Infinite Jest.* London: Abacus, 1996.

Warner, Marina. *From the Beast to the Blonde: On Fairy Tales and Their Tellers.* London: Chatto & Windus, 1994.

Watt, Adam. *The Cambridge Introduction to Marcel Proust.* Cambridge & New York: Cambridge University Press, 2011.

Webcowgirl. 'Life in the Cheap Seats'. Review of Punchdrunk's *The Masque of the Red Death*, 30 December 2007. https://webcowgirl.wordpress.com/2008/01/06/punchdrunk-productions-masque-of-the-red-death-battersea-arts-centre/

Weinstein, Philip. *Unknowing: the Work of Modernist Fiction*. Ithaca & London: Cornell University Press, 2005.

Weller, Sam. 'Ray Bradbury: The Art of Fiction, No. 203'. *The Paris Review* 192. 2010. http:/www.theparisreview.org/interviews/6012/the-art-of-fiction-no-203-ray-bradbury

Wick, Abigail. 'An Old-Fashioned *Infinite Jest* Invades Berlin'. *NPR Now*. US National Public Radio, 16 July 2012. http://www.npr.org/sections/nprberlinblog/2012/07/16/156853184/an-old-fashioned-infinite-jest-invades-berlin

Wiener, Aaron. '*Infinite Jest*! Live! On Stage! One Entire Day Only!' *Culturebox*, 18 June 2012. http://www.slate.com/articles/arts/culturebox/2012/06/infinite_jest_on_stage_berlin_theater_adaptation_of_david_foster_wallace_s_novel_.html

Wilson, Michael. *Storytelling and Theatre*. New York & Basingstoke: Palgrave Macmillan, 2009.

Woods, Michelle. *Kafka Translated: How Translators Have Shaped Our Reading of Kafka*. New York & London: Bloomsbury, 2014.

Woolf, Virginia. 'The Cinema'. *Collected Essays*, 4 Vols. (Vol. 2). London: Hogarth Press, 1966. 268–272.

Wozniak, Jan. 'The Value of Being Together? Audiences in Punchdrunk's *The Drowned Man*'. *Participations* 12:1. 2015. 318–332.

Zipes, Jack. *The Trials and Tribulations of Little Red Riding Hood*. London & New York: Routledge, 1993.

Zipes, Jack. *When Dreams Came True: Classical Fairy Tales and Their Tradition*. London & New York: Routledge, 1999.

Zipes, Jack. *Breaking the Magic Spell: Radical Theories of Folk and Fairy Tales*. New York: Palgrave Macmillan, 2002 (revised ed.).

Zipes, Jack. *Why Fairy Tales Stick: The Evolution and Relevance of a Genre*. New York & Abingdon: Routledge, 2006.

Index

Note: The letter 'n' following locators refers to notes.

CPSIA information can be obtained
at www.ICGtesting.com
Printed in the USA
LVHW021927060619
620412LV00014B/203/P

9 781472 531421